Music for U-U Choirs

by

Kenneth P. Langer

Music for U-U Choirs

by

Kenneth P. Langer

Music For U-U Choirs
by Kenneth P. Langer

Brass Bell Books

First Edition (Softcover)

ISBN: 13: 978-1-949464-04-7

Produced in the United States of America

Alphabetical Index

Parts Index

Order of Service Index

1. Opening Words/Welcome
    a. We Welcome You
2. Invocation
    a. Eternal Spirit
    b. Invocation
3. Hymns
    a. Seven Hymns
4. Chalice Lighting
    a. Hymn: The Growing Light
5. Singing the children out
    a. Go Now In Peace
6. Offertory
    a. (see General Music)
7. Meditation/Prayer/Blessing
    a. Peace Comes From Silence
8. Closing/Benediction
    a. Ten Benedictions

Special Days Index

- Flower Communion
    - There Are Flowers
- MLK Day
    - In Memory of MLK
- Easter (Springtime)
    - A Time of Jubilation
- Thanksgiving
    - Thanksgiving Round
    - Be Thankful
- Water Communion
    - Waters of the World
- National Holidays
    - Star Spangled Banner
- Commitment Sunday
    - Hey Yah
- Christmas
    - Season of Light
    - This Is The Night
- New Year Sunday
    - Ring Out Those New Year's Bells

A Time of Jubilation

Ken Langer

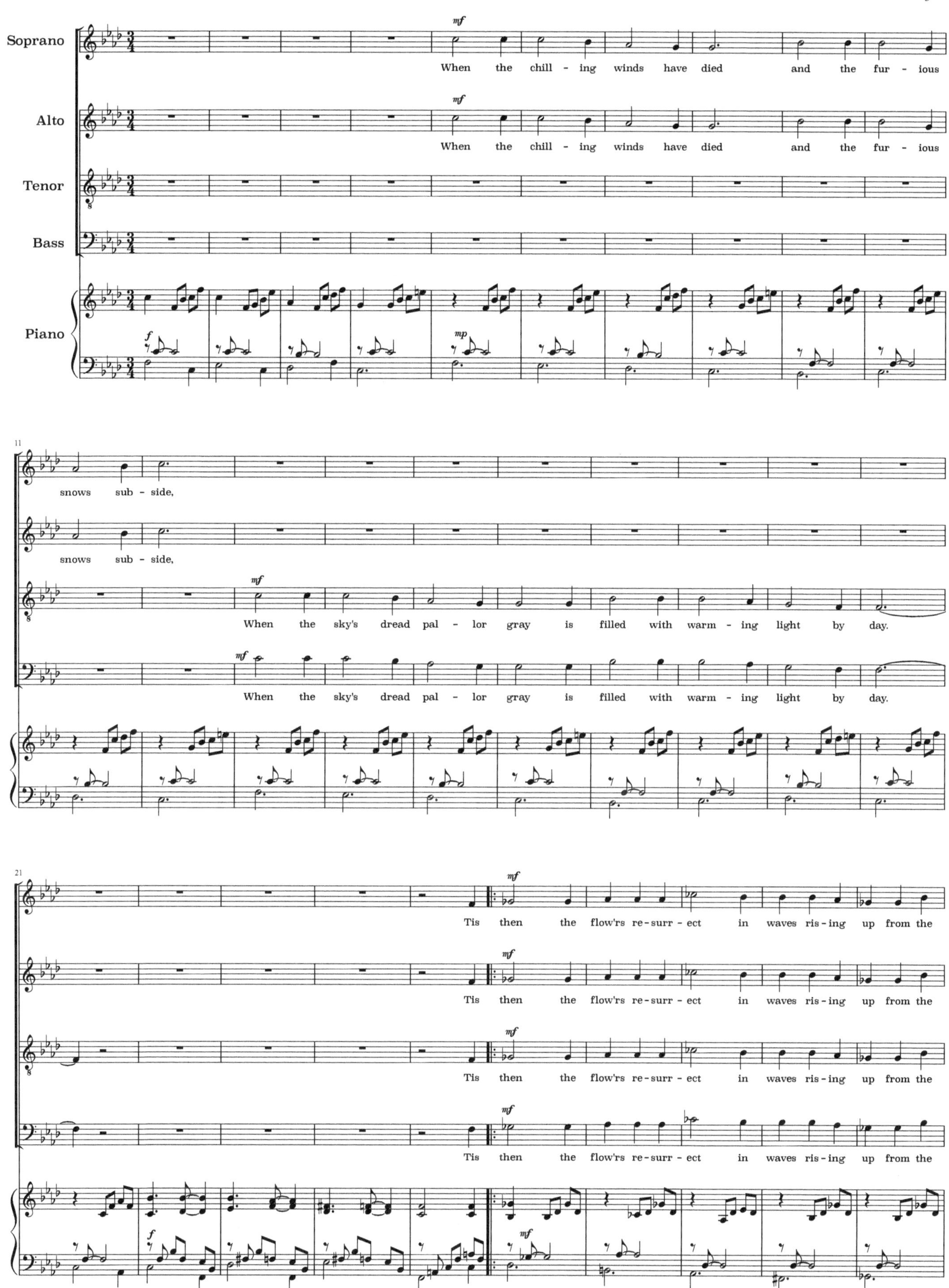

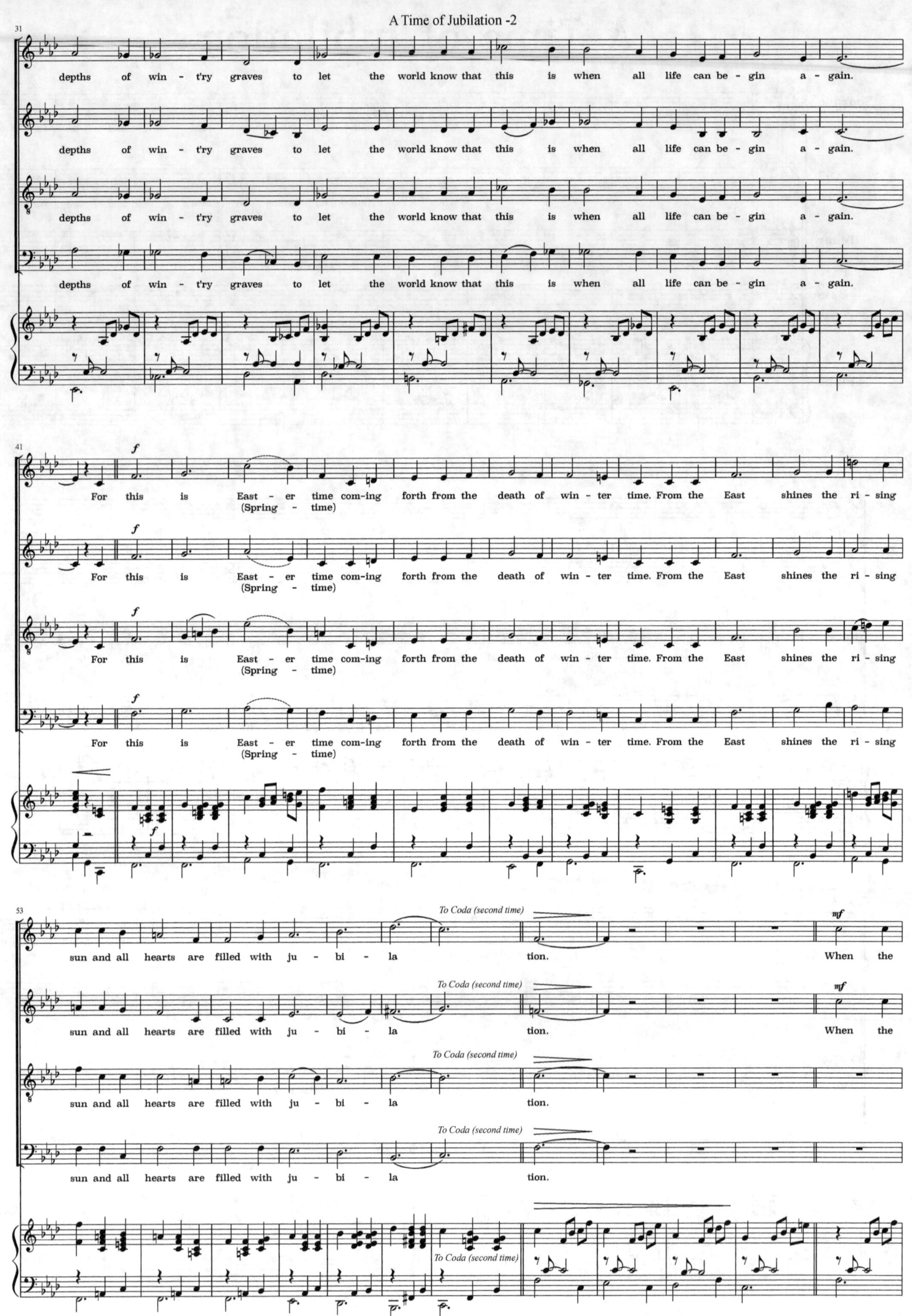
31
depths of win - t'ry graves to let the world know that this is when all life can be - gin a - gain.
41
For this is East - er time com-ing forth from the death of win - ter time. From the East shines the ri - sing
(Spring - time)
53
To Coda (second time)
sun and all hearts are filled with ju - bi - la tion.
When the

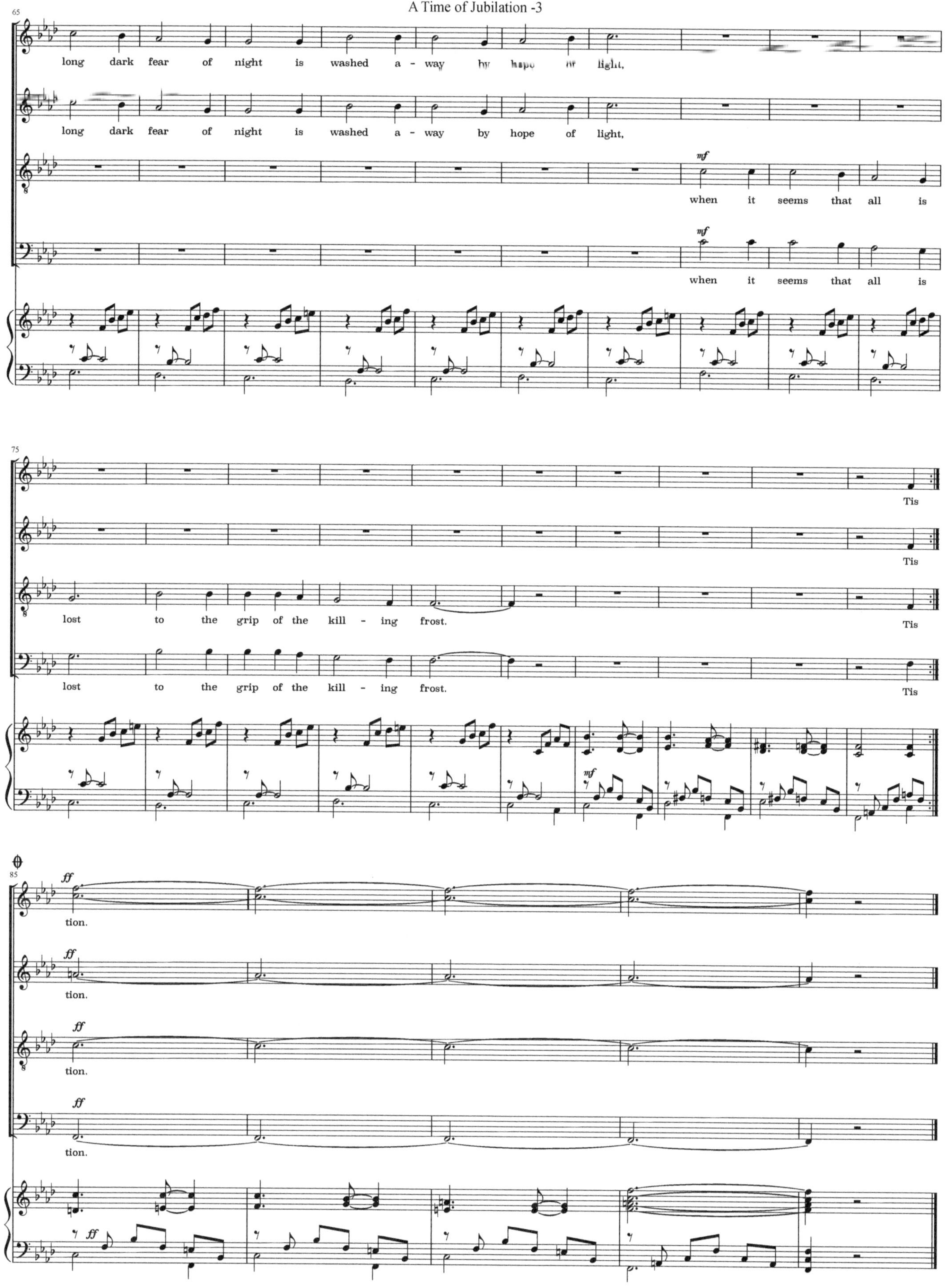
long dark fear of night is washed a - way by hope of light,
when it seems that all is lost to the grip of the kill - ing frost.
Tis
tion.

All The Best

Ken Langer

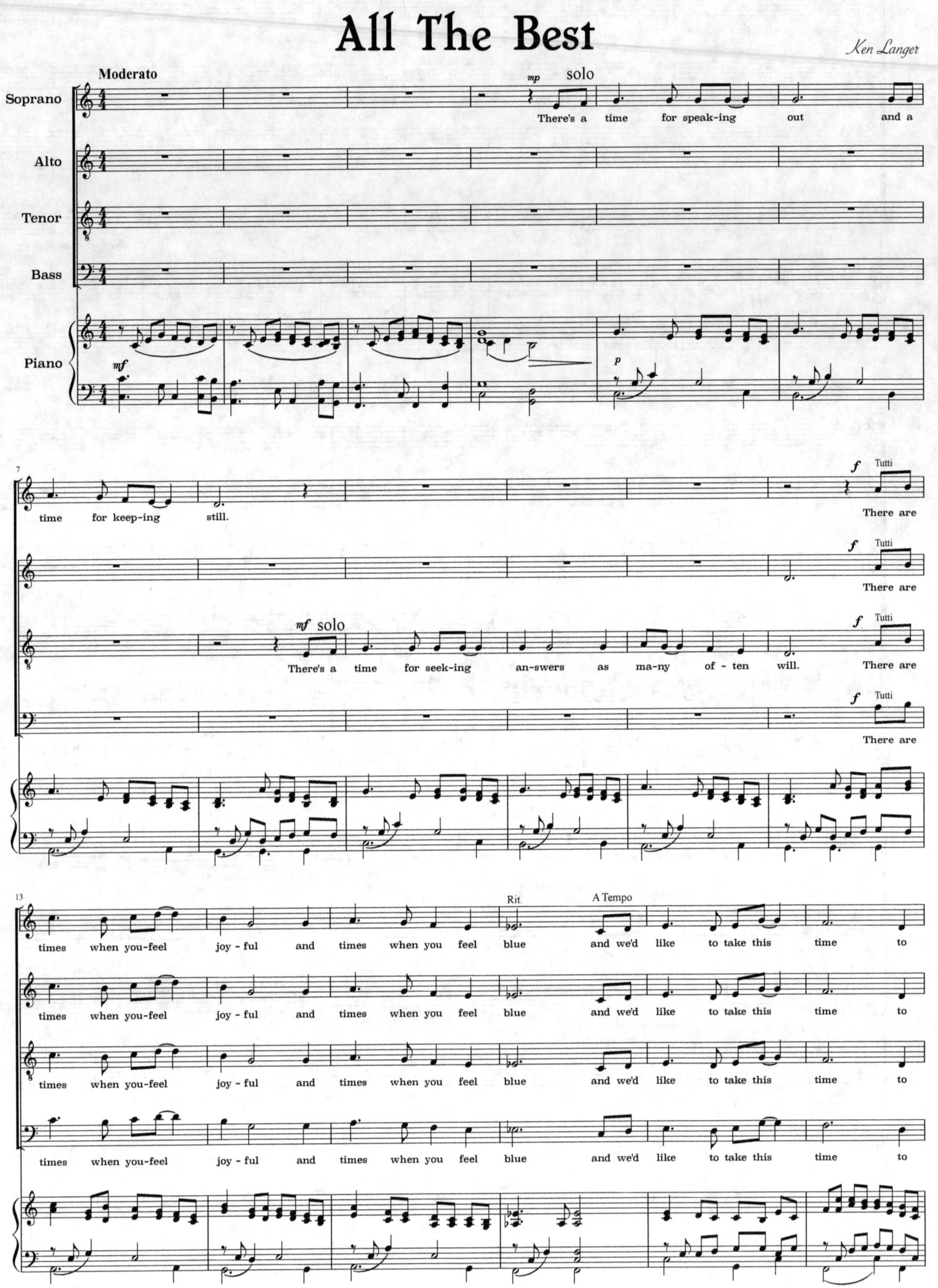

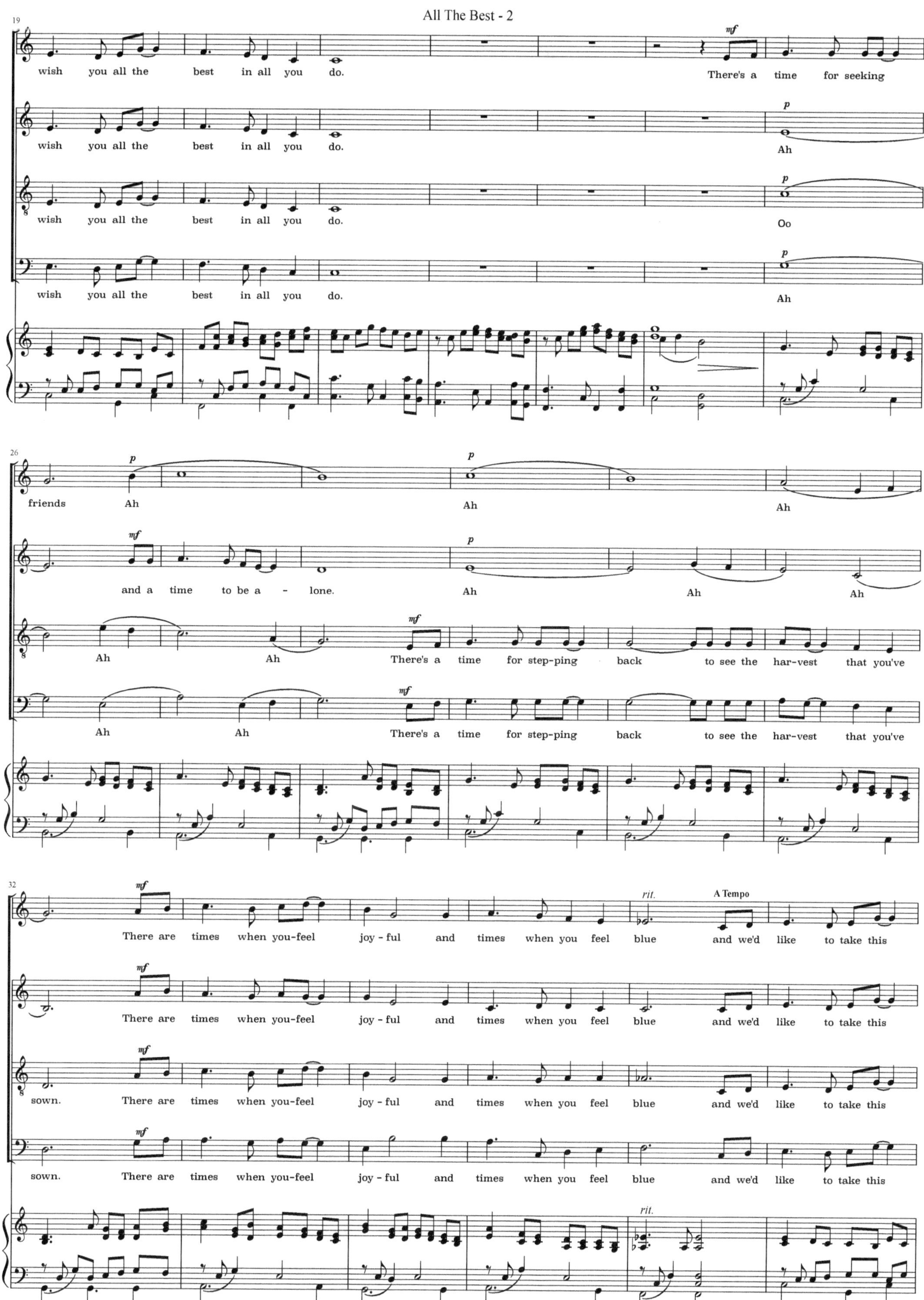
19
wish you all the best in all you do. There's a time for seeking
wish you all the best in all you do. Ah
wish you all the best in all you do. Oo
wish you all the best in all you do. Ah
26
friends Ah Ah Ah
and a time to be a - lone. Ah Ah Ah
Ah Ah There's a time for step-ping back to see the har-vest that you've
Ah Ah There's a time for step-ping back to see the har-vest that you've
32
rit.
A Tempo
There are times when you-feel joy - ful and times when you feel blue and we'd like to take this
There are times when you-feel joy - ful and times when you feel blue and we'd like to take this
sown. There are times when you-feel joy - ful and times when you feel blue and we'd like to take this
sown. There are times when you-feel joy - ful and times when you feel blue and we'd like to take this
rit.

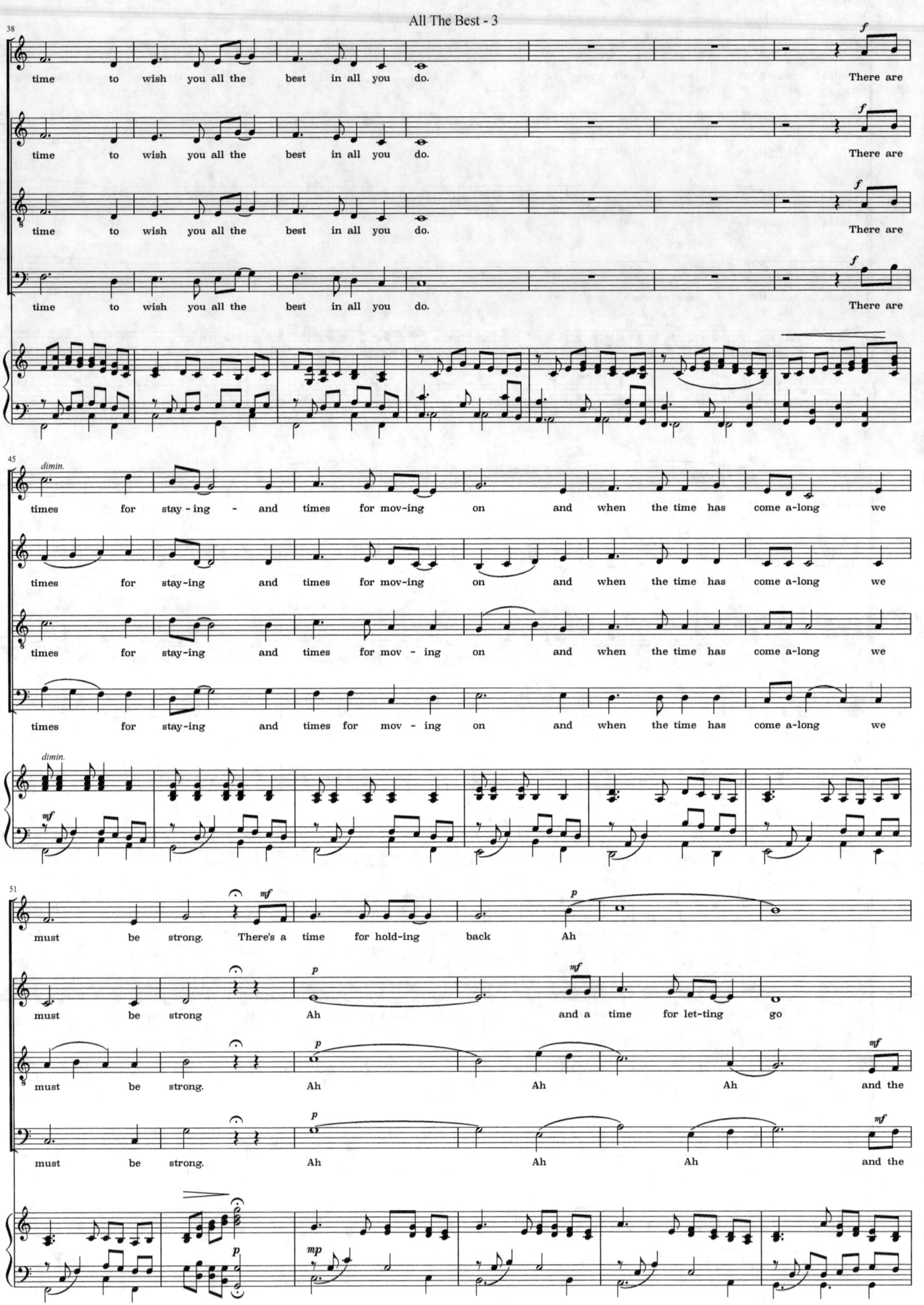
38
time to wish you all the best in all you do. There are
time to wish you all the best in all you do. There are
time to wish you all the best in all you do. There are
time to wish you all the best in all you do. There are
45
dimin.
times for stay-ing - and times for mov-ing on and when the time has come a-long we
times for stay-ing and times for mov-ing on and when the time has come a-long we
times for stay-ing and times for mov - ing on and when the time has come a-long we
times for stay-ing and times for mov - ing on and when the time has come a-long we
dimin.
51
must be strong. There's a time for hold-ing back Ah
must be strong Ah and a time for let-ting go
must be strong. Ah Ah Ah and the
must be strong. Ah Ah Ah and the

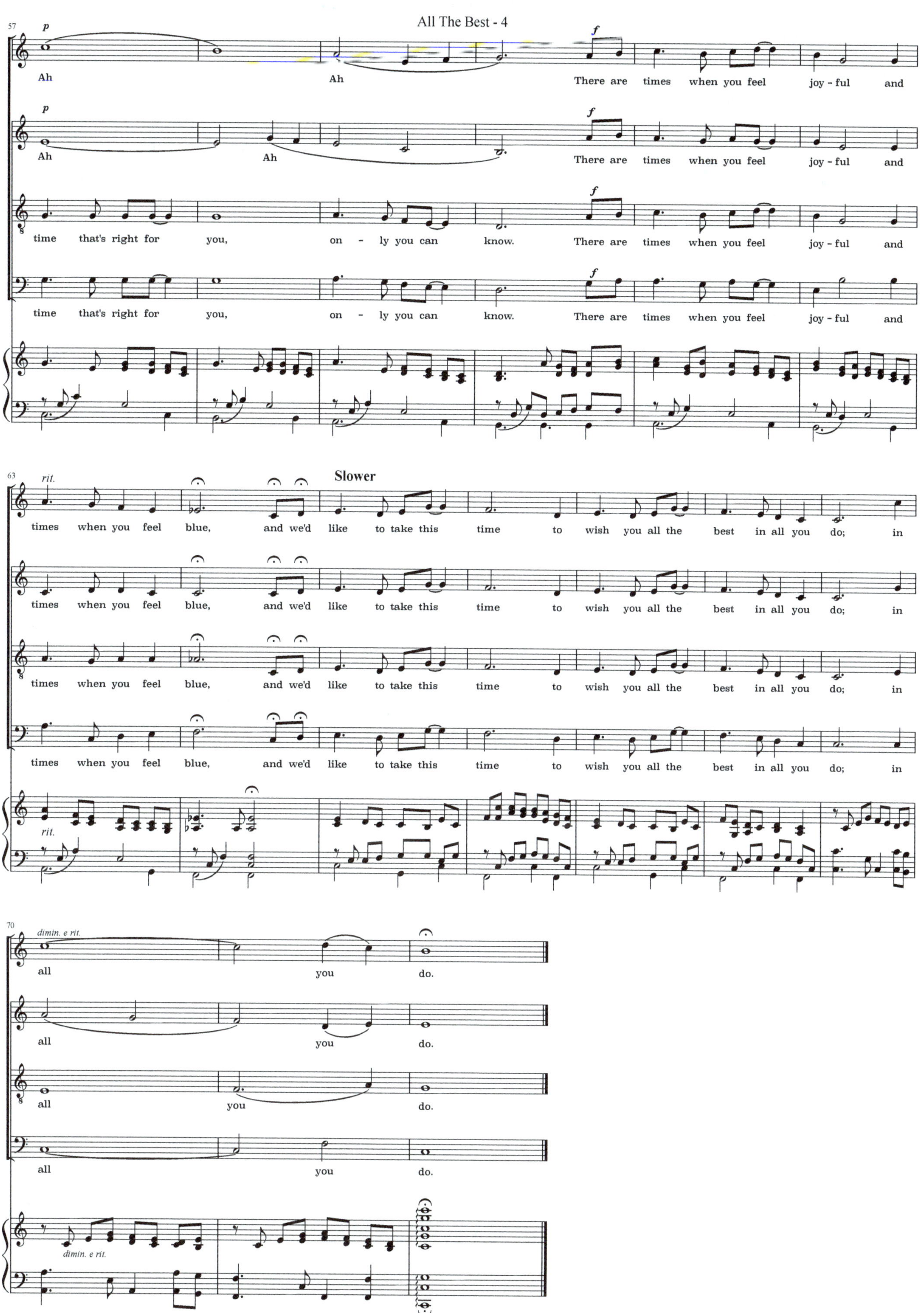
57
p
Ah Ah There are times when you feel joy - ful and
Ah Ah There are times when you feel joy - ful and
time that's right for you, on - ly you can know. There are times when you feel joy - ful and
f
63
rit.
Slower
times when you feel blue, and we'd like to take this time to wish you all the best in all you do; in
70
dimin. e rit.
all you do.

Be Thankful

Ken Langer

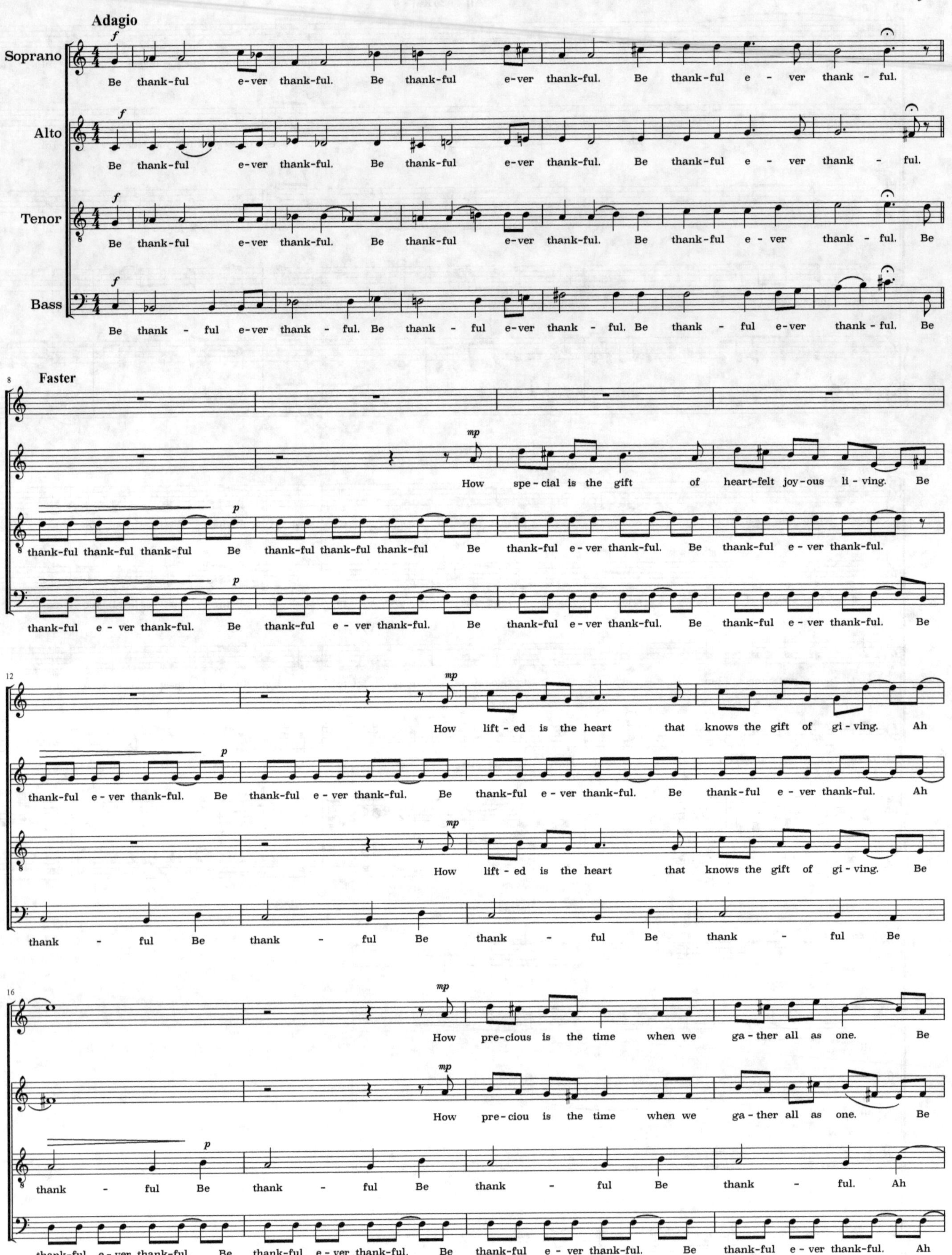

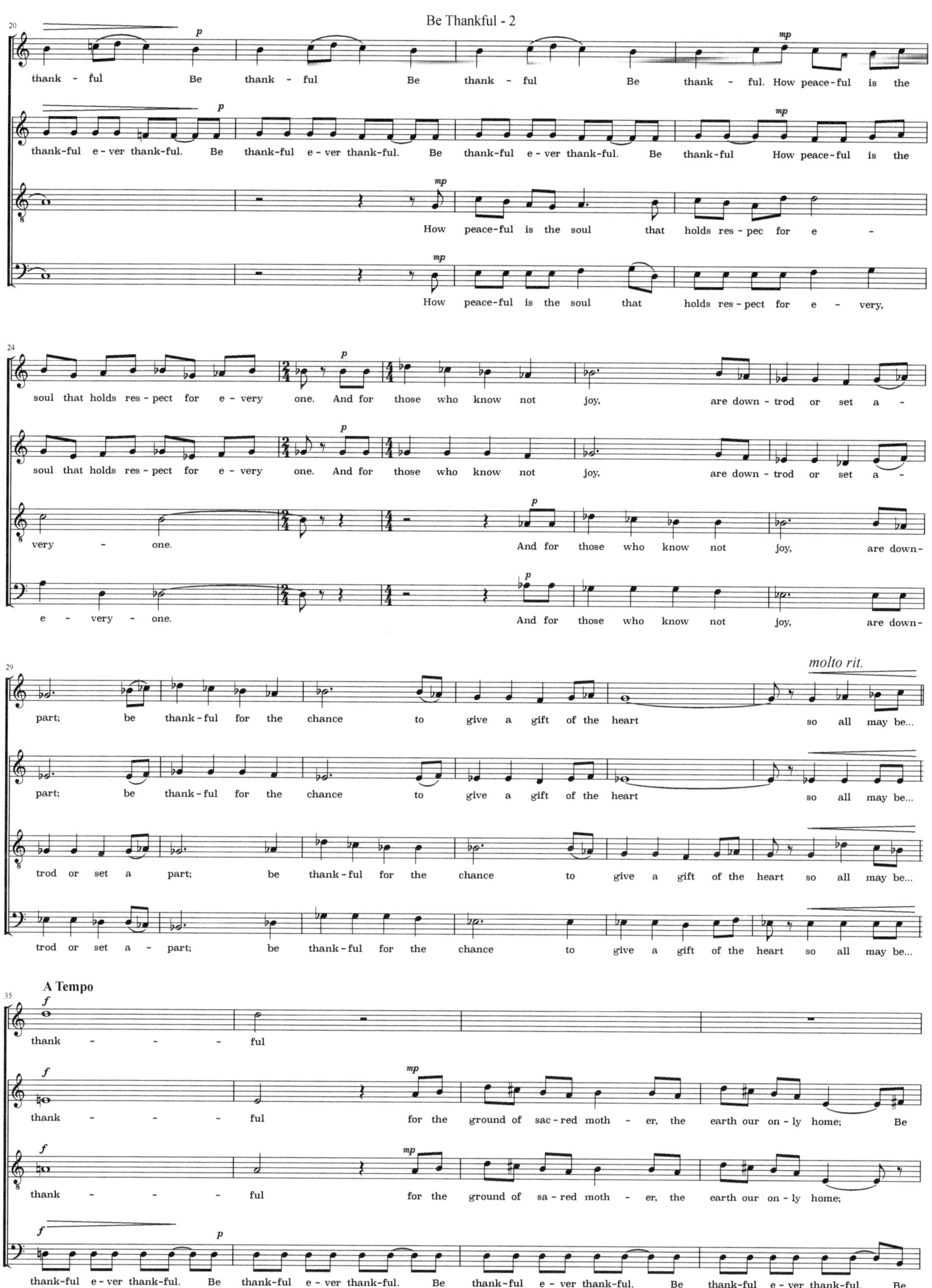
thank - ful Be thank - ful Be thank - ful Be thank - ful. How peace-ful is the
thank-ful e-ver thank-ful. Be thank-ful e-ver thank-ful. Be thank-ful e-ver thank-ful. Be thank-ful How peace-ful is the
How peace-ful is the soul that holds res-pec for e -
How peace-ful is the soul that holds res-pect for e - very,
soul that holds res-pect for e-very one. And for those who know not joy, are down-trod or set a -
soul that holds res-pect for e-very one. And for those who know not joy, are down-trod or set a -
very - one. And for those who know not joy, are down-
e - very - one. And for those who know not joy, are down-
molto rit.
part; be thank-ful for the chance to give a gift of the heart so all may be...
part; be thank-ful for the chance to give a gift of the heart so all may be...
trod or set a part; be thank-ful for the chance to give a gift of the heart so all may be...
trod or set a - part; be thank-ful for the chance to give a gift of the heart so all may be...
A Tempo
thank - - - ful
thank - - - ful for the ground of sac-red moth - er, the earth our on-ly home; Be
thank - - - ful for the ground of sa-red moth - er, the earth our on-ly home;
thank-ful e-ver thank-ful. Be thank-ful e-ver thank-ful. Be thank-ful e-ver thank-ful. Be thank-ful e-ver thank-ful. Be

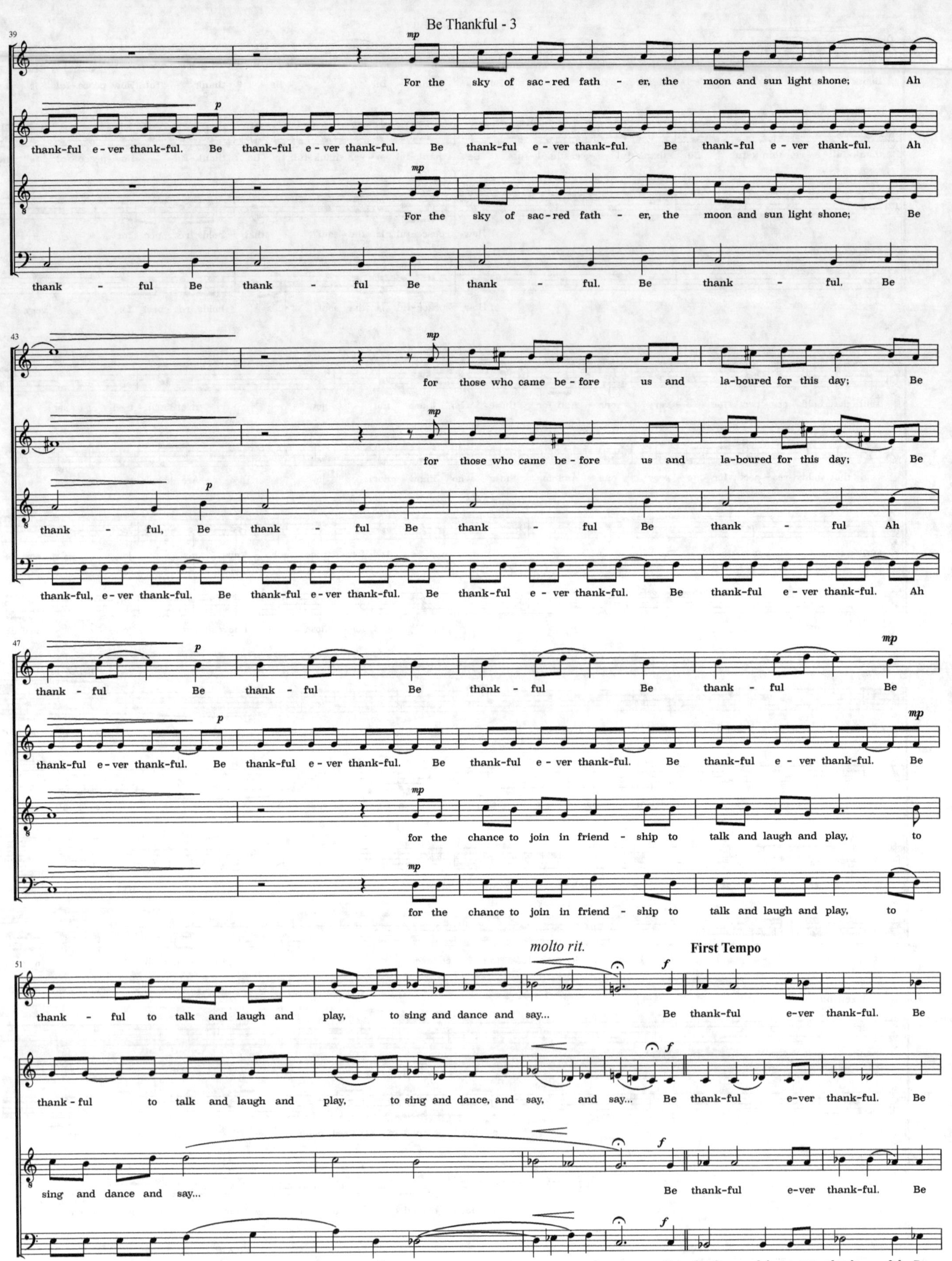
Be Thankful - 3
For the sky of sac-red fath - er, the moon and sun light shone; Ah
thank-ful e-ver thank-ful. Be thank-ful e-ver thank-ful. Be thank-ful e-ver thank-ful. Be thank-ful e-ver thank-ful. Ah
For the sky of sac-red fath - er, the moon and sun light shone; Be
thank - ful Be thank - ful Be thank - ful. Be thank - ful. Be
for those who came be-fore us and la-boured for this day; Be
for those who came be-fore us and la-boured for this day; Be
thank - ful, Be thank - ful Be thank - ful Be thank - ful Ah
thank-ful, e-ver thank-ful. Be thank-ful e-ver thank-ful. Be thank-ful e-ver thank-ful. Be thank-ful e-ver thank-ful. Ah
thank - ful Be thank - ful Be thank - ful Be thank - ful Be
thank-ful e-ver thank-ful. Be thank-ful e-ver thank-ful. Be thank-ful e-ver thank-ful. Be thank-ful e-ver thank-ful. Be
for the chance to join in friend - ship to talk and laugh and play, to
for the chance to join in friend - ship to talk and laugh and play, to
molto rit.
First Tempo
thank - ful to talk and laugh and play, to sing and dance and say... Be thank-ful e-ver thank-ful. Be
thank - ful to talk and laugh and play, to sing and dance, and say, and say... Be thank-ful e-ver thank-ful. Be
sing and dance and say... Be thank-ful e-ver thank-ful. Be
sing and dance and say, and say, and say... Be thank - ful e-ver thank - ful. Be

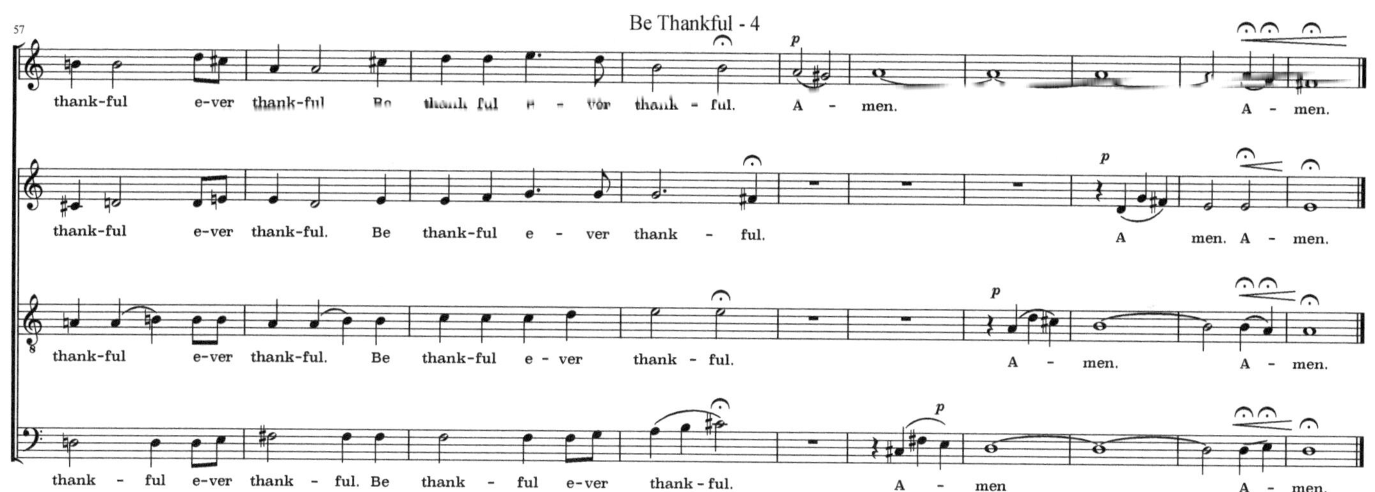
57
p
thank-ful e-ver thank-ful Be thank-ful e - ver thank - ful. A - men. A - men.
thank-ful e-ver thank-ful. Be thank-ful e - ver thank - ful. A men. A - men.
thank-ful e-ver thank-ful. Be thank-ful e - ver thank - ful. A - men. A - men.
thank - ful e-ver thank - ful. Be thank - ful e-ver thank-ful. A - men A - men.

Dancing In Circles

Ken Langer

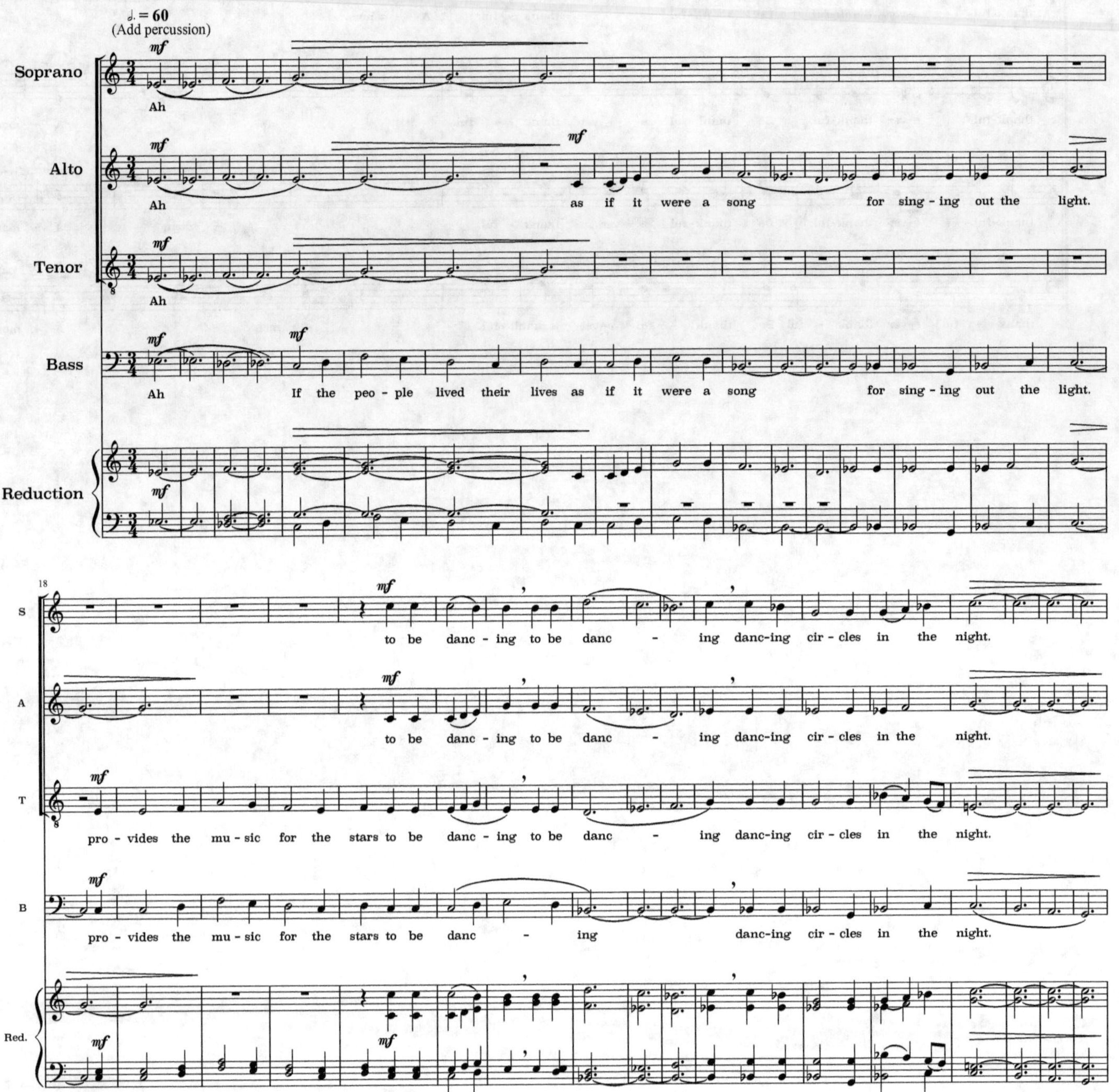

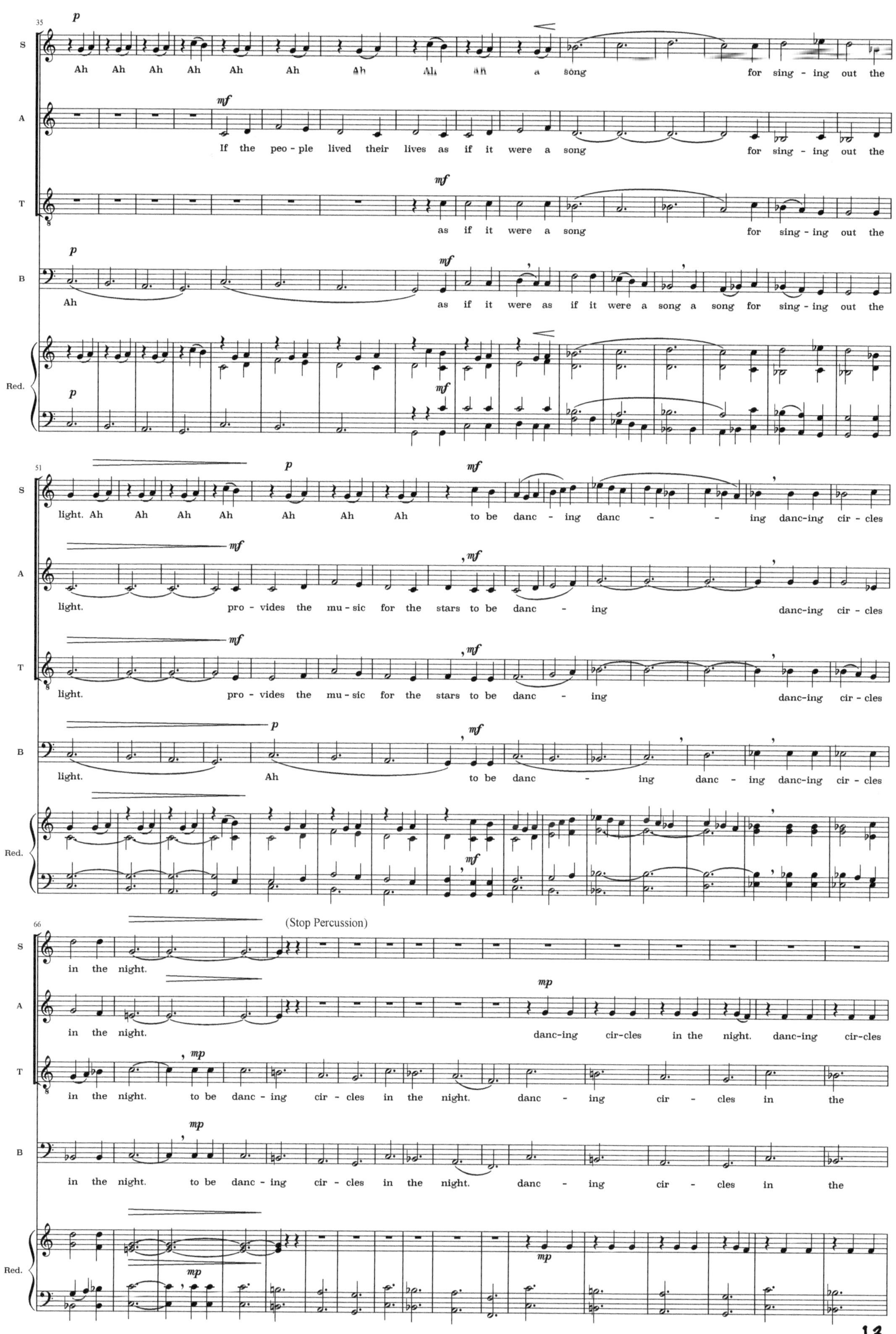
35
S
A
T
B
Red.
Ah Ah Ah Ah Ah Ah Ah Ah Ah a song for sing - ing out the
If the peo - ple lived their lives as if it were a song for sing - ing out the
as if it were a song for sing - ing out the
Ah as if it were as if it were a song a song for sing - ing out the
51
light. Ah Ah Ah Ah Ah Ah Ah to be danc - ing danc - - ing danc-ing cir - cles
light. pro - vides the mu - sic for the stars to be danc - ing danc-ing cir - cles
light. pro - vides the mu - sic for the stars to be danc - ing danc-ing cir - cles
light. Ah to be danc - ing danc - ing danc-ing cir - cles
66
(Stop Percussion)
in the night.
in the night. danc-ing cir-cles in the night. danc-ing cir-cles
in the night. to be danc - ing cir - cles in the night. danc - ing cir - cles in the
in the night. to be danc - ing cir - cles in the night. danc - ing cir - cles in the

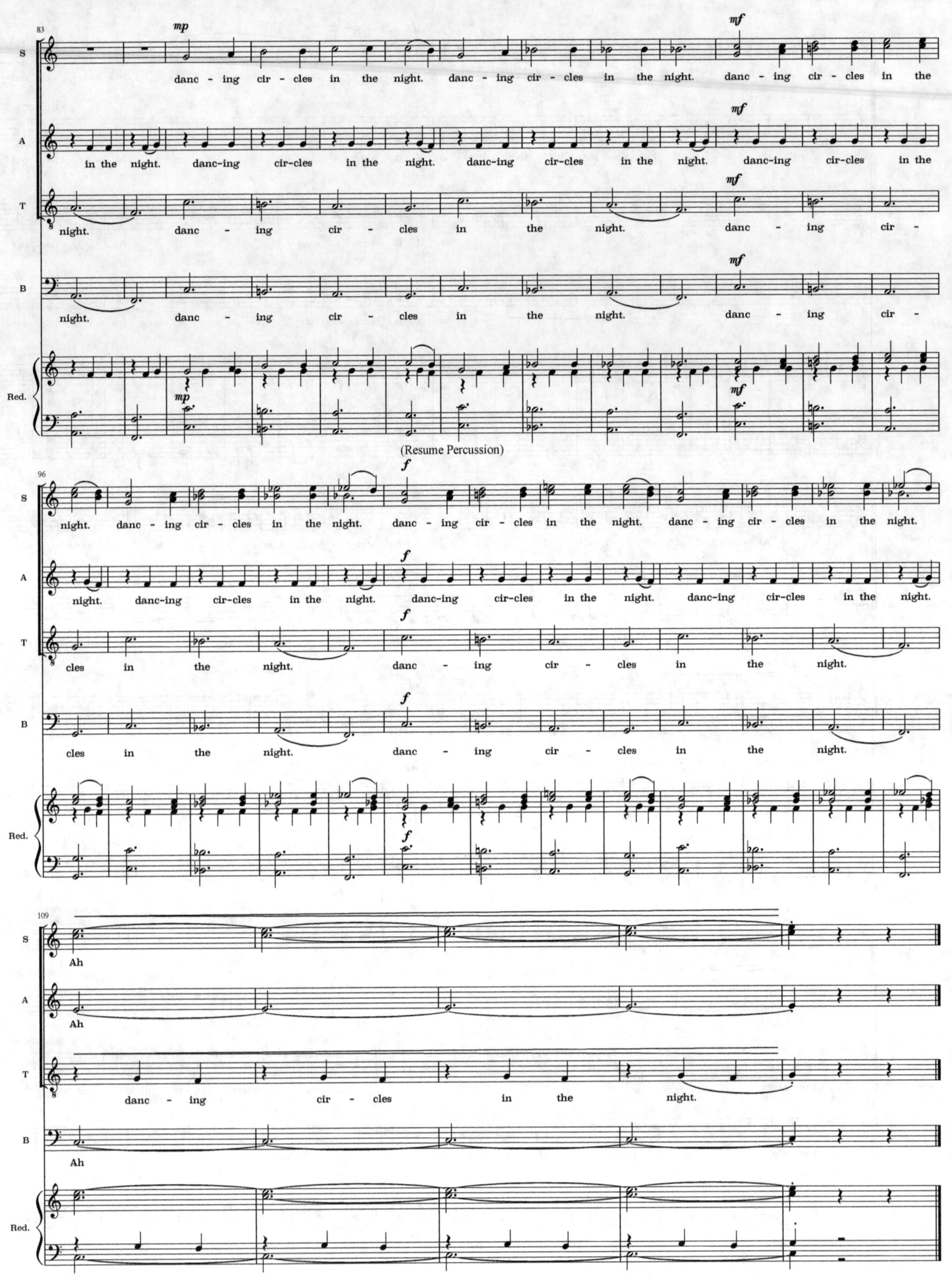
83
S
A
T
B
Red.
mp
mf
dranc - ing cir - cles in the night. danc - ing cir - cles in the night. danc - ing cir - cles in the
in the night. danc-ing cir-cles in the night. danc-ing cir-cles in the night. danc-ing cir-cles in the
night. danc - ing cir - cles in the night. danc - ing cir -
(Resume Percussion)
96
f
night. danc - ing cir - cles in the night. danc - ing cir - cles in the night. danc - ing cir - cles in the night.
night. danc-ing cir-cles in the night. danc-ing cir-cles in the night. danc-ing cir-cles in the night.
cles in the night. danc - ing cir - cles in the night.
109
Ah
danc - ing cir - cles in the night.

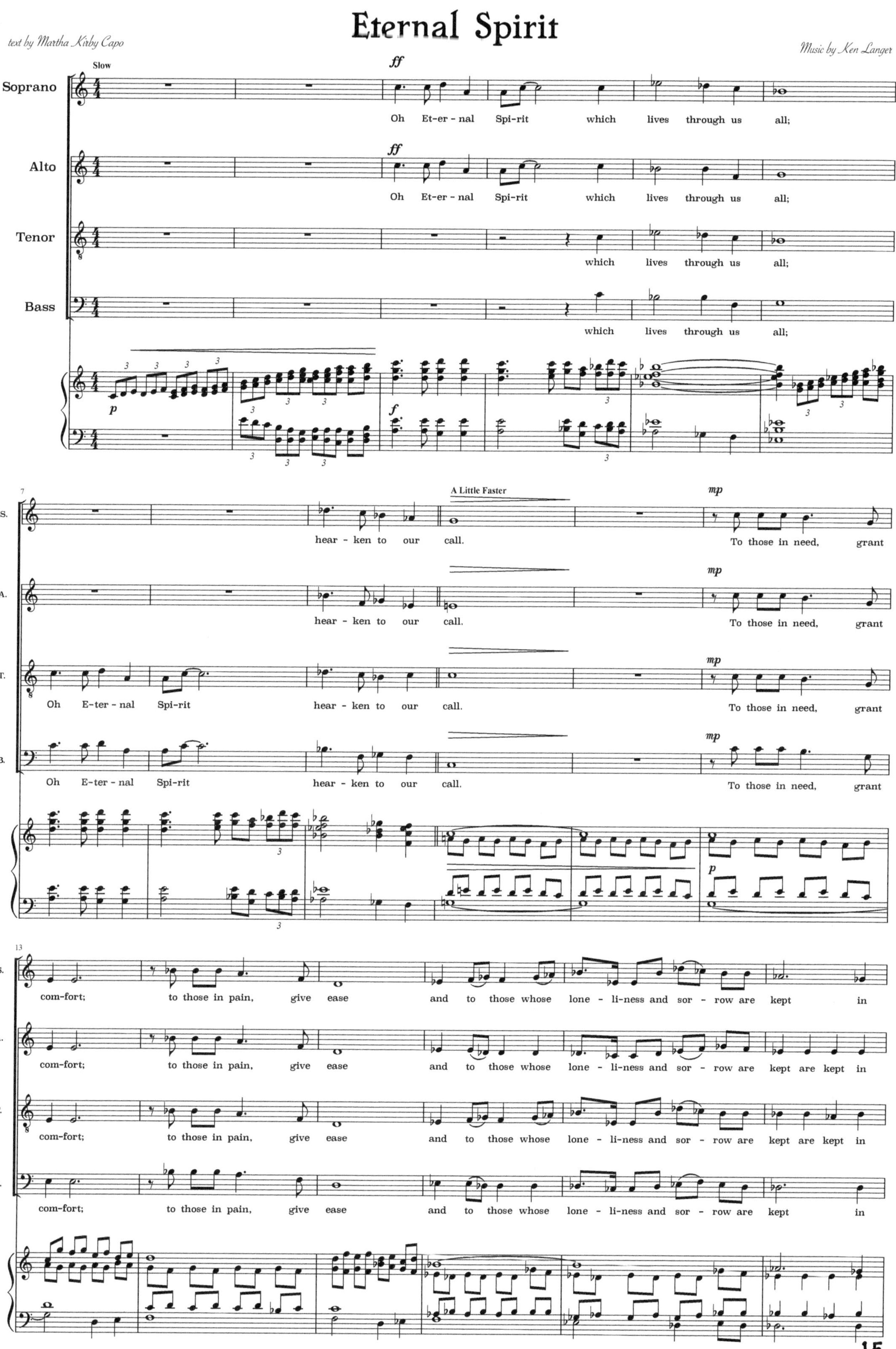
Eternal Spirit
text by Martha Kirby Capo
Music by Ken Langer
Slow
Soprano
Alto
Tenor
Bass
ff
Oh Et-er-nal Spi-rit which lives through us all;
which lives through us all;
p
f
7
hear-ken to our call.
Oh E-ter-nal Spi-rit hear-ken to our call.
A Little Faster
mp
To those in need, grant
S.
A.
T.
B.
13
com-fort; to those in pain, give ease and to those whose lone-li-ness and sor-row are kept in
com-fort; to those in pain, give ease and to those whose lone-li-ness and sor-row are kept are kept in
15

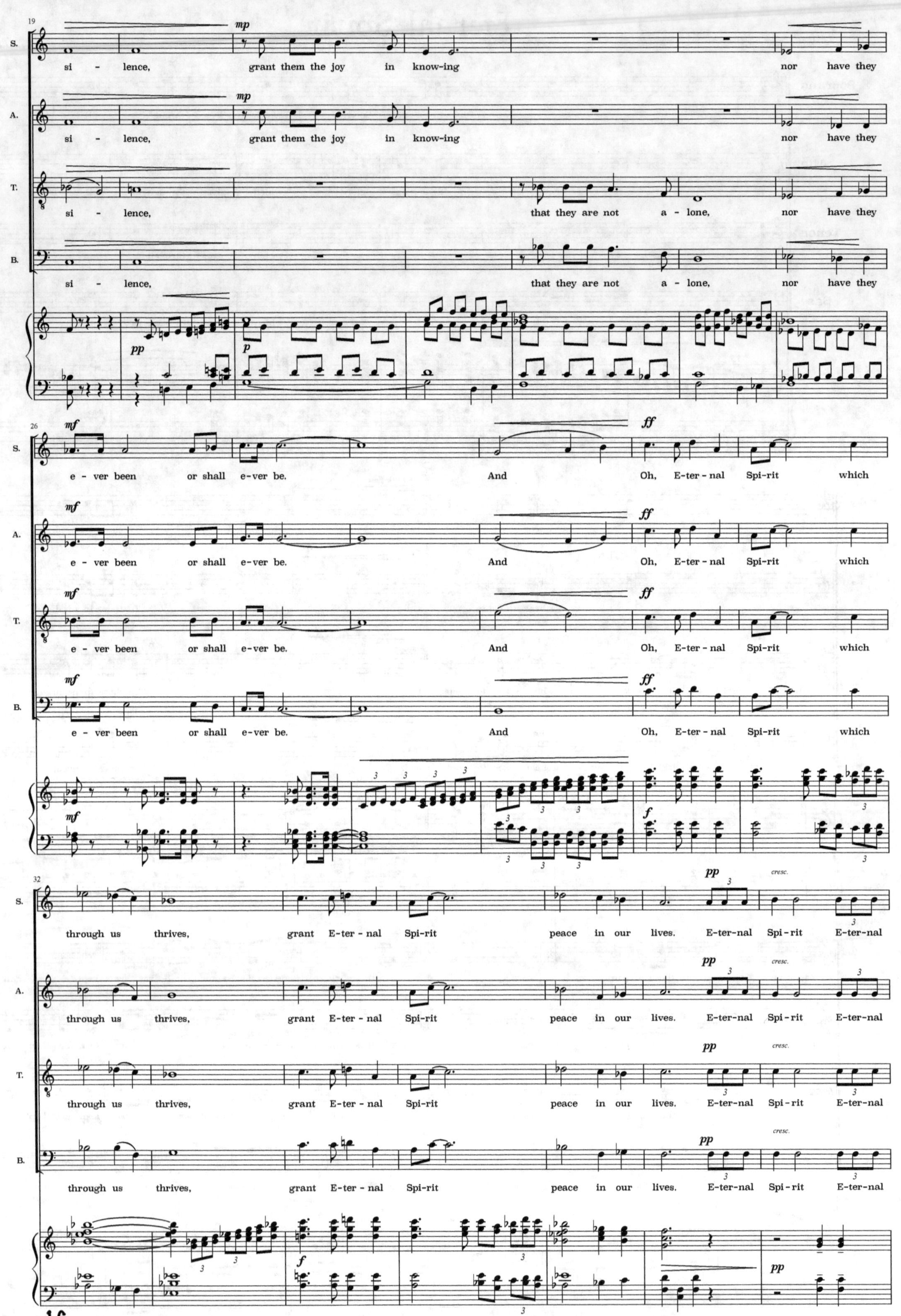
19
S.
A.
T.
B.
mp
si - lence, grant them the joy in know-ing nor have they
si - lence, that they are not a - lone, nor have they
pp
p
26
mf
e - ver been or shall e-ver be. And
ff
Oh, E-ter - nal Spi-rit which
f
32
through us thrives, grant E-ter - nal Spi-rit peace in our lives. E-ter-nal Spi-rit E-ter-nal
pp
cresc.

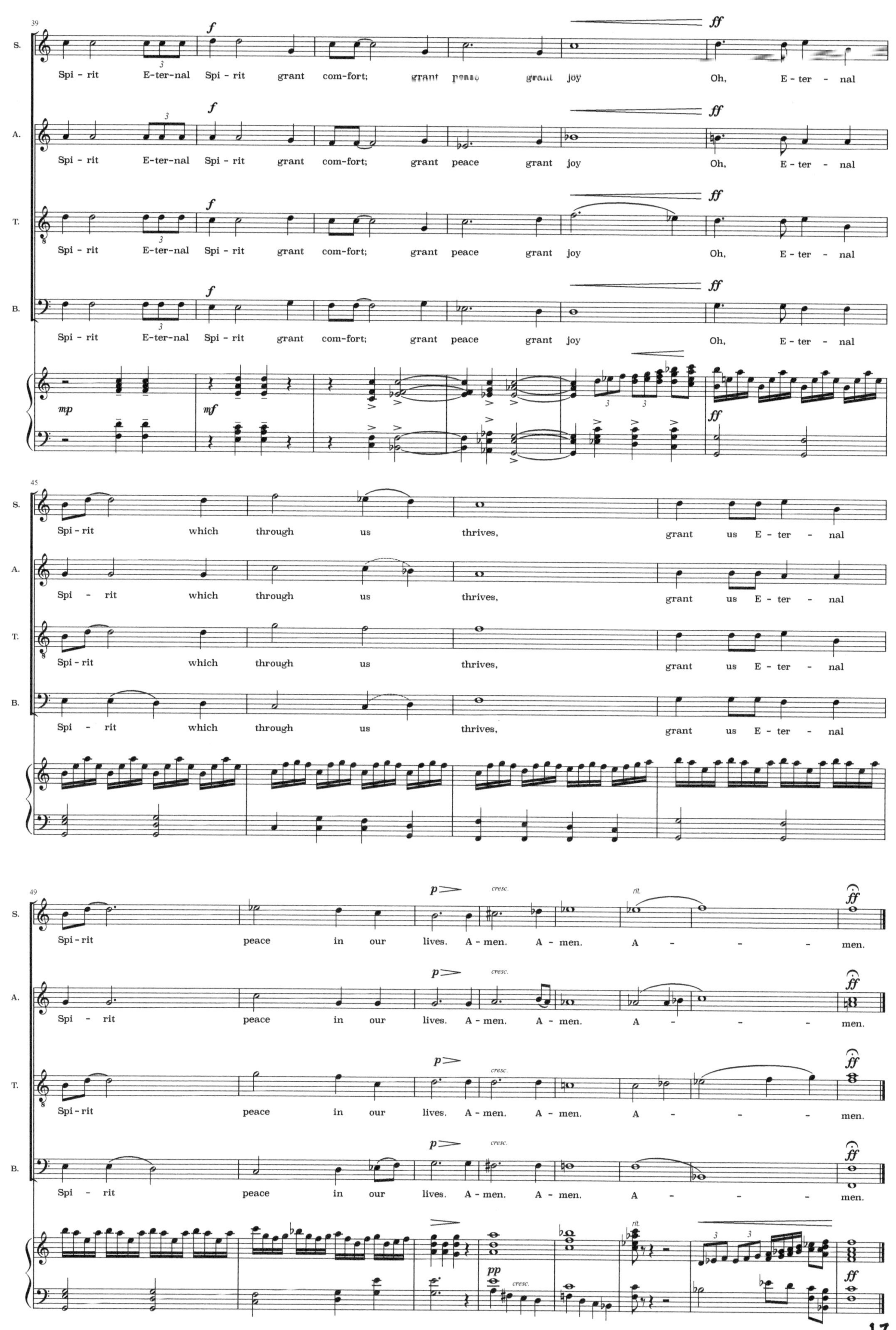
39
S.
A.
T.
B.
f
ff
mp
mf
Spi - rit E-ter-nal Spi - rit grant com-fort; grant peace grant joy Oh, E - ter - nal
45
Spi - rit which through us thrives, grant us E - ter - nal
49
p
cresc.
rit.
pp
Spi - rit peace in our lives. A - men. A - men. A - - - men.

Go Now In Peace

Ken Langer

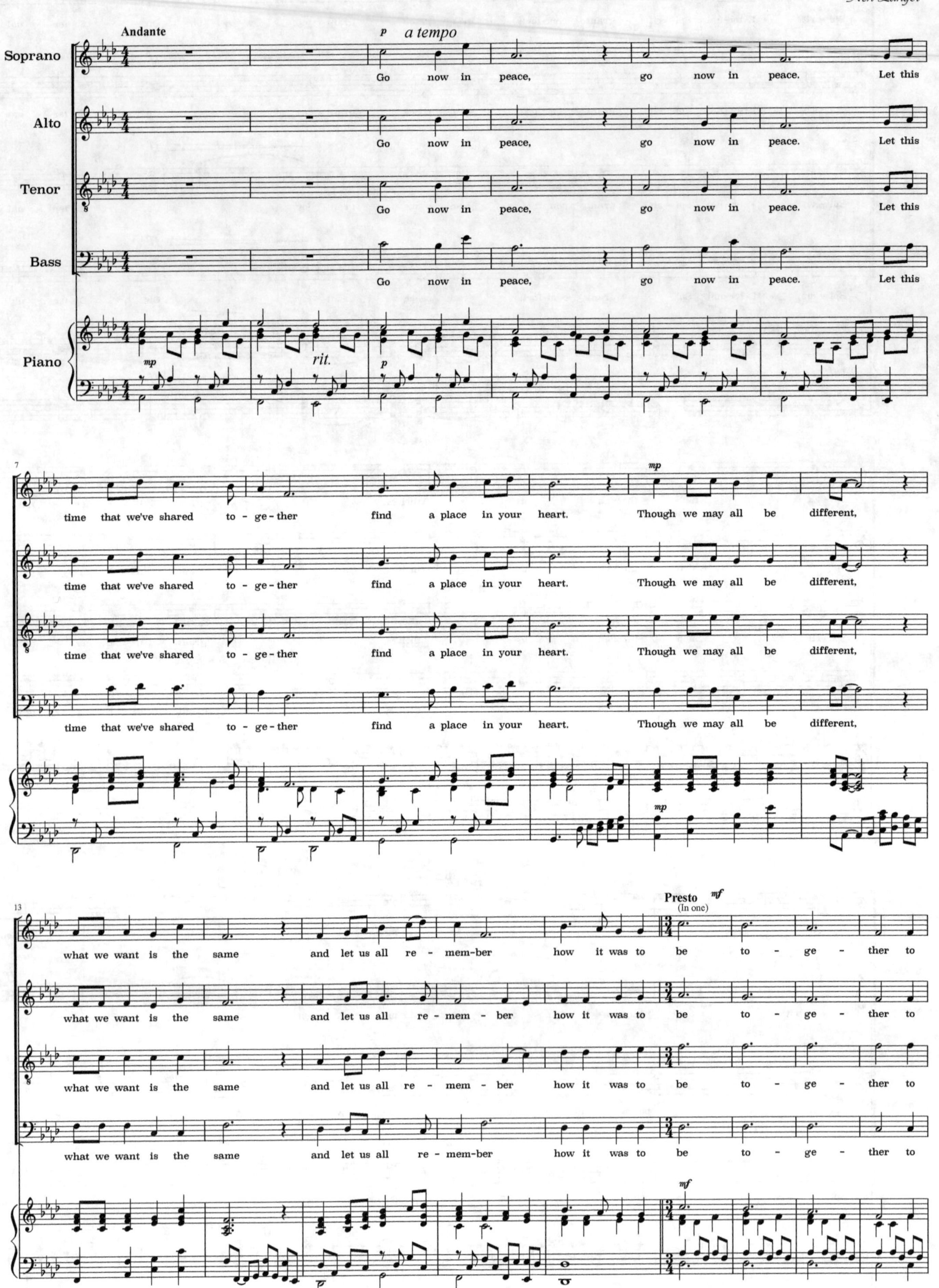

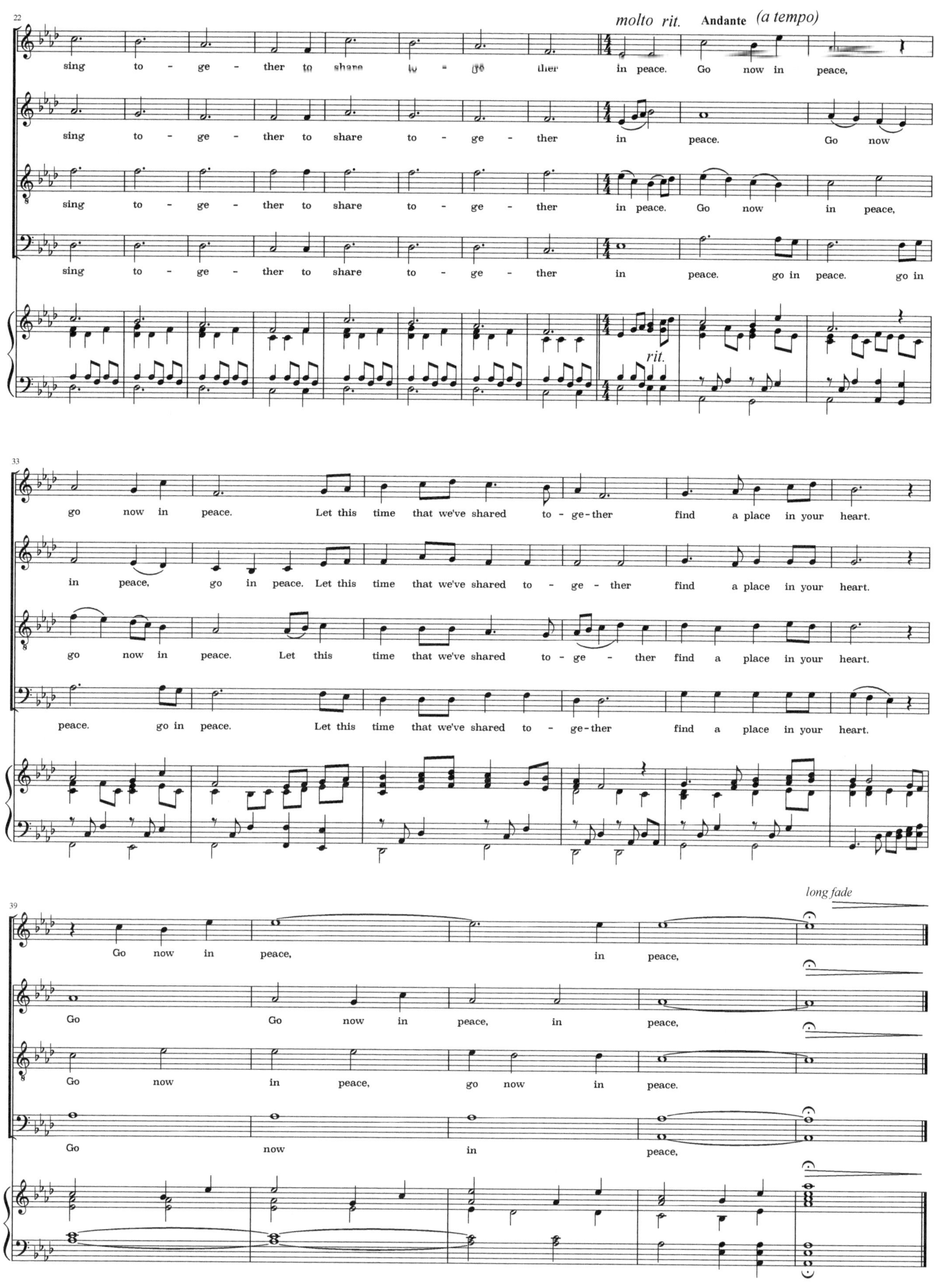
22
molto rit.
Andante
(a tempo)
sing to - ge - ther to
ther in peace. Go now in peace,
sing to - ge - ther to share to - ge - ther in peace. Go now
sing to - ge - ther to share to - ge - ther in peace. Go now in peace,
sing to - ge - ther to share to - ge - ther in peace. go in peace. go in
rit.
33
go now in peace. Let this time that we've shared to - ge - ther find a place in your heart.
in peace, go in peace. Let this time that we've shared to - ge - ther find a place in your heart.
go now in peace. Let this time that we've shared to - ge - ther find a place in your heart.
peace. go in peace. Let this time that we've shared to - ge - ther find a place in your heart.
39
long fade
Go now in peace, in peace,
Go Go now in peace, in peace,
Go now in peace, go now in peace.
Go now in peace,

Hey Yah

the text may be changed
to suit the occasion

Ken Langer

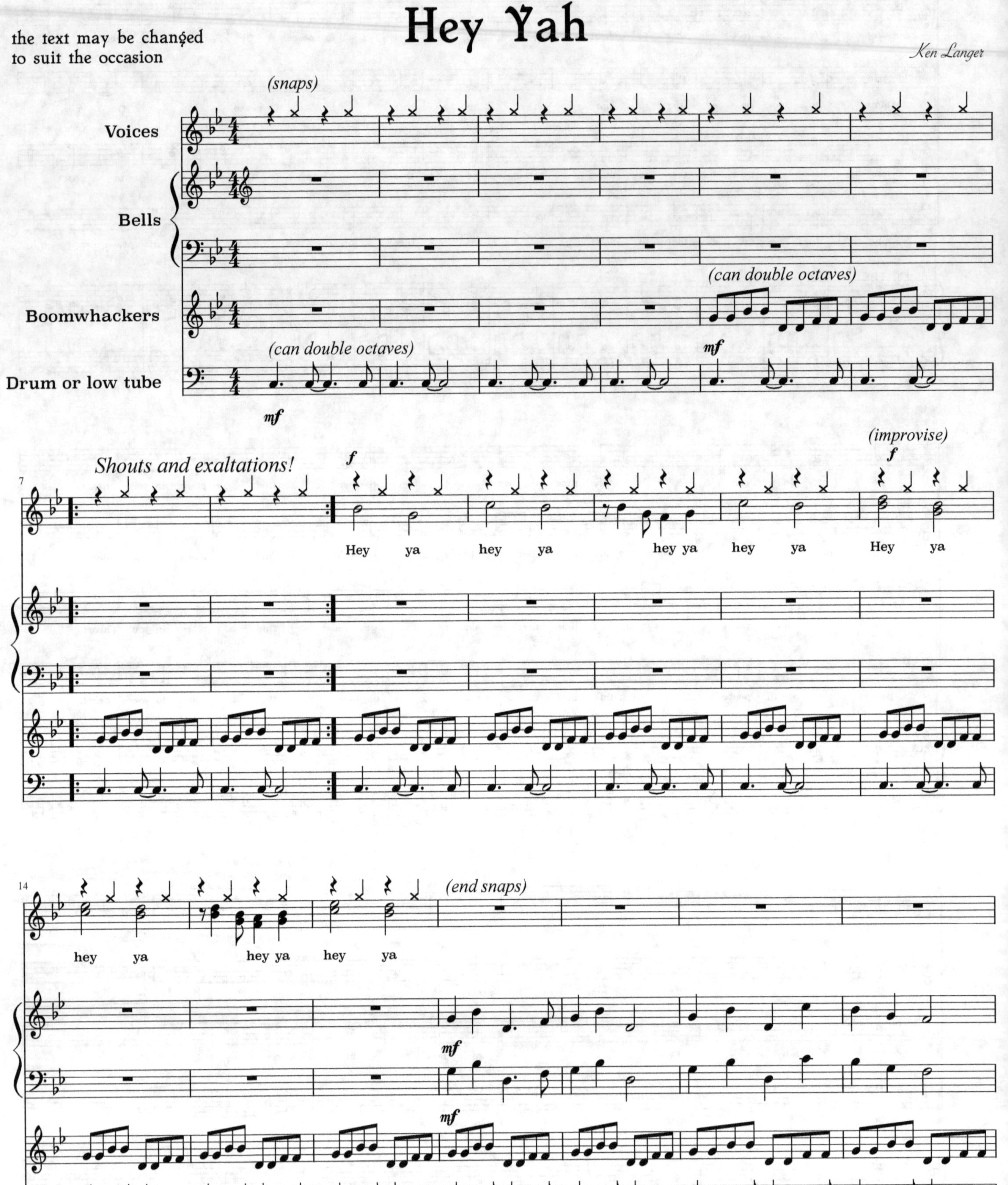

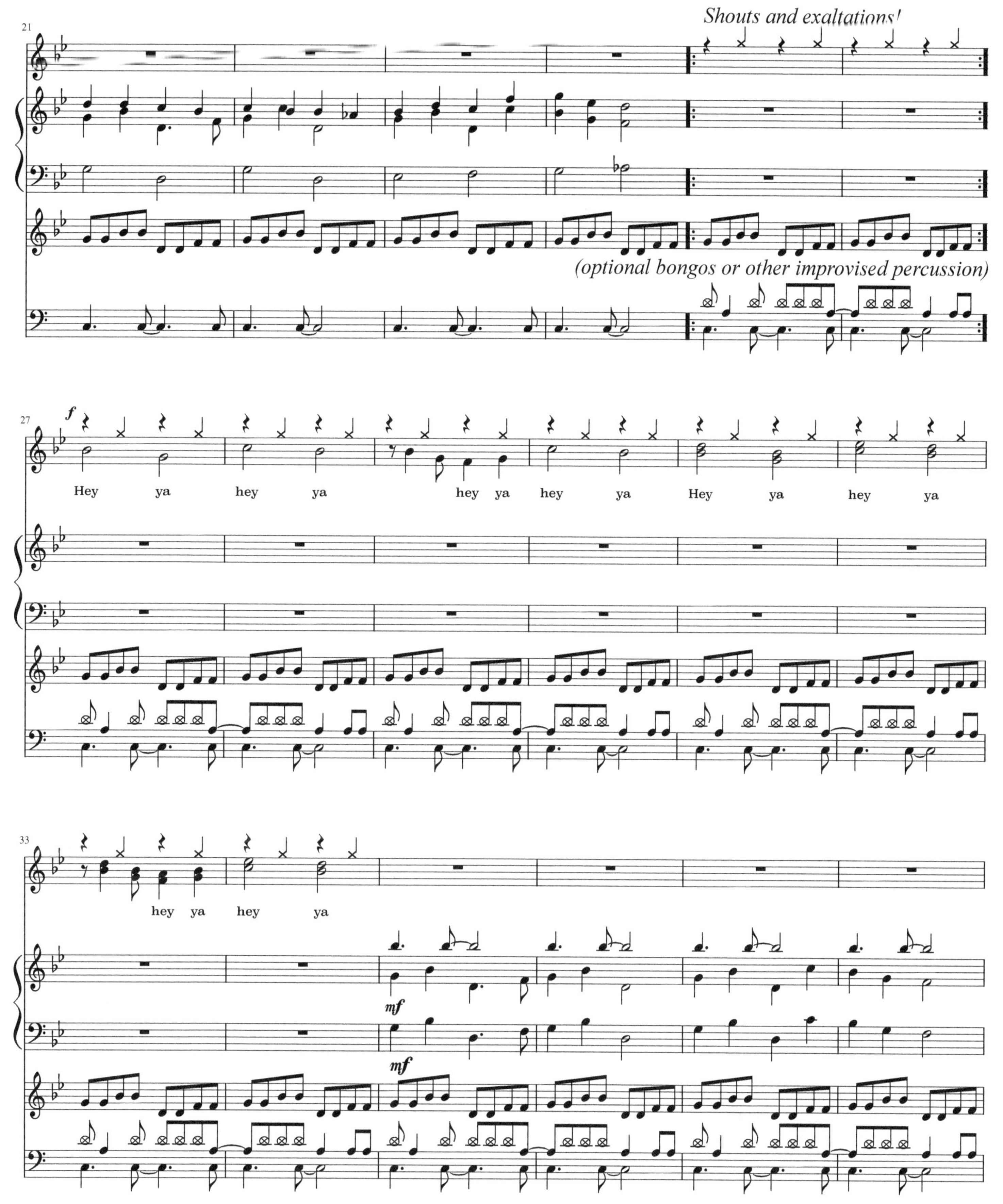
Shouts and exaltations!
Hey ya hey ya hey ya hey ya Hey ya hey ya
hey ya hey ya
(optional bongos or other improvised percussion)

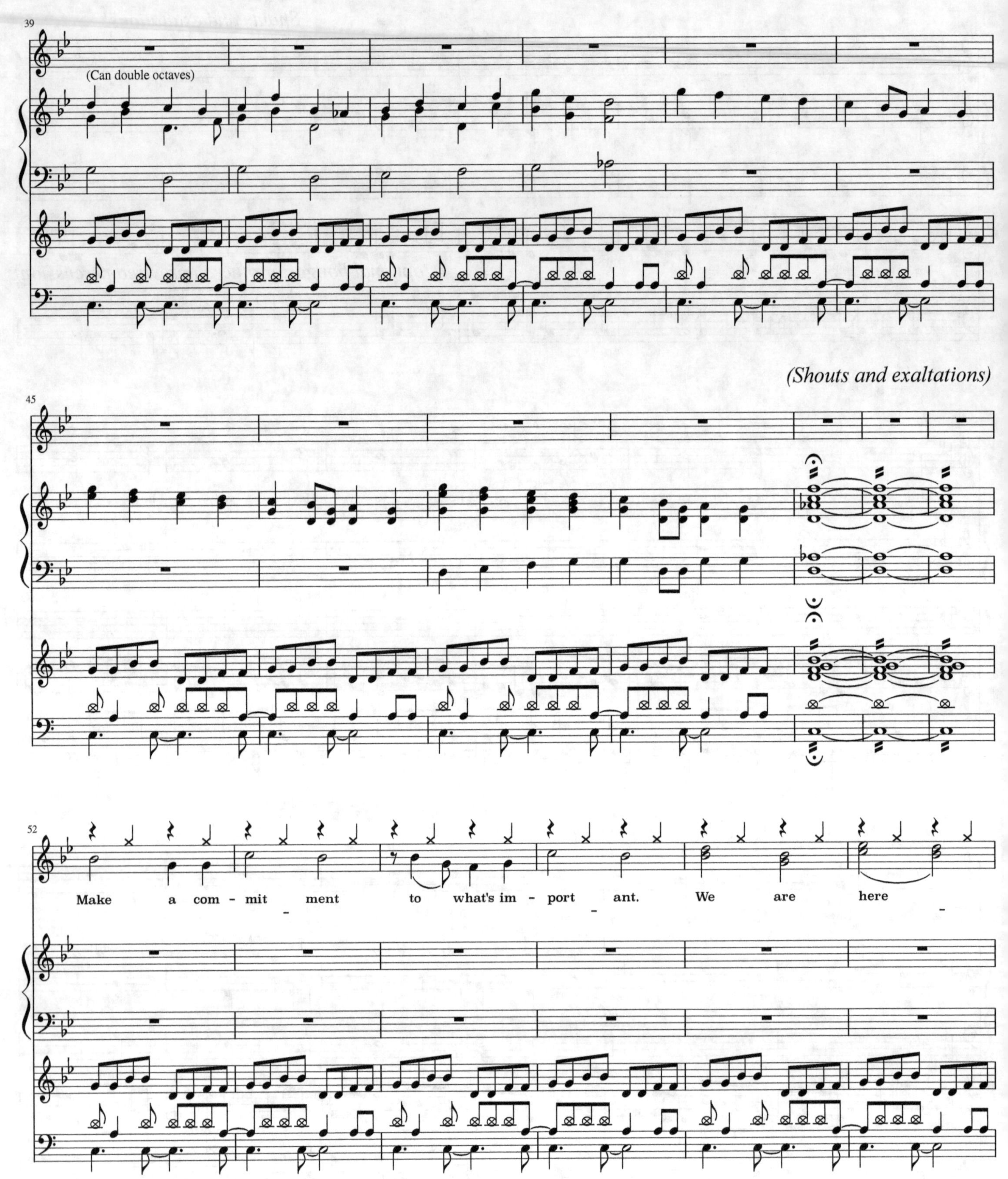

39
(Can double octaves)
(Shouts and exaltations)
45
52
Make a com - mit - ment to what's im - port - ant. We are here -

3

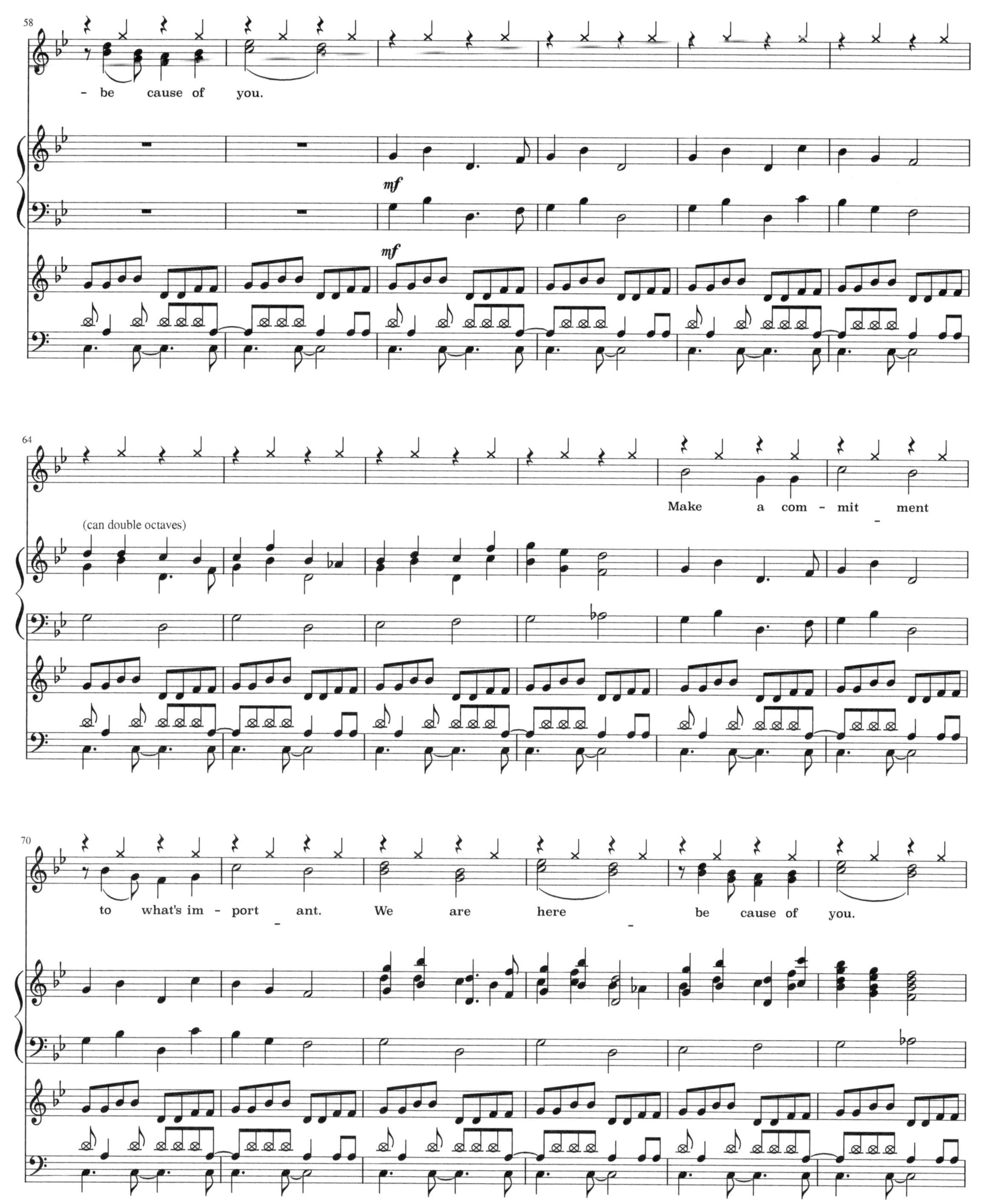
58
be cause of you.
mf
mf
64
(can double octaves)
Make a com - mit - ment
70
to what's im - port ant. We are here be cause of you.

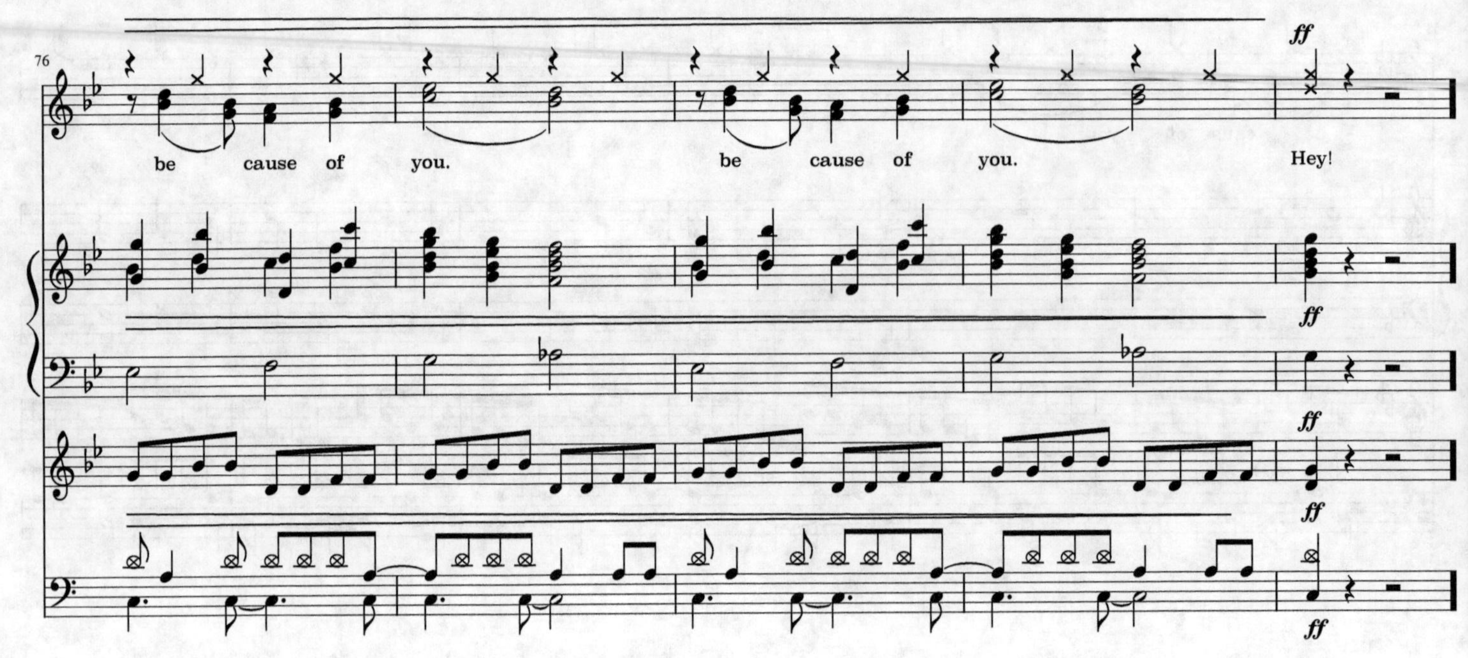
76
ff
be cause of you. be cause of you.
Hey!
ff
ff
ff
ff

I Believe In Love

Ken Langer

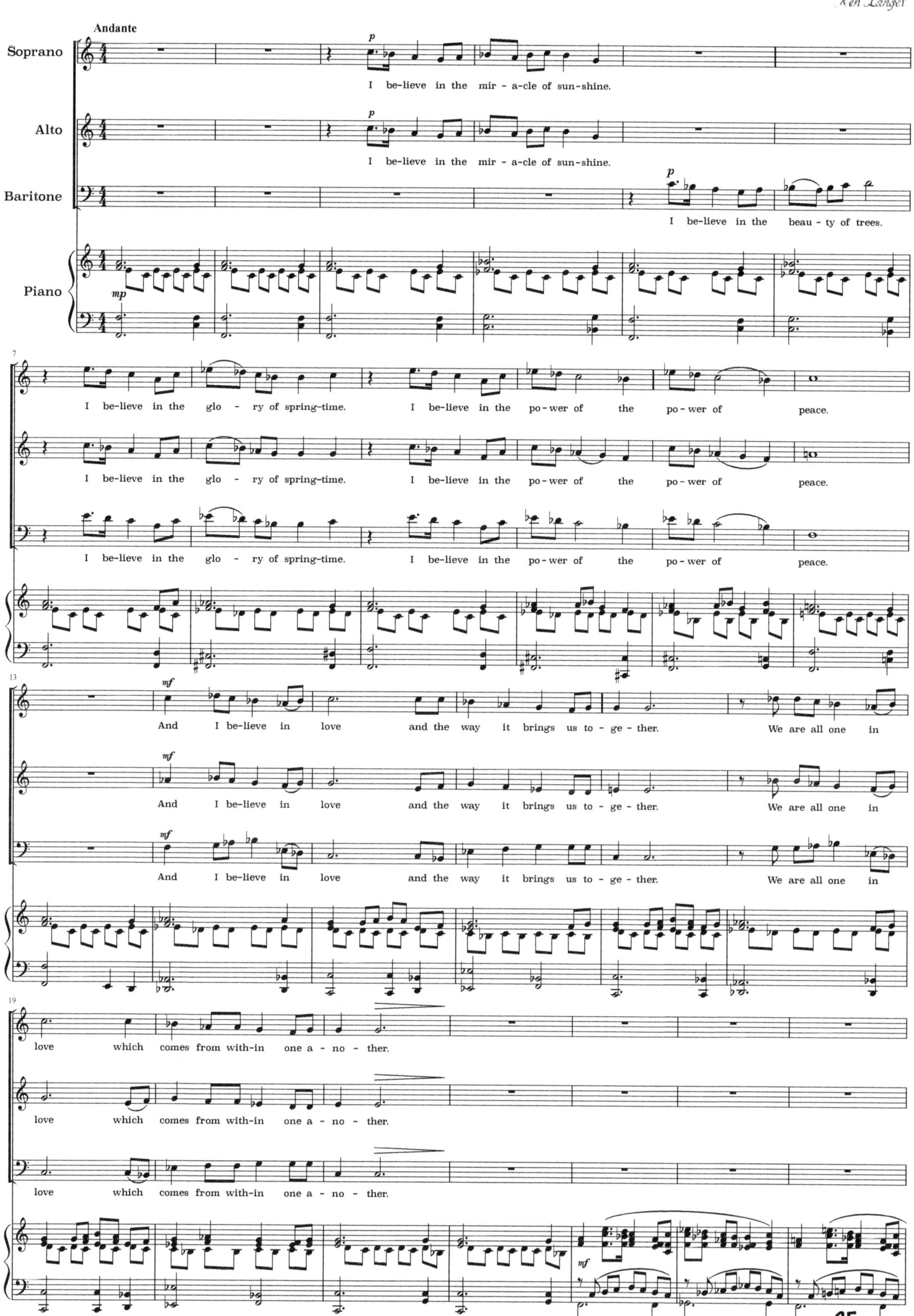

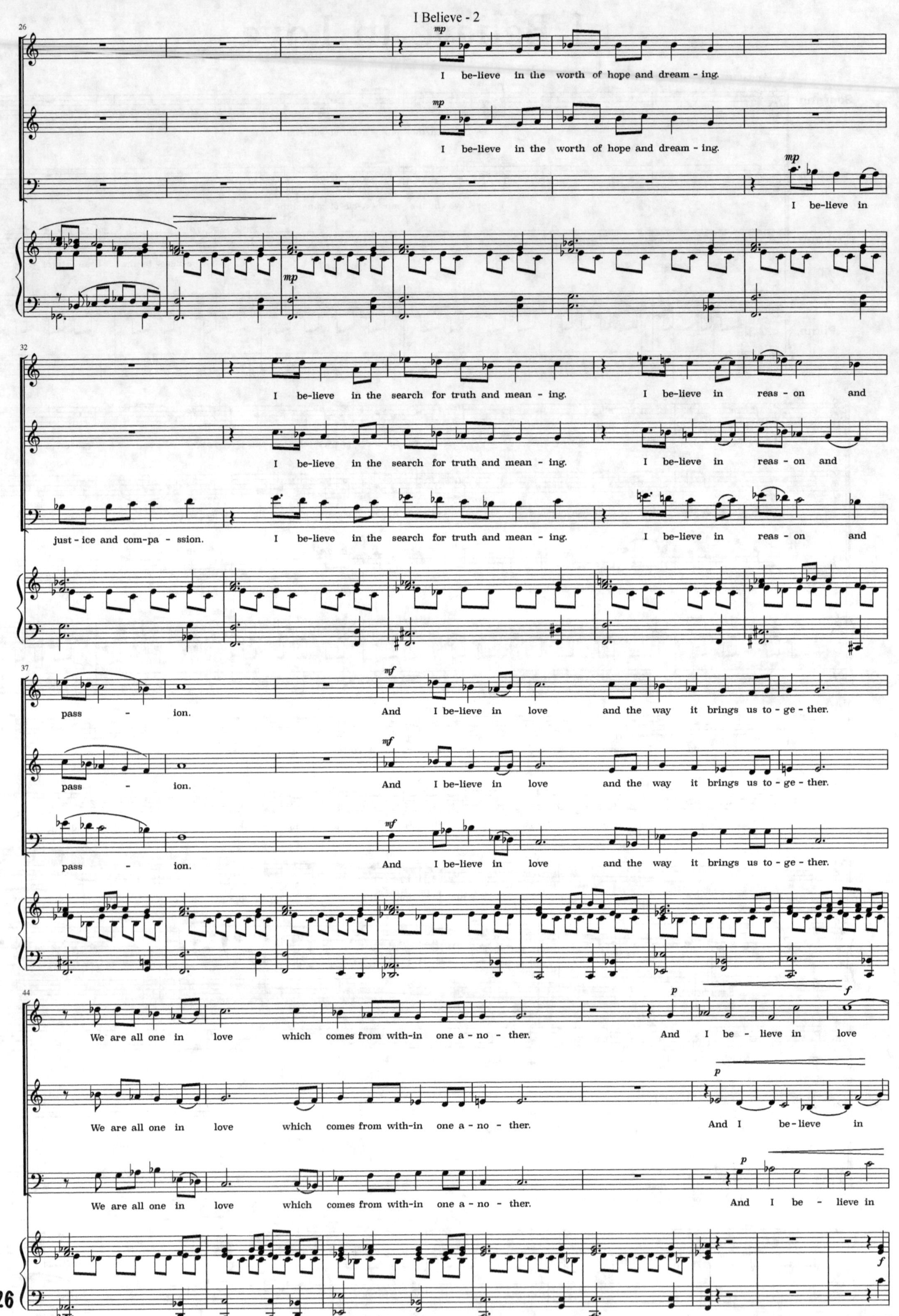
26
mp
I be-lieve in the worth of hope and dream - ing.
mp
I be-lieve in the worth of hope and dream - ing.
mp
I be-lieve in
mp
32
I be-lieve in the search for truth and mean - ing. I be-lieve in reas - on and
I be-lieve in the search for truth and mean - ing. I be-lieve in reas - on and
just - ice and com-pa - ssion. I be-lieve in the search for truth and mean - ing. I be-lieve in reas - on and
37
mf
pass - ion. And I be-lieve in love and the way it brings us to - ge - ther.
mf
pass - ion. And I be-lieve in love and the way it brings us to - ge - ther.
mf
pass - ion. And I be-lieve in love and the way it brings us to - ge - ther.
44
p
f
We are all one in love which comes from with-in one a - no - ther. And I be - lieve in love
p
We are all one in love which comes from with-in one a - no - ther. And I be-lieve in
p
We are all one in love which comes from with-in one a - no - ther. And I be - lieve in
f

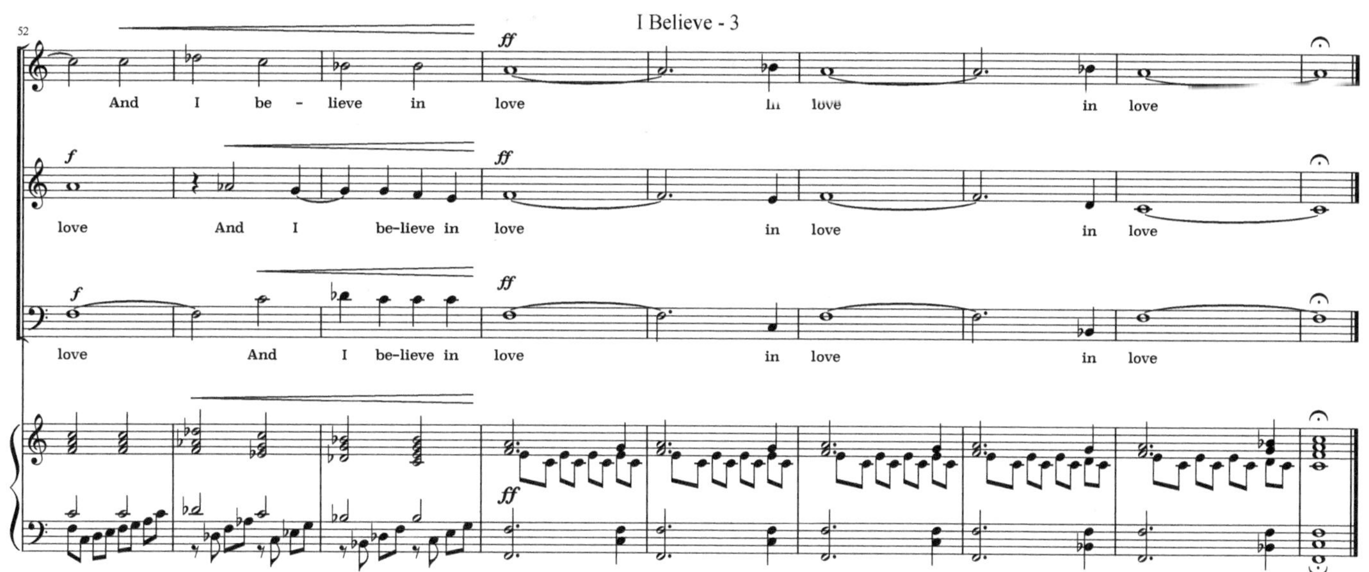
52
ff
And
I
be
-
lieve
in
love
in
love
in
love
f
love
And
I
be-lieve
in
love
in
love
in
love
f
love
And
I
be-lieve
in
love
in
love
in
love
ff

In Dream Time

Ken Langer

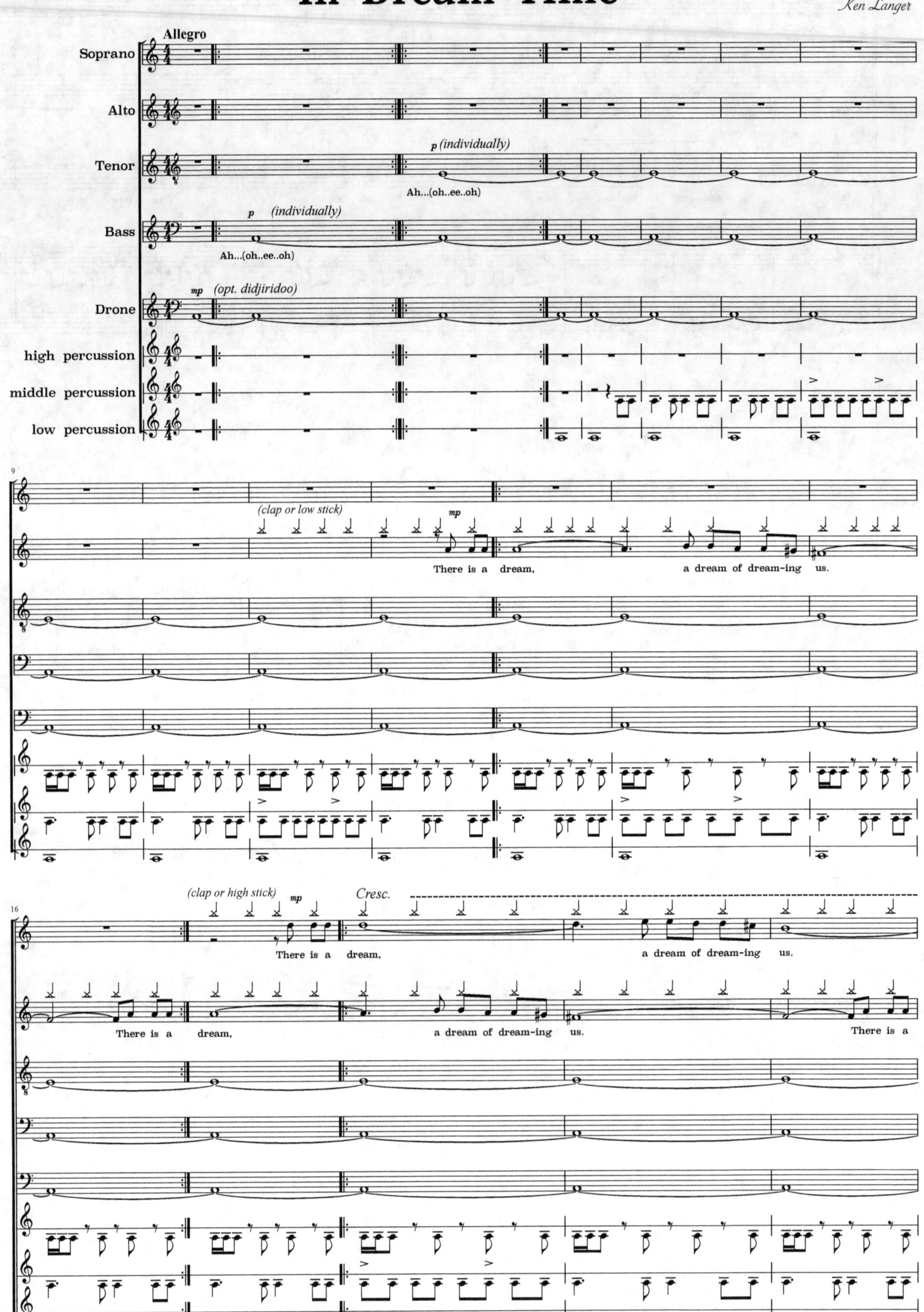

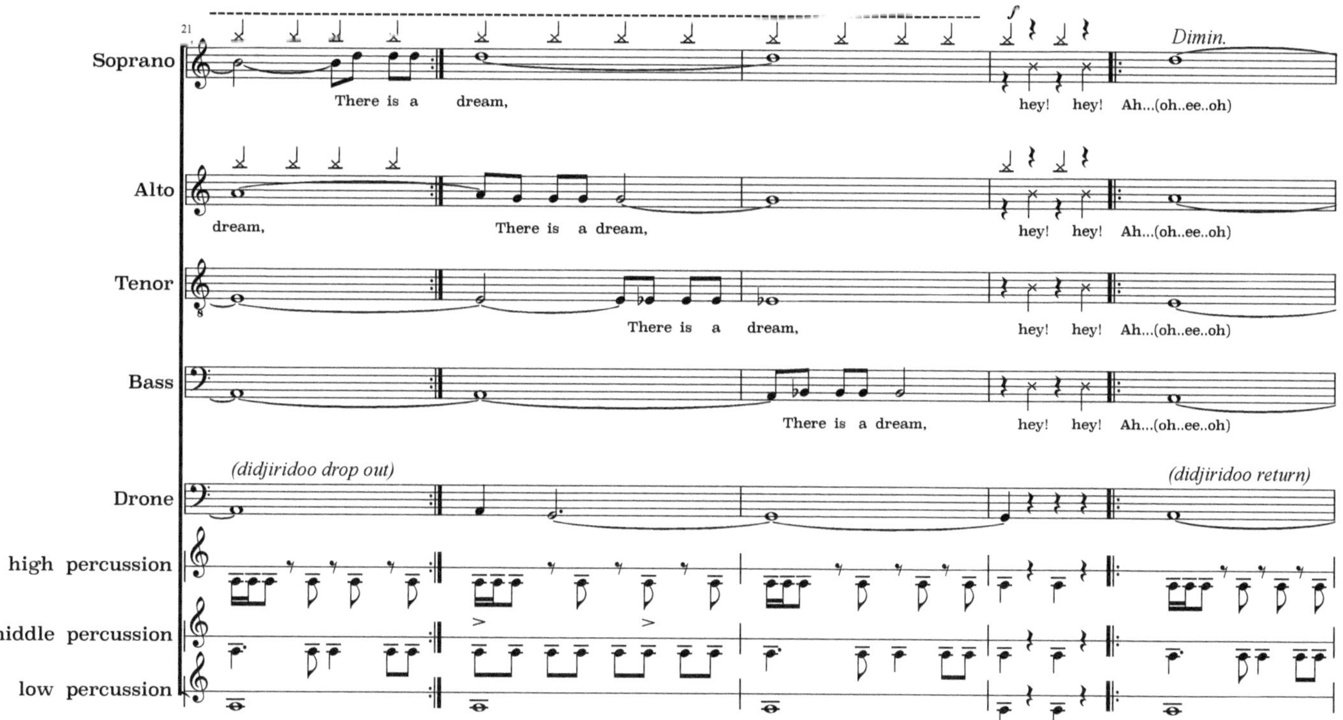

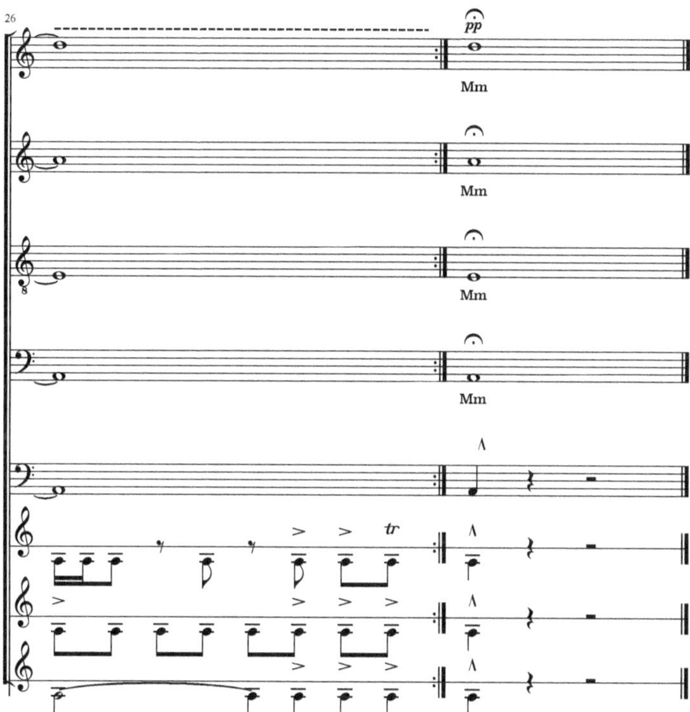

Performance Note: When the voices are directed to sing "Ah...(oh..ee..oh)" they should attempt to imitate the sound of the didjeridoo each at their own pace to create a vocal montage.

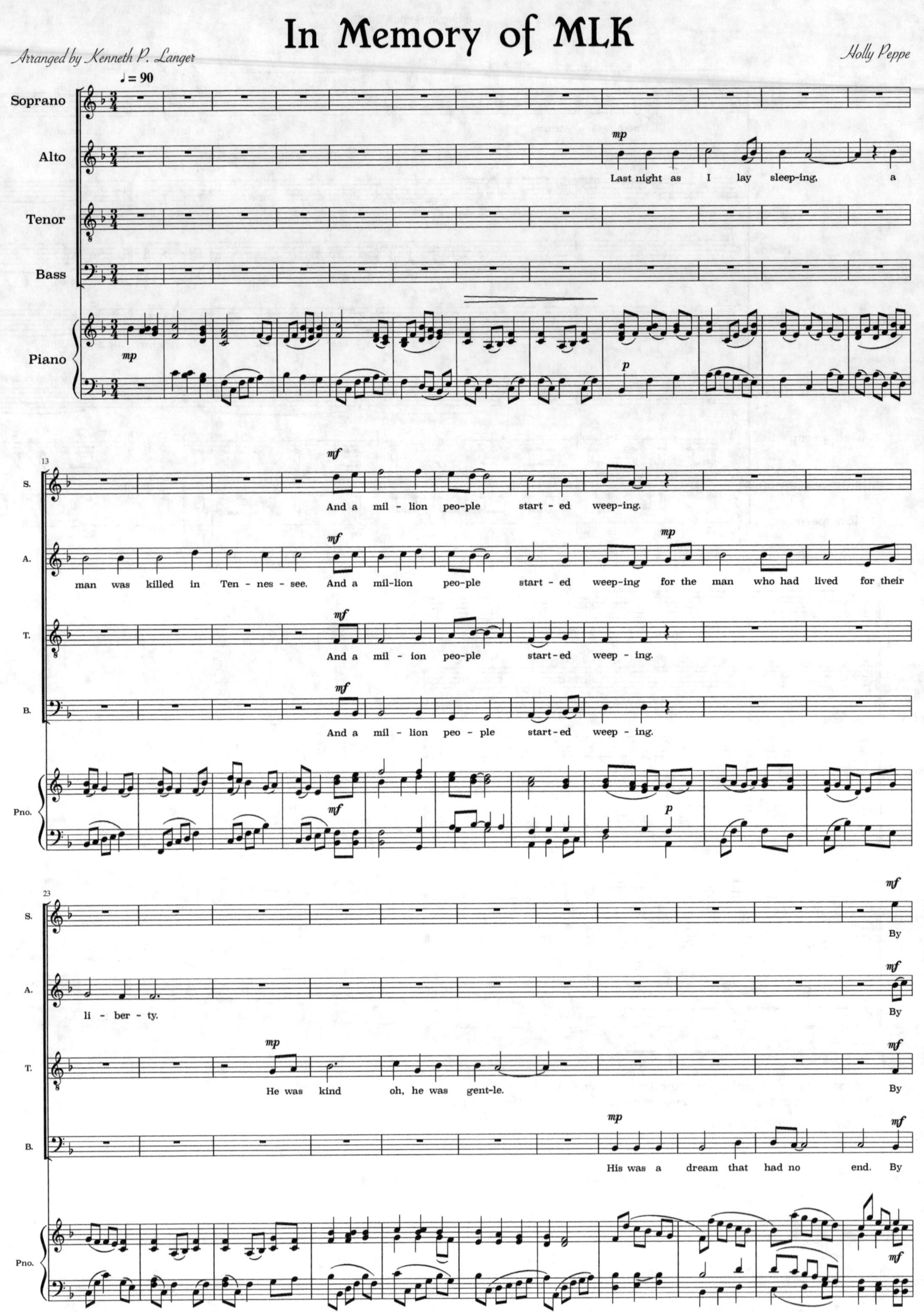

In Memory of MLK
Arranged by Kenneth P. Langer
Holly Peppe
♩ = 90
Soprano
Alto
Tenor
Bass
Piano
mp
p
mf
Last night as I lay sleep-ing, a man was killed in Ten-nes-see. And a mil-lion peo-ple start-ed weep-ing for the man who had lived for their li-ber-ty.
And a mil-lion peo-ple start-ed weep-ing.
He was kind oh, he was gent-le.
His was a dream that had no end.
By
S.
A.
T.
B.
Pno.

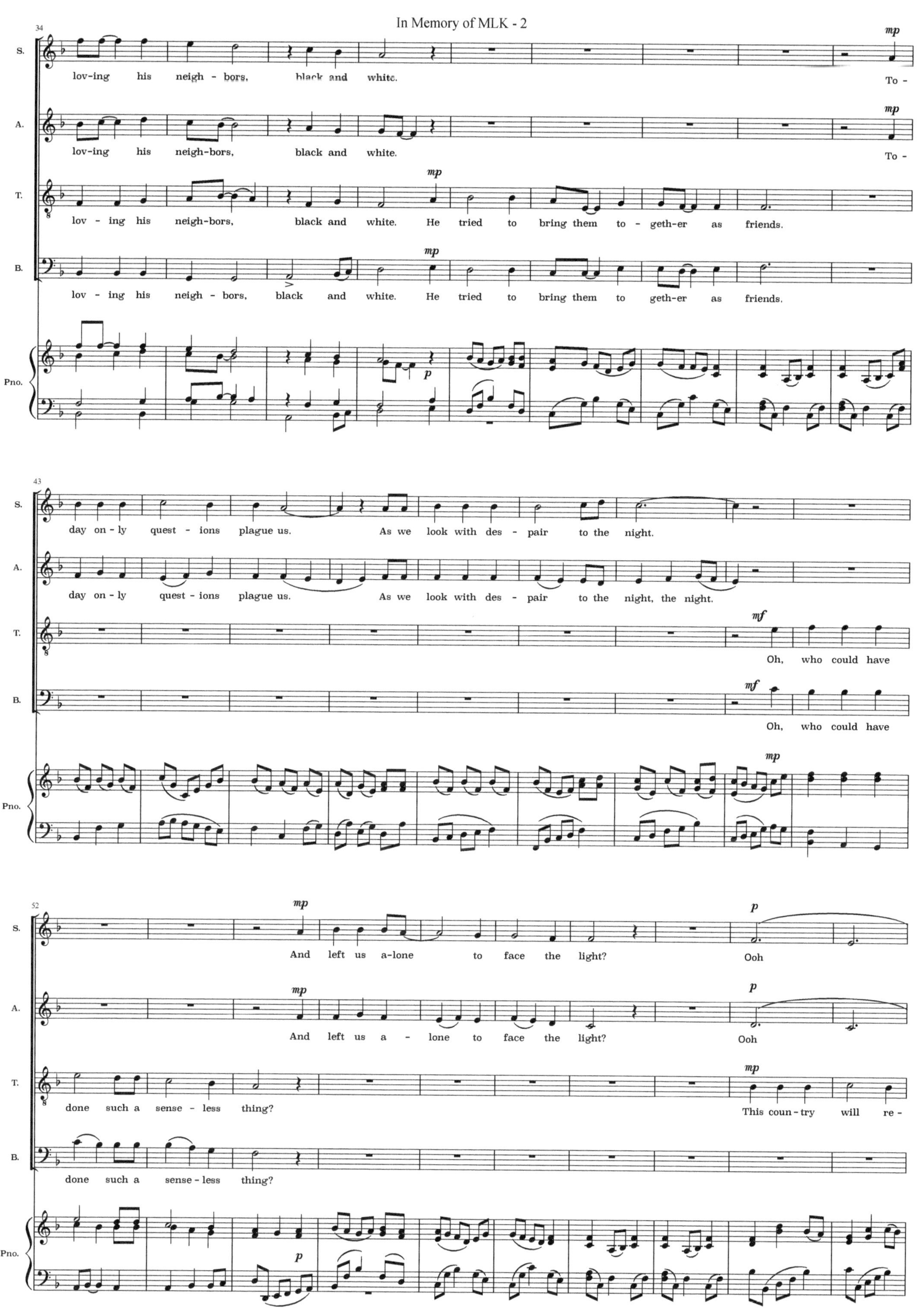
34
S.
lov-ing his neigh - bors, black and white. To -
A.
lov-ing his neigh-bors, black and white. To -
T.
lov - ing his neigh-bors, black and white. He tried to bring them to - geth-er as friends.
B.
lov - ing his neigh - bors, black and white. He tried to bring them to geth-er as friends.
Pno.
43
S.
day on - ly quest - ions plague us. As we look with des - pair to the night.
A.
day on - ly quest - ions plague us. As we look with des - pair to the night, the night.
T.
Oh, who could have
B.
Oh, who could have
Pno.
52
S.
And left us a-lone to face the light? Ooh
A.
And left us a - lone to face the light? Ooh
T.
done such a sense - less thing? This coun - try will re -
B.
done such a sense - less thing?
Pno.

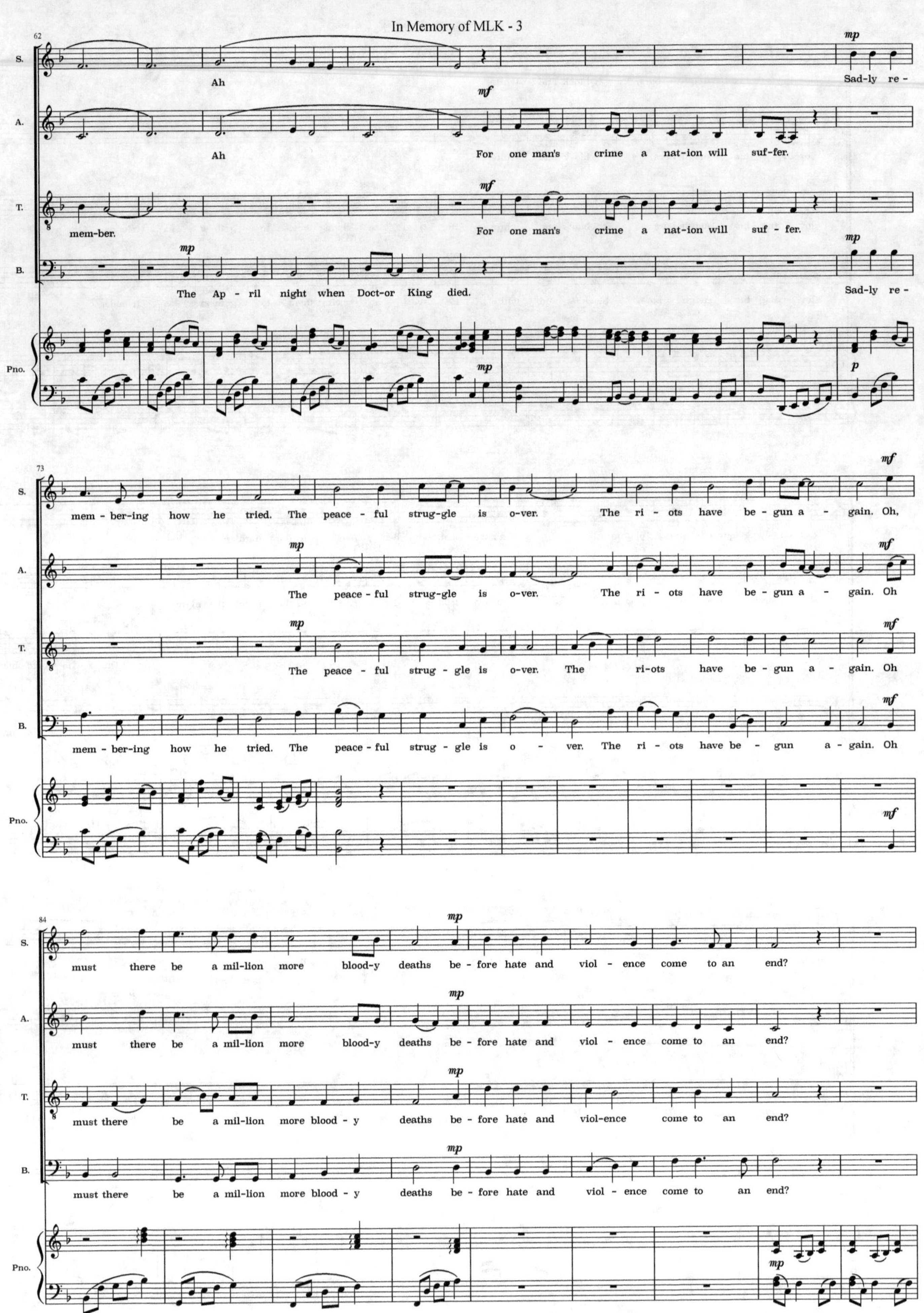
62
S.
A.
T.
B.
Pno.
mp
mf
p
Ah
Sad-ly re-
Ah
For one man's crime a nat-ion will suf-fer.
mem-ber.
For one man's crime a nat-ion will suf-fer.
The Ap-ril night when Doct-or King died.
Sad-ly re-
73
mem-ber-ing how he tried. The peace-ful strug-gle is o-ver. The ri-ots have be-gun a-gain. Oh,
The peace-ful strug-gle is o-ver. The ri-ots have be-gun a-gain. Oh
The peace-ful strug-gle is o-ver. The ri-ots have be-gun a-gain. Oh
mem-ber-ing how he tried. The peace-ful strug-gle is o-ver. The ri-ots have be-gun a-gain. Oh
84
must there be a mil-lion more blood-y deaths be-fore hate and viol-ence come to an end?
must there be a mil-lion more blood-y deaths be-fore hate and viol-ence come to an end?
must there be a mil-lion more blood-y deaths be-fore hate and viol-ence come to an end?
must there be a mil-lion more blood-y deaths be-fore hate and viol-ence come to an end?

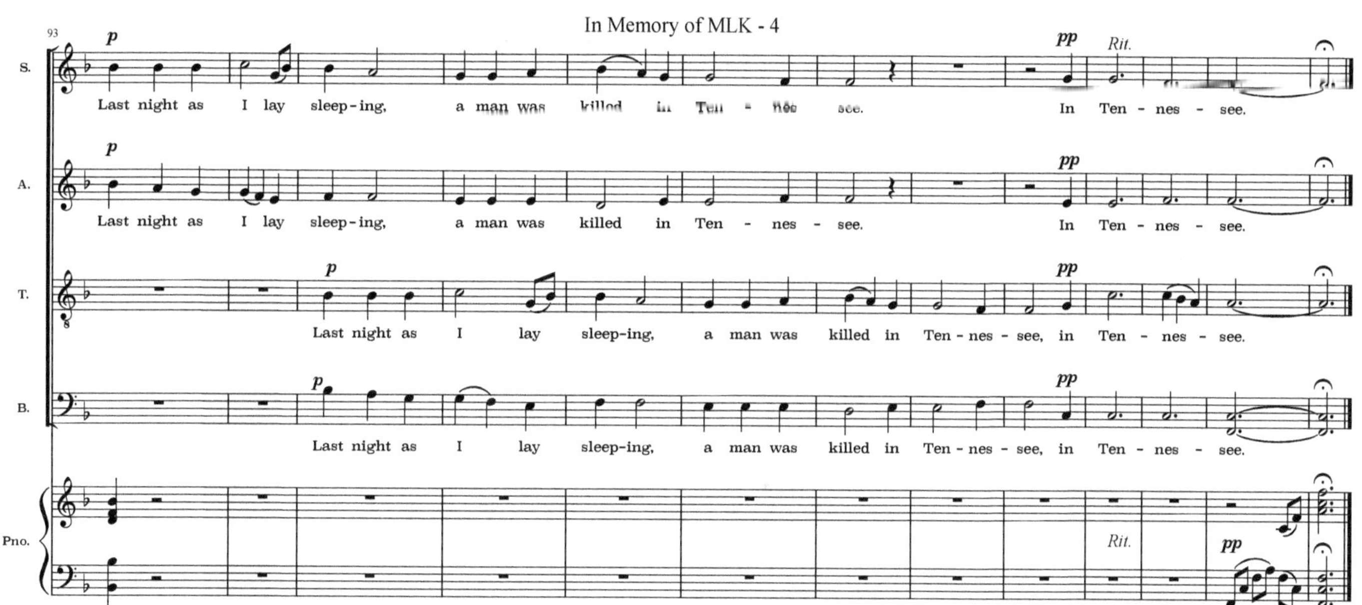
93
S.
Last night as I lay sleep-ing, a man was killed in Ten - nes - see. In Ten - nes - see.
A.
Last night as I lay sleep-ing, a man was killed in Ten - nes - see. In Ten - nes - see.
T.
Last night as I lay sleep-ing, a man was killed in Ten - nes - see, in Ten - nes - see.
B.
Last night as I lay sleep-ing, a man was killed in Ten - nes - see, in Ten - nes - see.
Pno.
Rit.

Invocation

Ken Langer

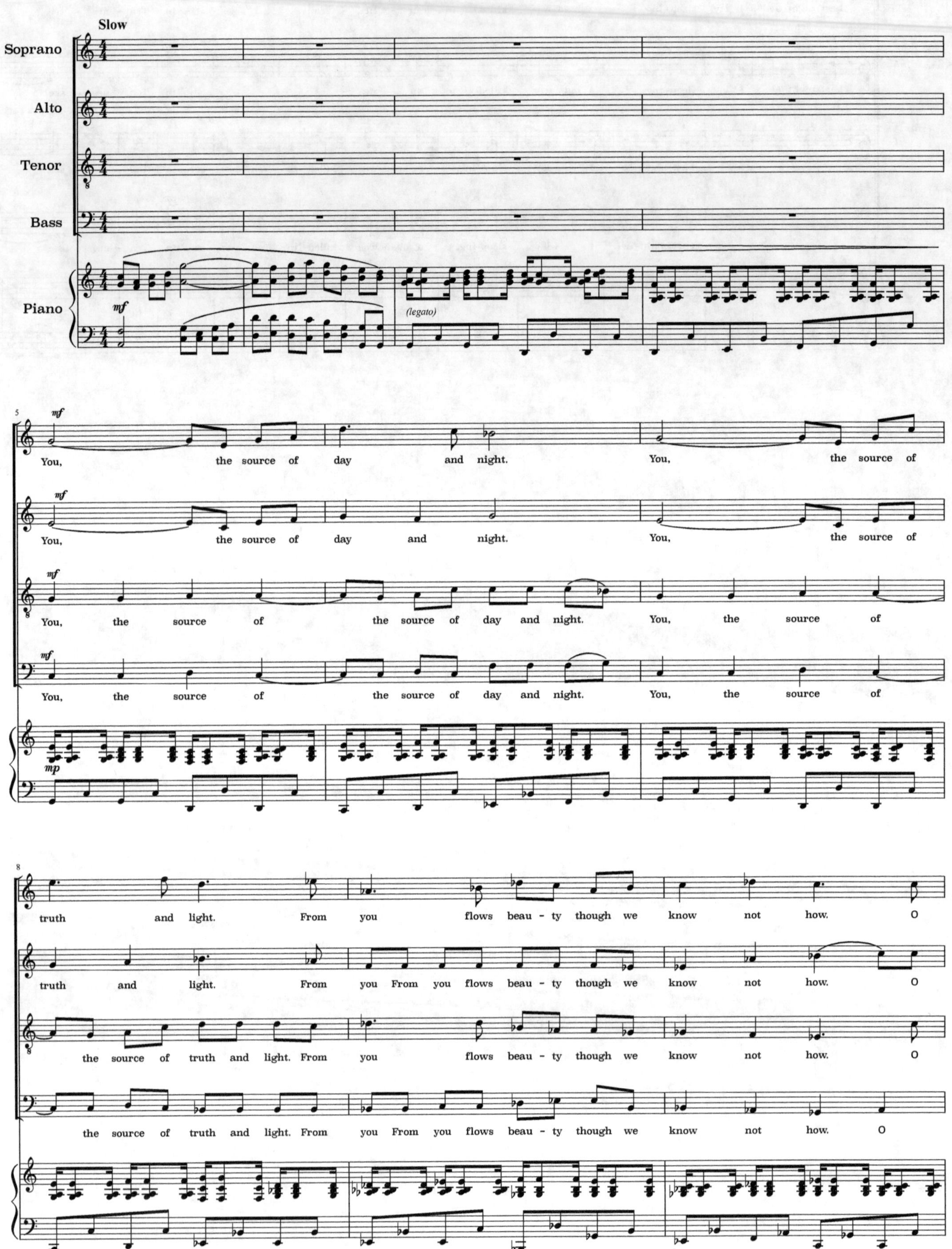

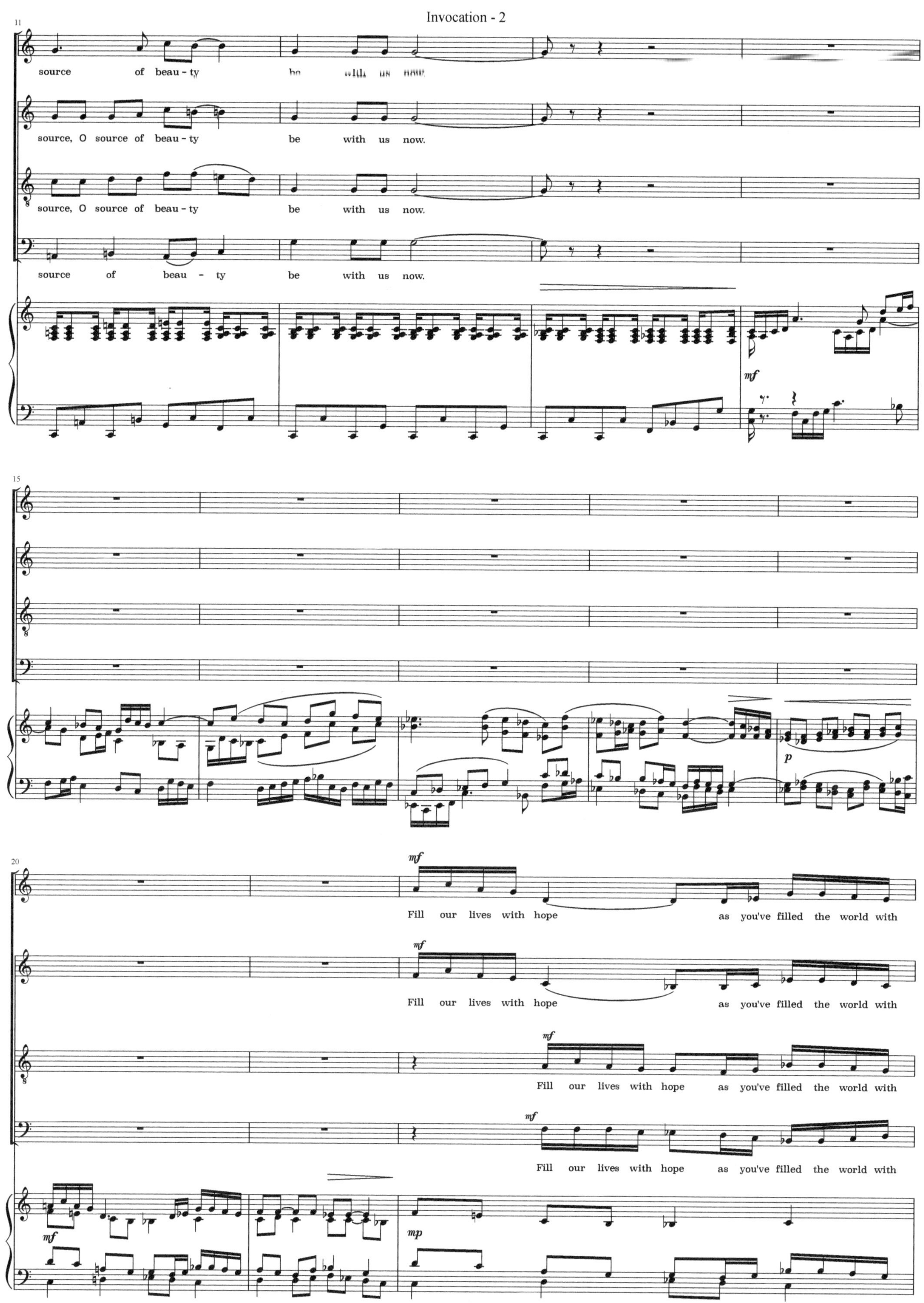
11
source of beau - ty be with us now.
source, O source of beau - ty be with us now.
source, O source of beau - ty be with us now.
source of beau - ty be with us now.
mf
15
p
20
mf
Fill our lives with hope as you've filled the world with
mf
Fill our lives with hope as you've filled the world with
mf
Fill our lives with hope as you've filled the world with
mf
Fill our lives with hope as you've filled the world with
mf
mp

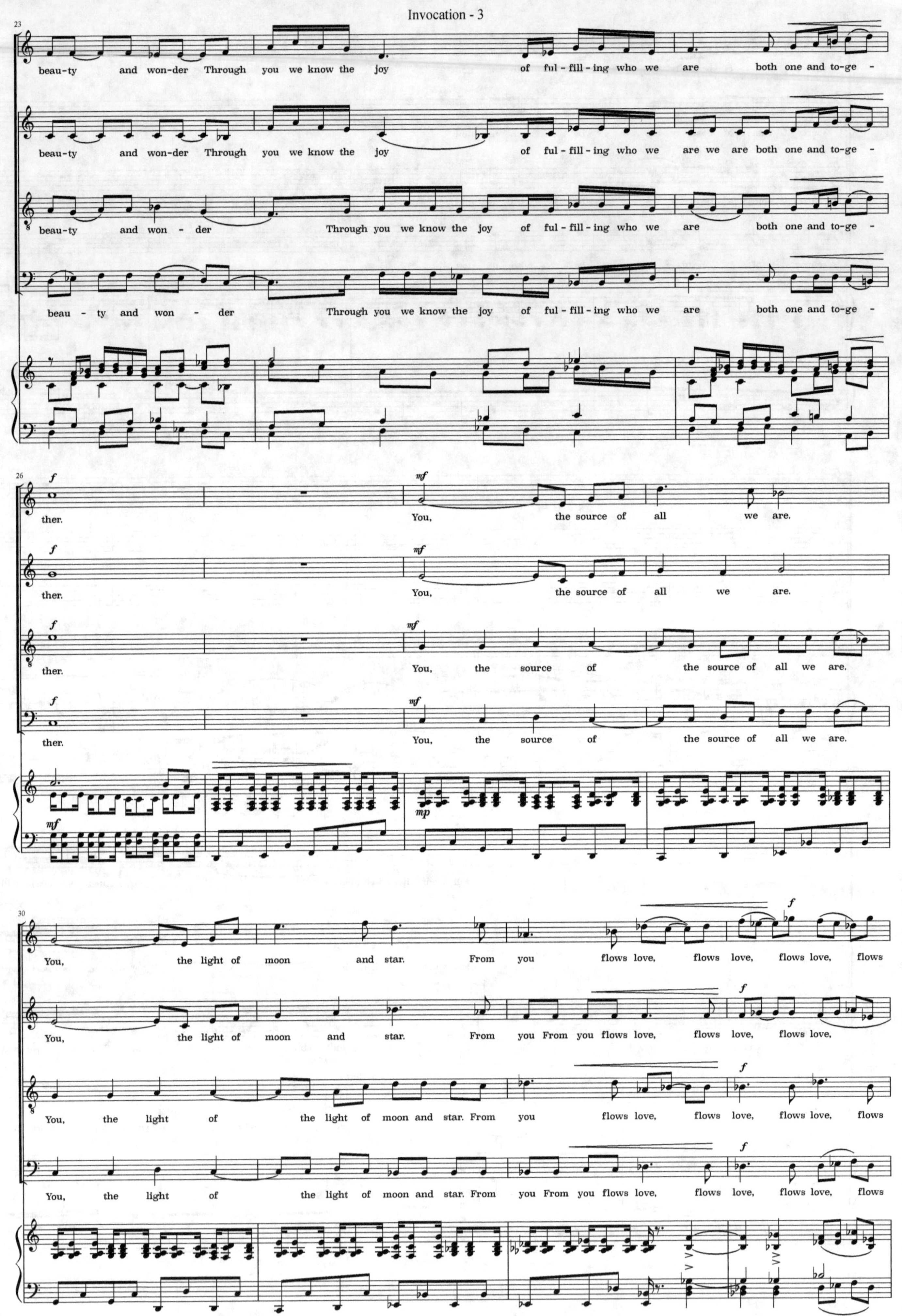
23
beau-ty and won-der Through you we know the joy of ful-fill-ing who we are both one and to-ge -
beau-ty and won-der Through you we know the joy of ful-fill-ing who we are we are both one and to-ge -
beau-ty and won - der Through you we know the joy of ful-fill-ing who we are both one and to-ge -
beau - ty and won - der Through you we know the joy of ful-fill-ing who we are both one and to-ge -
26
f
ther. mf You, the source of all we are.
ther. mf You, the source of all we are.
ther. mf You, the source of the source of all we are.
ther. mf You, the source of the source of all we are.
mf
mp
30
You, the light of moon and star. From you flows love, f flows love, flows love, flows
You, the light of moon and star. From you From you flows love, f flows love, flows love,
You, the light of the light of moon and star. From you flows love, f flows love, flows love, flows
You, the light of the light of moon and star. From you From you flows love, f flows love, flows love, flows

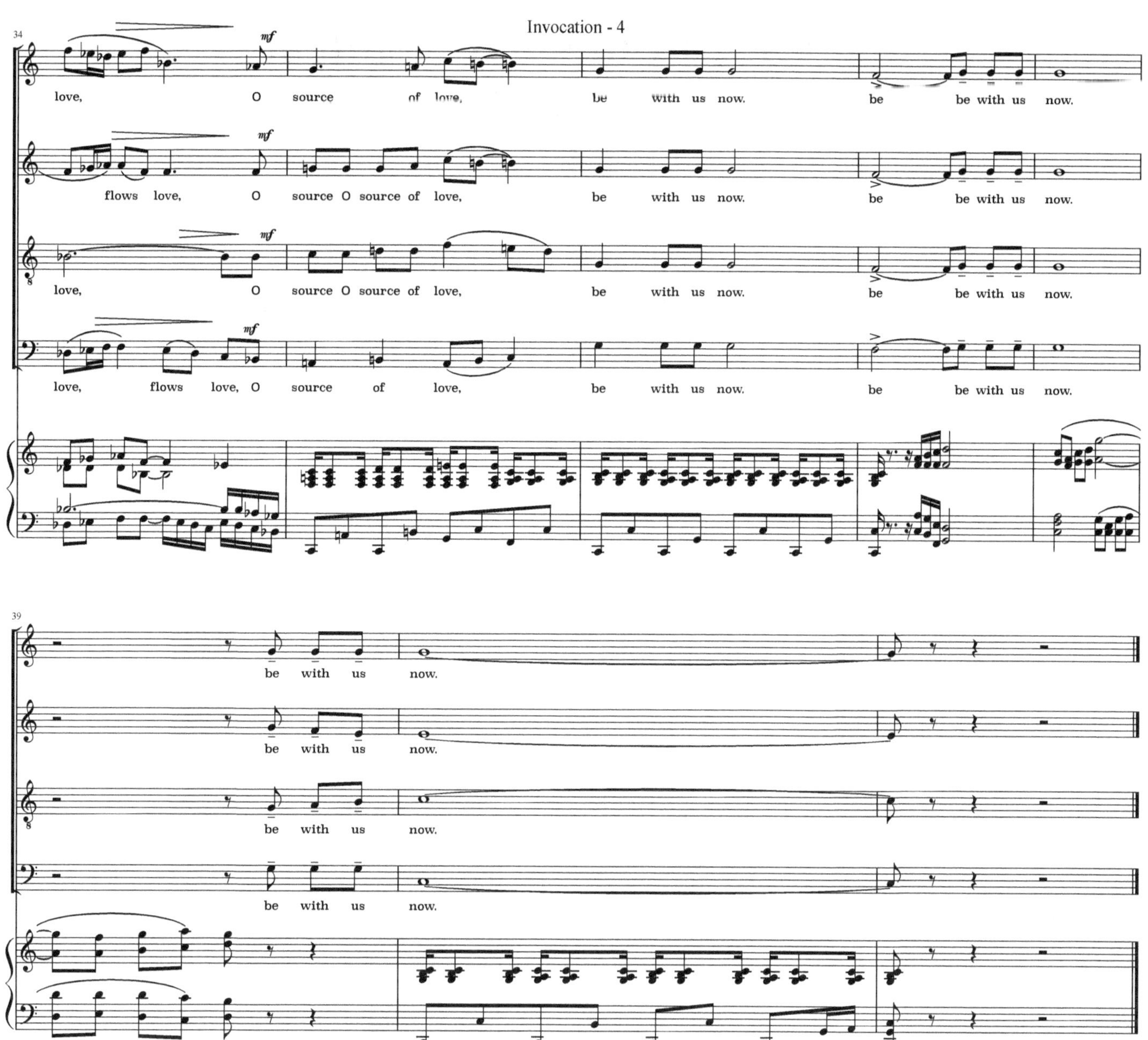
34
mf
love, O source of love, be with us now. be be with us now.
mf
flows love, O source O source of love, be with us now. be be with us now.
mf
love, O source O source of love, be with us now. be be with us now.
mf
love, flows love, O source of love, be with us now. be be with us now.
39
be with us now.
be with us now.
be with us now.
be with us now.

Peace Comes From Silence

Ken Langer

This work was written on the 4th anniversary of the Iraq War (March 2007). In it, I wanted to express the sorrow of all countries involved in the war who have lost children and relatives. The piece includes some unusual performance ideas. In the first two measures, the choir is asked to sing the shown three notes (E, F, and G with an emphasis on E) not together as it appears in the music. Instead, the choir should hum the E and move briefly to the other two notes on an individual basis. The rhythm should be done freely. It might be even more effective if the choir actually started doing this as they move to their singing positions. The effect should be that the sound starts quietly and mysteriously rather than as a directed opening. The first two measures and the effect of the mysterious voices should continue until the director cues measure 3 after which the piece is conducted as normal. The ending should have the same mysterious effect as voices slowly are asked to do the same effect done in the first 2 measures. At the end, voices should be allowed to slowly drop out. If this could be done without the director actually conducting the ending, it would be more effective.

The beginning should build slowly and carefully to measure 28 which should then be done forcefully. The remainder of the piece should feel like a gradual release of that force all the way to the end.

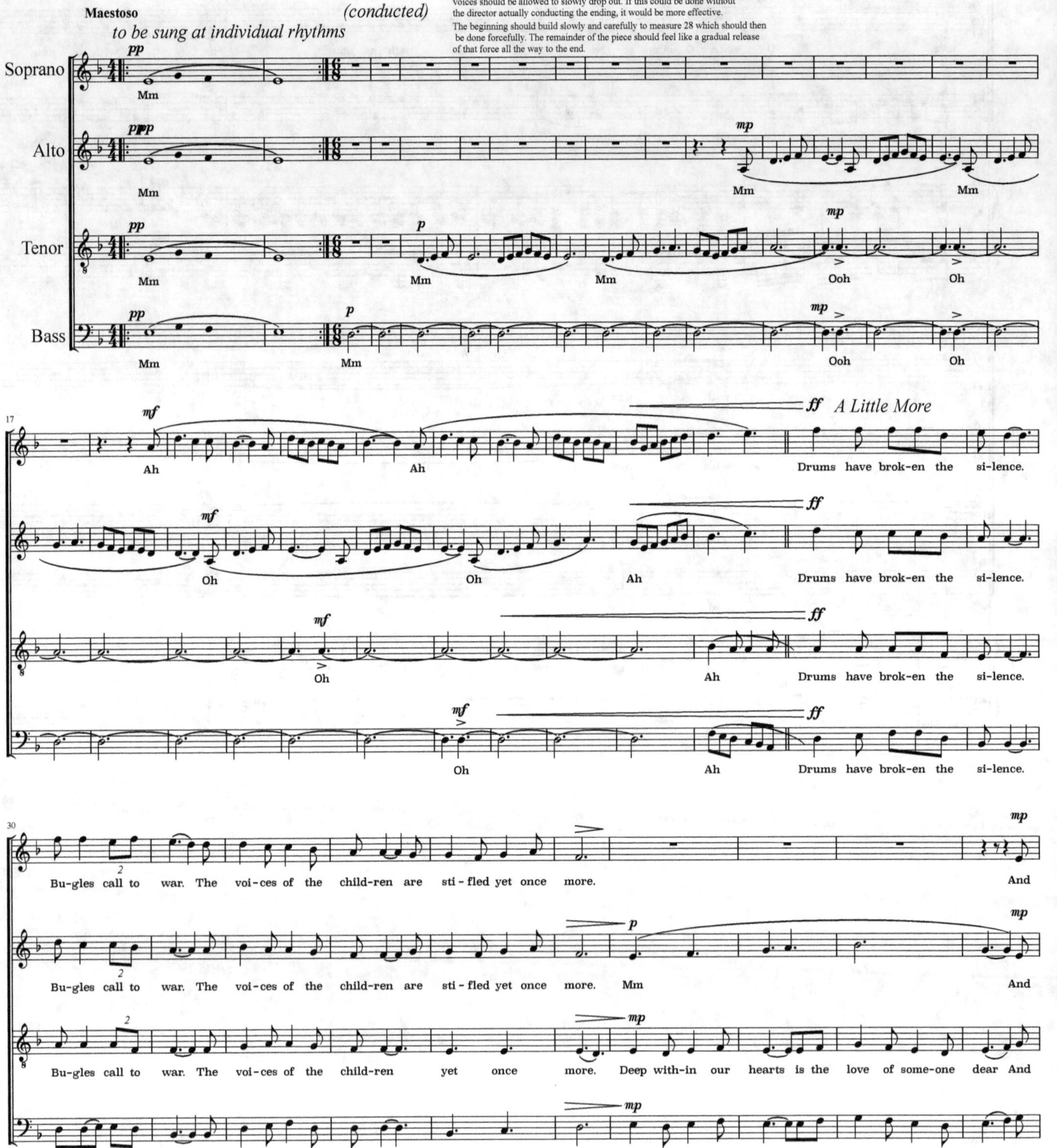

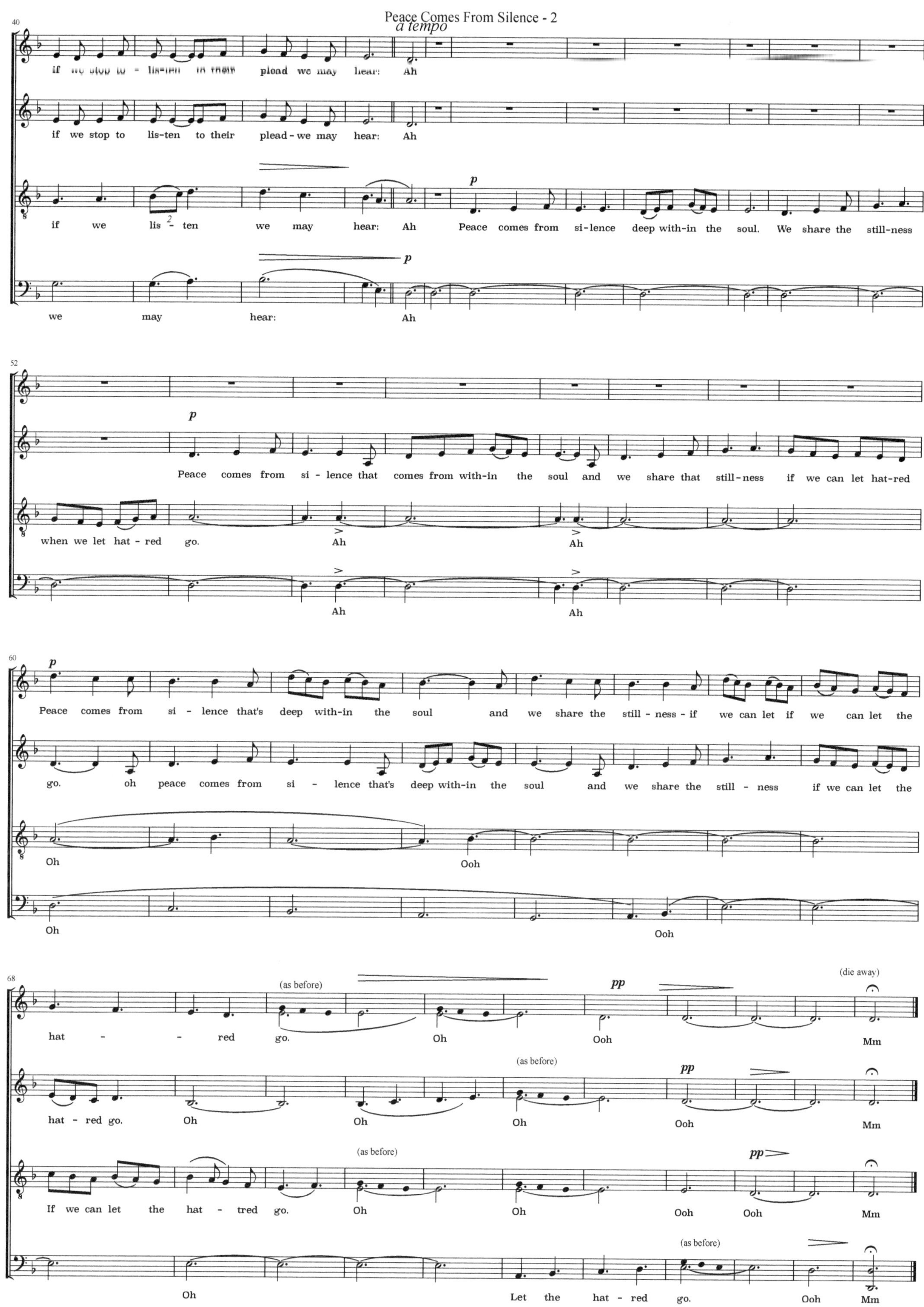
40
a tempo
if we stop to - lis-ten to their plead we may hear: Ah
if we stop to lis-ten to their plead - we may hear: Ah
if we lis - ten we may hear: Ah Peace comes from si-lence deep with-in the soul. We share the still-ness
we may hear: Ah
p
52
Peace comes from si - lence that comes from with-in the soul and we share that still-ness if we can let hat-red
when we let hat - red go. Ah Ah
Ah Ah
60
Peace comes from si - lence that's deep with-in the soul and we share the still - ness - if we can let if we can let the
go. oh peace comes from si - lence that's deep with-in the soul and we share the still - ness if we can let the
Oh Ooh
Oh Ooh
68
(as before)
(die away)
pp
hat - - red go. Oh Ooh Mm
hat - red go. Oh Oh Oh Ooh Mm
If we can let the hat - tred go. Oh Oh Ooh Ooh Mm
Oh Let the hat - red go. Ooh Mm

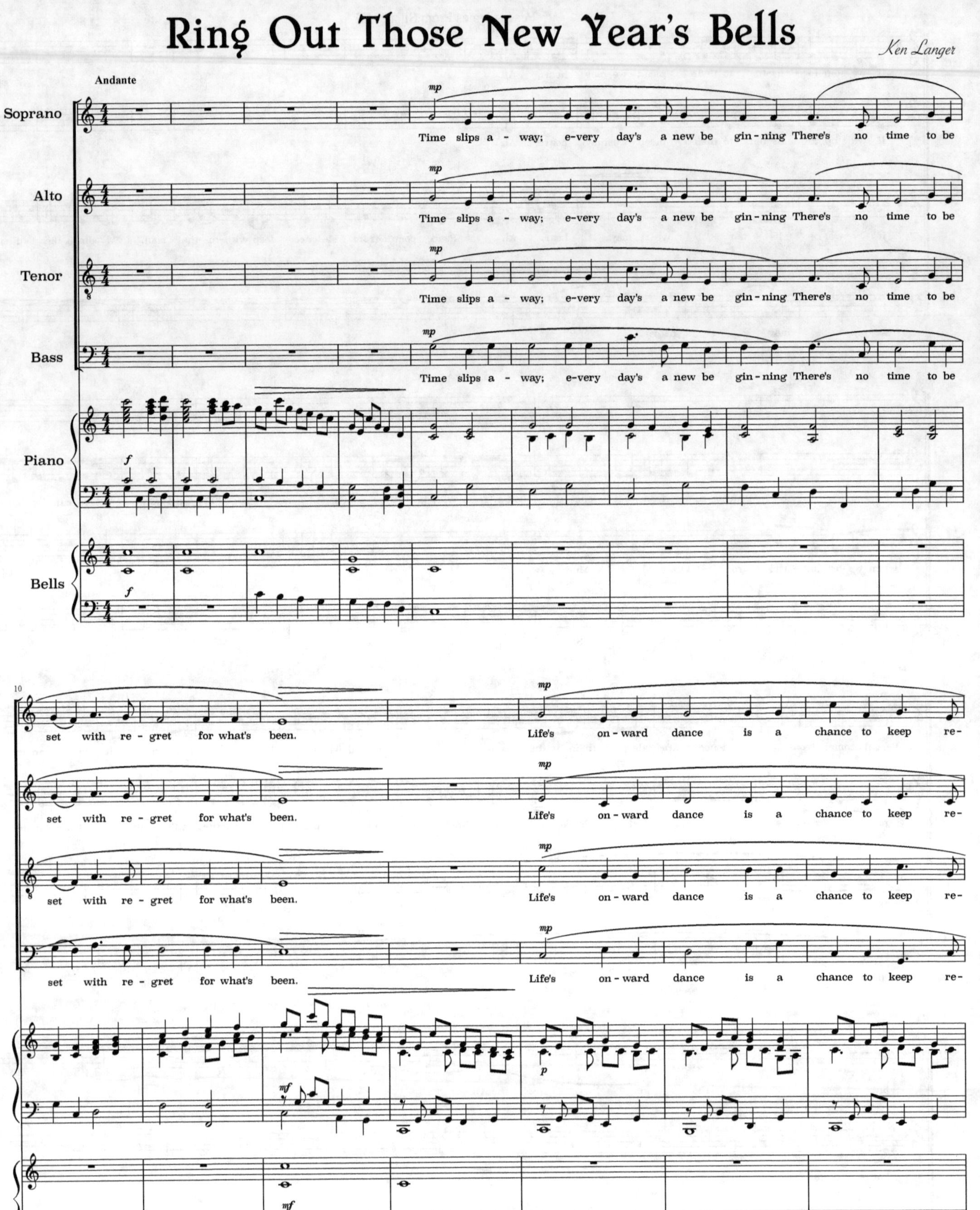
Ring Out Those New Year's Bells
Ken Langer
Andante
Soprano
Alto
Tenor
Bass
Piano
Bells
Time slips a - way; e-very day's a new be gin-ning There's no time to be
set with re - gret for what's been.
Life's on - ward dance is a chance to keep re-

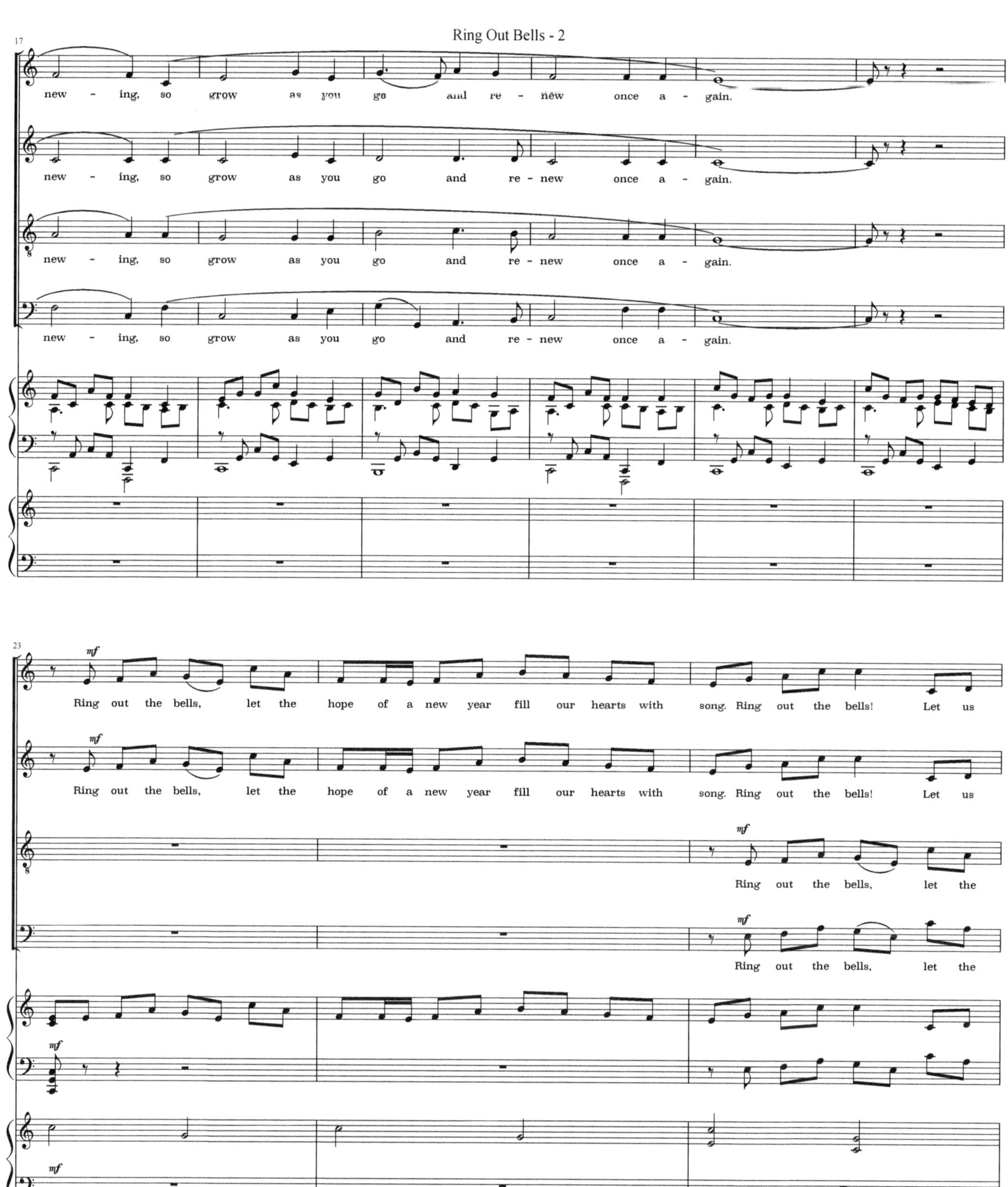
17
new - ing, so grow as you go and re - new once a - gain.
new - ing, so grow as you go and re - new once a - gain.
new - ing, so grow as you go and re - new once a - gain.
new - ing, so grow as you go and re - new once a - gain.
23
mf
Ring out the bells, let the hope of a new year fill our hearts with song. Ring out the bells! Let us
mf
Ring out the bells, let the hope of a new year fill our hearts with song. Ring out the bells! Let us
mf
Ring out the bells, let the
mf
Ring out the bells, let the
mf
mf

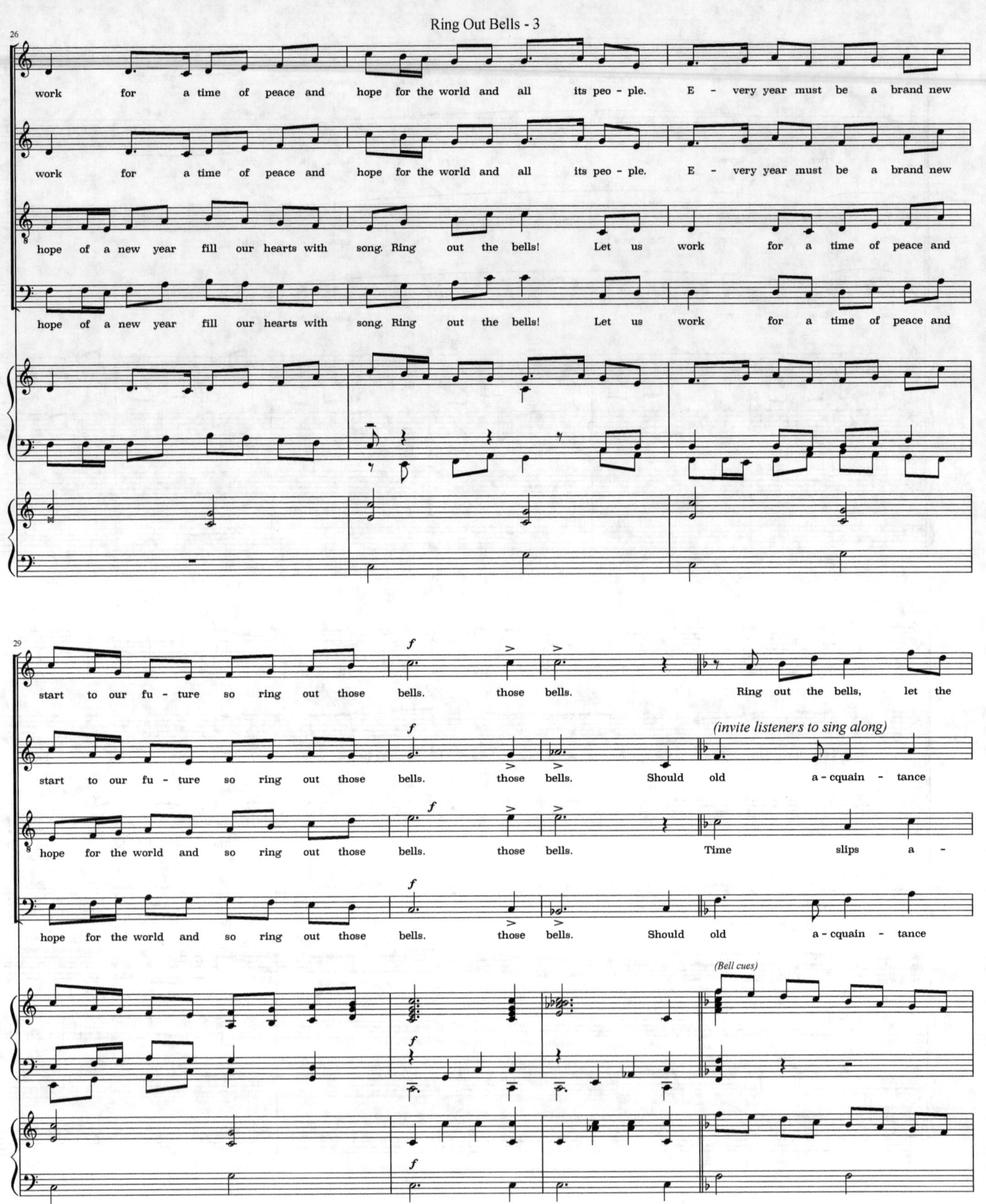
26
work for a time of peace and hope for the world and all its peo - ple. E - very year must be a brand new
work for a time of peace and hope for the world and all its peo - ple. E - very year must be a brand new
hope of a new year fill our hearts with song. Ring out the bells! Let us work for a time of peace and
hope of a new year fill our hearts with song. Ring out the bells! Let us work for a time of peace and
29
f
start to our fu - ture so ring out those bells. those bells. Ring out the bells, let the
(invite listeners to sing along)
start to our fu - ture so ring out those bells. those bells. Should old a - cquain - tance
hope for the world and so ring out those bells. those bells. Time slips a -
hope for the world and so ring out those bells. those bells. Should old a - cquain - tance
(Bell cues)

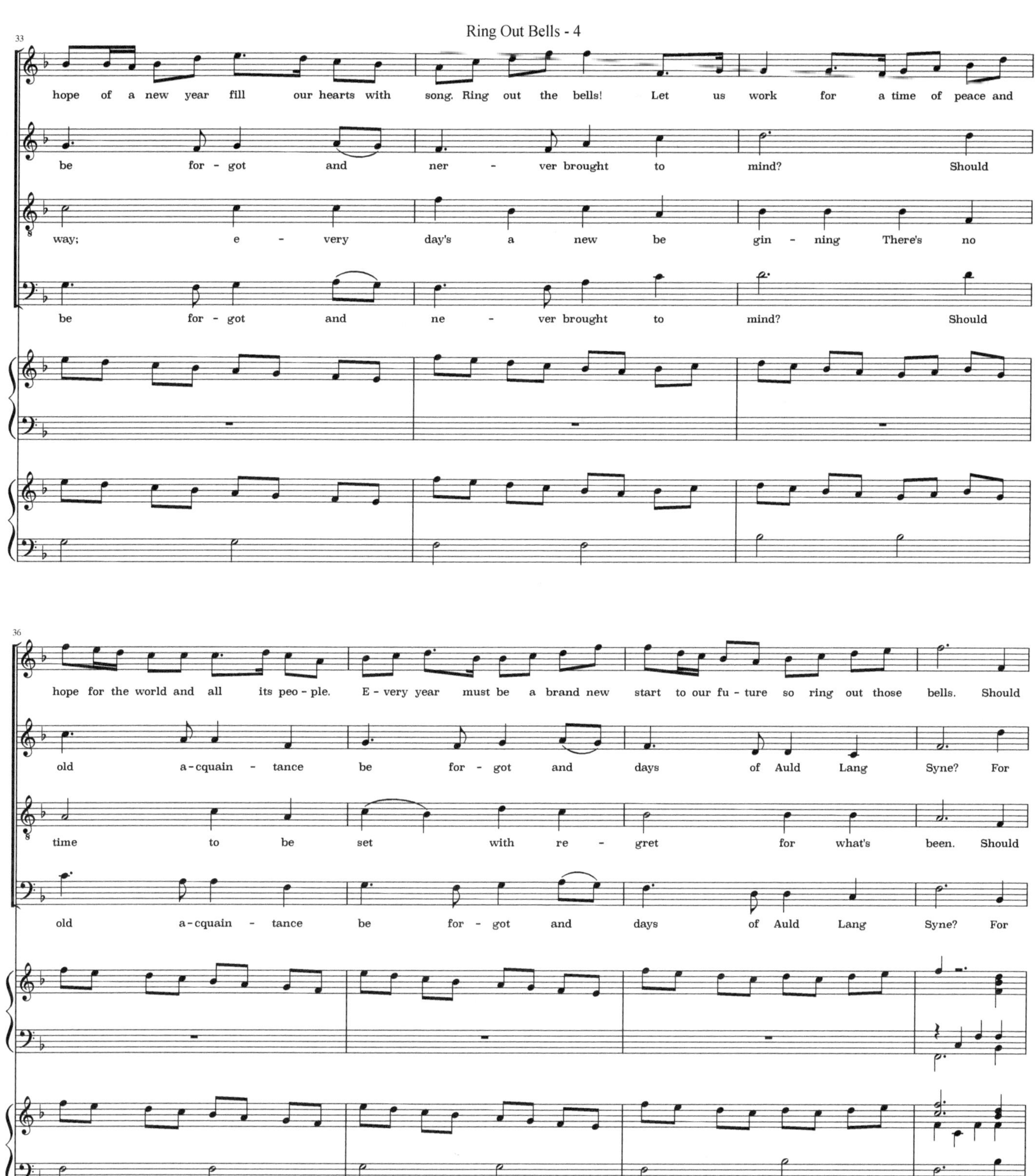
33
hope of a new year fill our hearts with song. Ring out the bells! Let us work for a time of peace and
be for - got and ner - ver brought to mind? Should
way; e - very day's a new be gin - ning There's no
be for - got and ne - ver brought to mind? Should
36
hope for the world and all its peo - ple. E - very year must be a brand new start to our fu - ture so ring out those bells. Should
old a - cquain - tance be for - got and days of Auld Lang Syne? For
time to be set with re - gret for what's been. Should
old a - cquain - tance be for - got and days of Auld Lang Syne? For

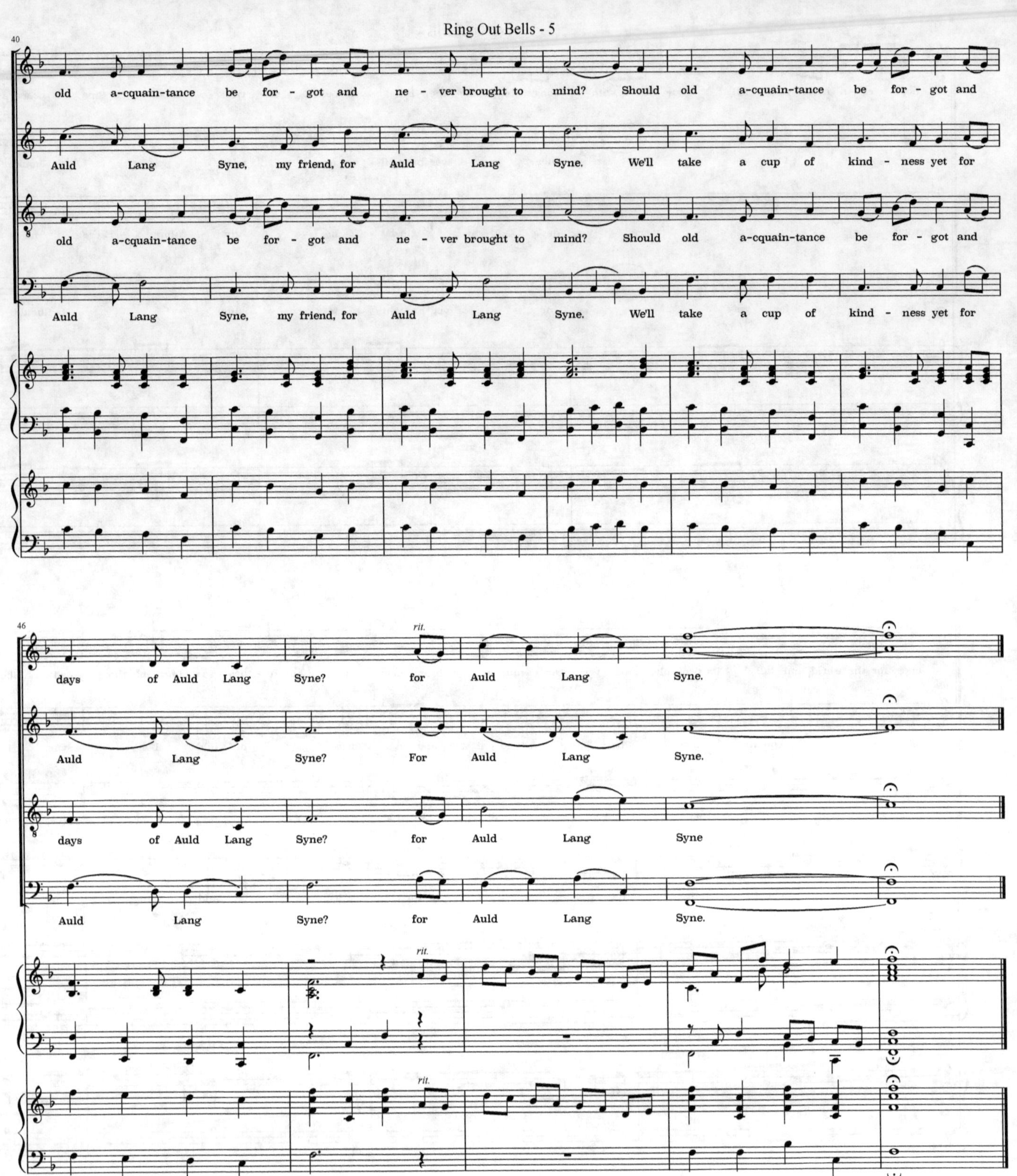
40
old a-cquain-tance be for - got and ne - ver brought to mind? Should old a-cquain-tance be for - got and
Auld Lang Syne, my friend, for Auld Lang Syne. We'll take a cup of kind - ness yet for
old a-cquain-tance be for - got and ne - ver brought to mind? Should old a-cquain-tance be for - got and
Auld Lang Syne, my friend, for Auld Lang Syne. We'll take a cup of kind - ness yet for
46
rit.
days of Auld Lang Syne? for Auld Lang Syne.
Auld Lang Syne? For Auld Lang Syne.
days of Auld Lang Syne? for Auld Lang Syne
Auld Lang Syne? for Auld Lang Syne.
rit.
rit.

Sacred Dawn

Kenneth P. Langer

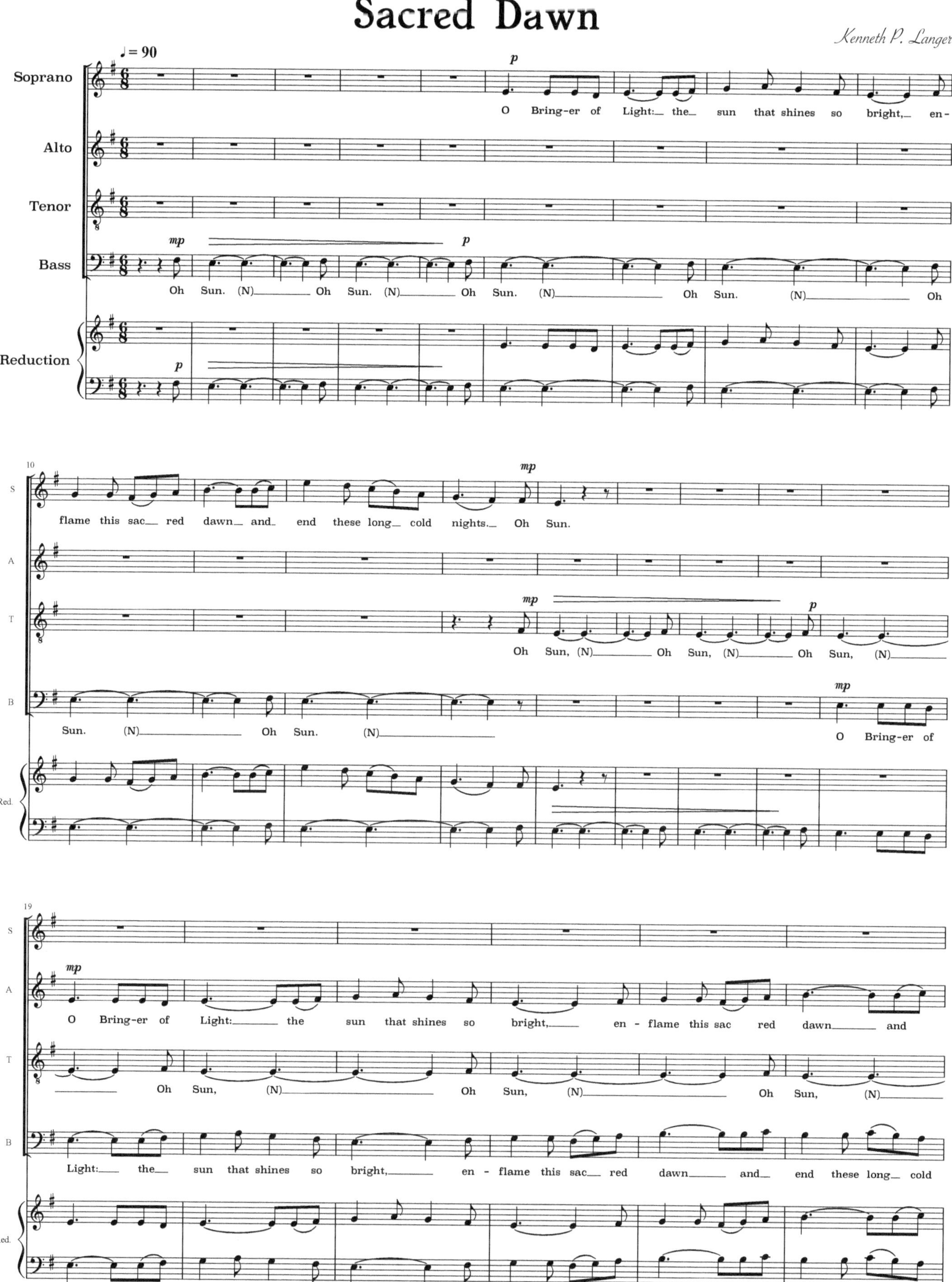

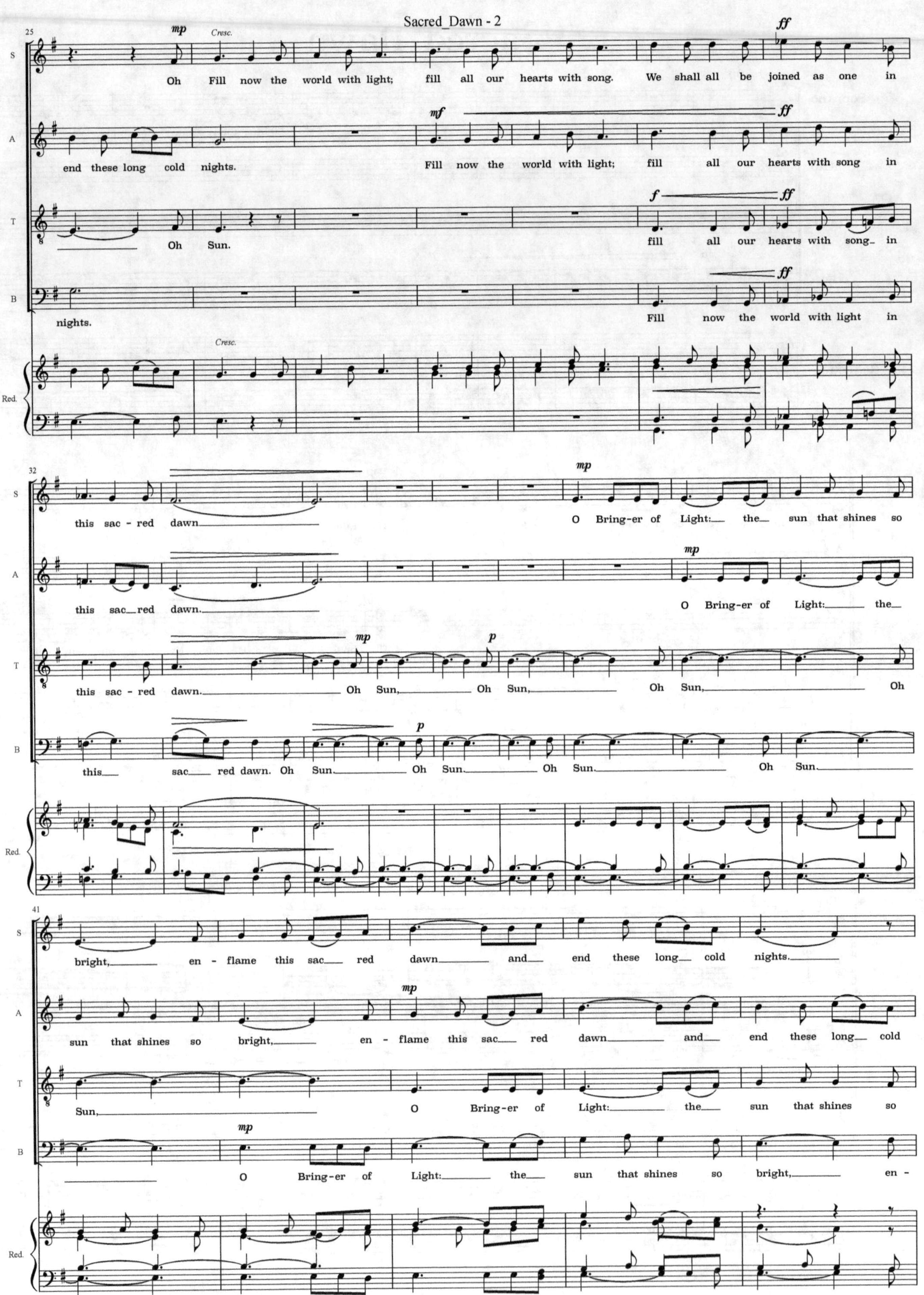
25
S
A
T
B
Red.
mp
Cresc.
Oh Fill now the world with light; fill all our hearts with song. We shall all be joined as one in
mf
ff
end these long cold nights. Fill now the world with light; fill all our hearts with song in
f
ff
Oh Sun. fill all our hearts with song_ in
ff
nights. Fill now the world with light in
Cresc.
32
this sac - red dawn
mp
O Bring-er of Light:_ the_ sun that shines so
this sac_ red dawn.
mp
O Bring-er of Light: the_
mp
p
this sac - red dawn. Oh Sun, Oh Sun, Oh Sun, Oh
p
this_ sac_ red dawn. Oh Sun. Oh Sun. Oh Sun. Oh Sun.
41
bright, en - flame this sac_ red dawn and_ end these long_ cold nights.
mp
sun that shines so bright, en - flame this sac_ red dawn and_ end these long_ cold
Sun, O Bring-er of Light: the_ sun that shines so
mp
O Bring-er of Light: the_ sun that shines so bright, en -

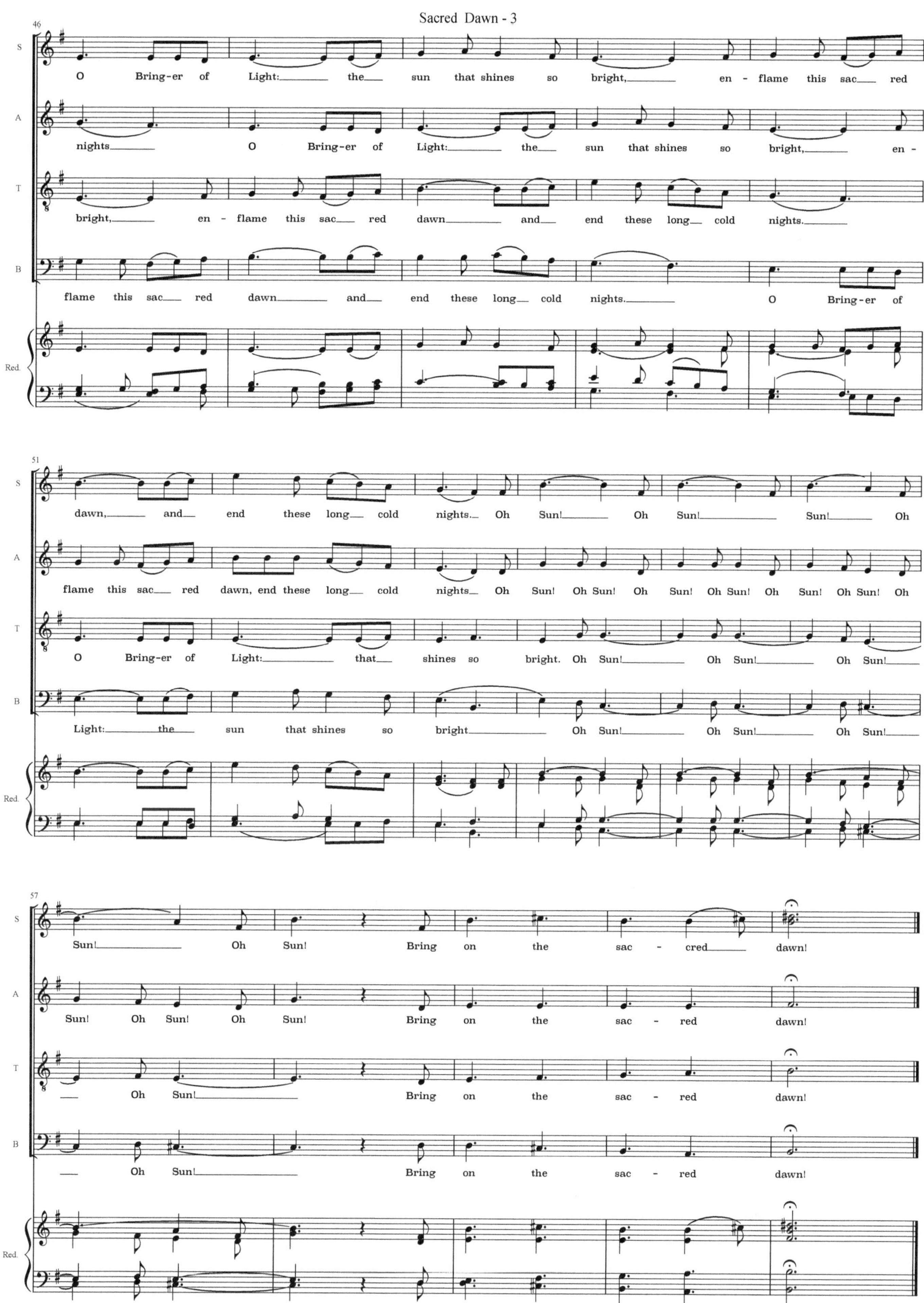
46
S
O Bring-er of Light: the sun that shines so bright, en - flame this sac red
A
nights O Bring-er of Light: the sun that shines so bright, en -
T
bright, en - flame this sac red dawn and end these long cold nights.
B
flame this sac red dawn and end these long cold nights. O Bring-er of
Red.
51
S
dawn, and end these long cold nights. Oh Sun! Oh Sun! Sun! Oh
A
flame this sac red dawn, end these long cold nights Oh Sun! Oh Sun! Oh Sun! Oh Sun! Oh Sun! Oh Sun! Oh
T
O Bring-er of Light: that shines so bright. Oh Sun! Oh Sun! Oh Sun!
B
Light: the sun that shines so bright Oh Sun! Oh Sun! Oh Sun!
Red.
57
S
Sun! Oh Sun! Bring on the sac - cred dawn!
A
Sun! Oh Sun! Oh Sun! Bring on the sac - red dawn!
T
Oh Sun! Bring on the sac - red dawn!
B
Oh Sun! Bring on the sac - red dawn!
Red.

The Season of Light

Ken Langer

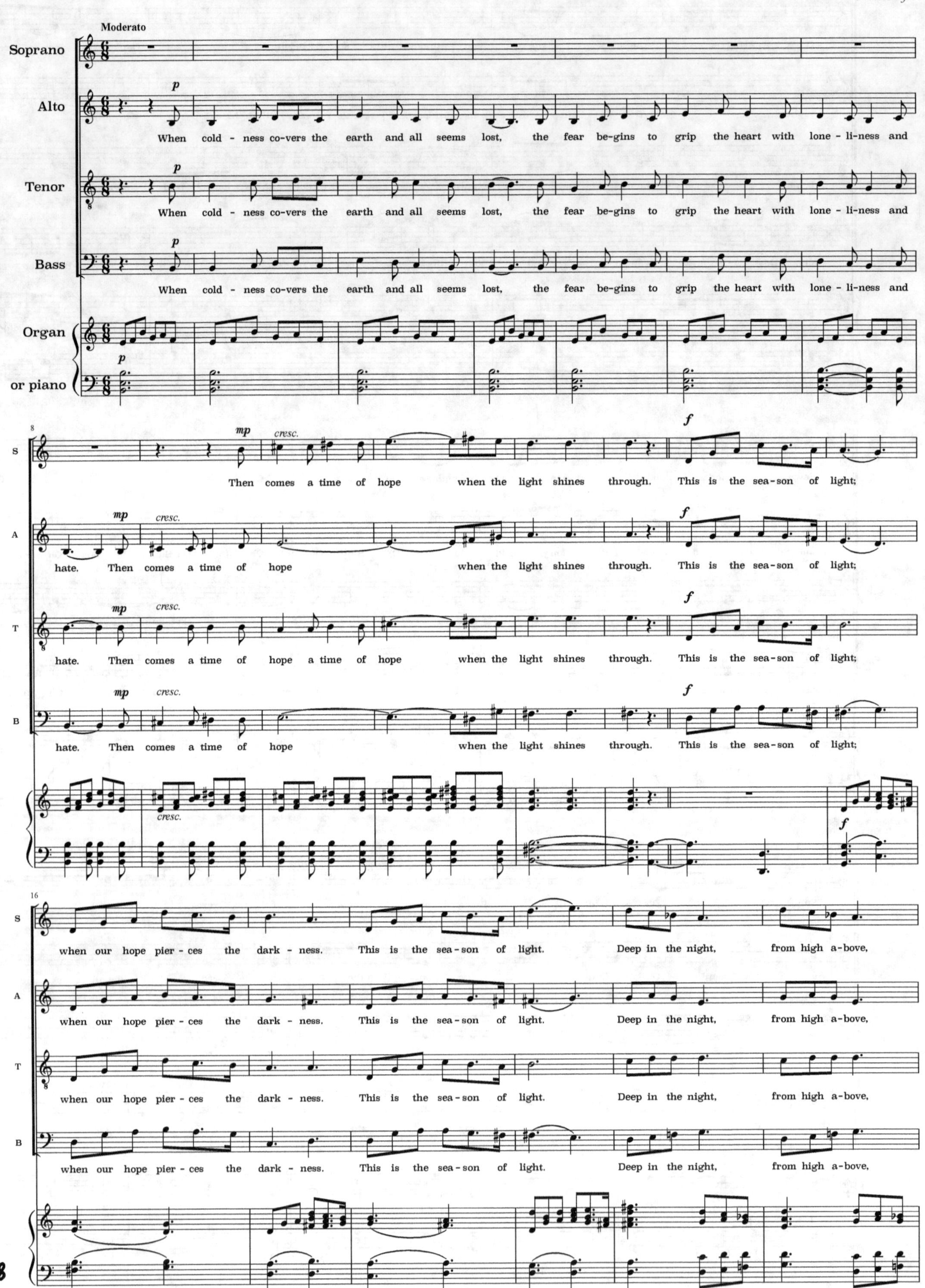

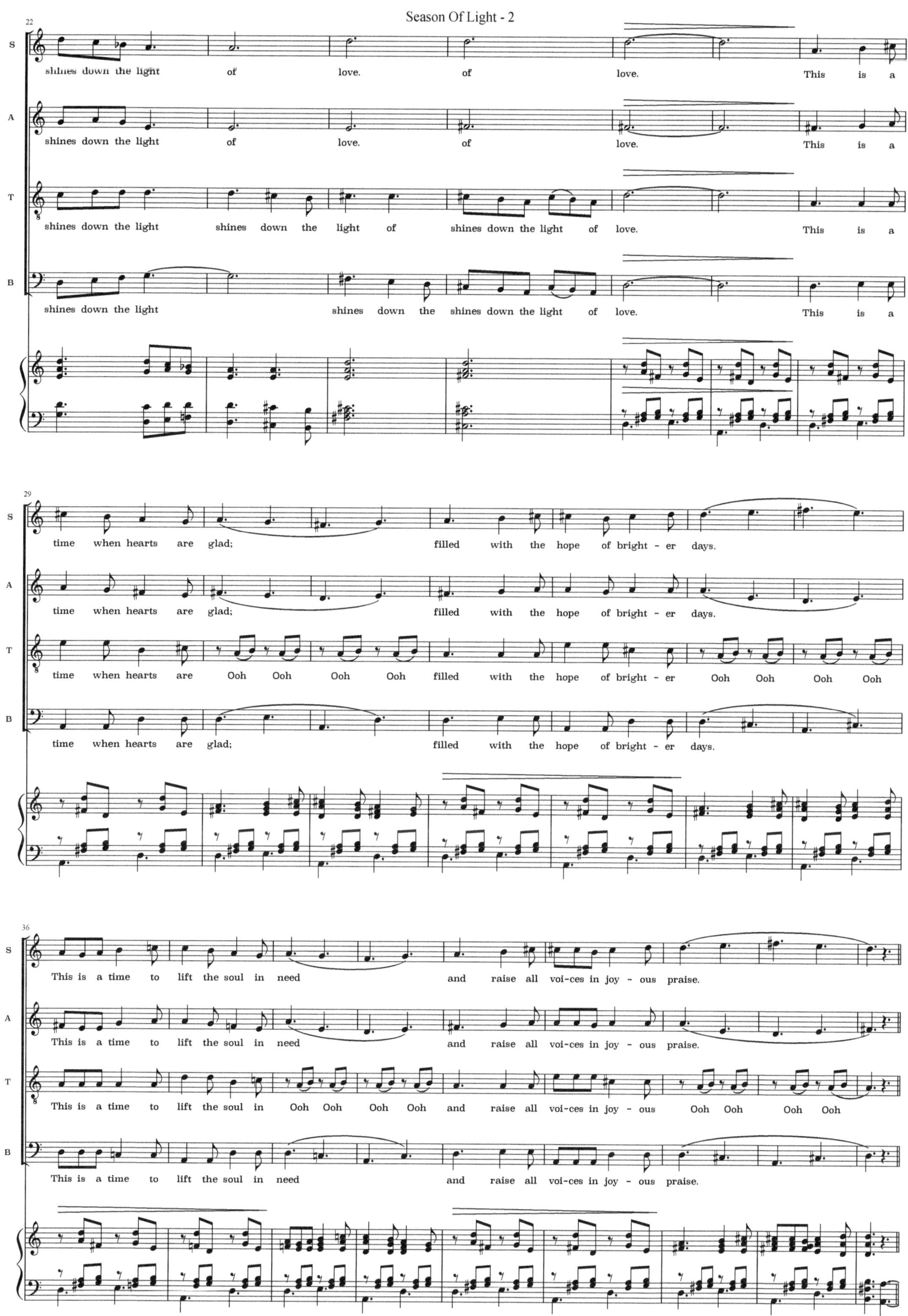
22
S
shines down the light of love. of love. This is a
A
shines down the light of love. of love. This is a
T
shines down the light shines down the light of shines down the light of love. This is a
B
shines down the light shines down the shines down the light of love. This is a
29
S
time when hearts are glad; filled with the hope of bright - er days.
A
time when hearts are glad; filled with the hope of bright - er days.
T
time when hearts are Ooh Ooh Ooh Ooh filled with the hope of bright - er Ooh Ooh Ooh Ooh
B
time when hearts are glad; filled with the hope of bright - er days.
36
S
This is a time to lift the soul in need and raise all voi-ces in joy - ous praise.
A
This is a time to lift the soul in need and raise all voi-ces in joy - ous praise.
T
This is a time to lift the soul in Ooh Ooh Ooh Ooh and raise all voi-ces in joy - ous Ooh Ooh Ooh Ooh
B
This is a time to lift the soul in need and raise all voi-ces in joy - ous praise.

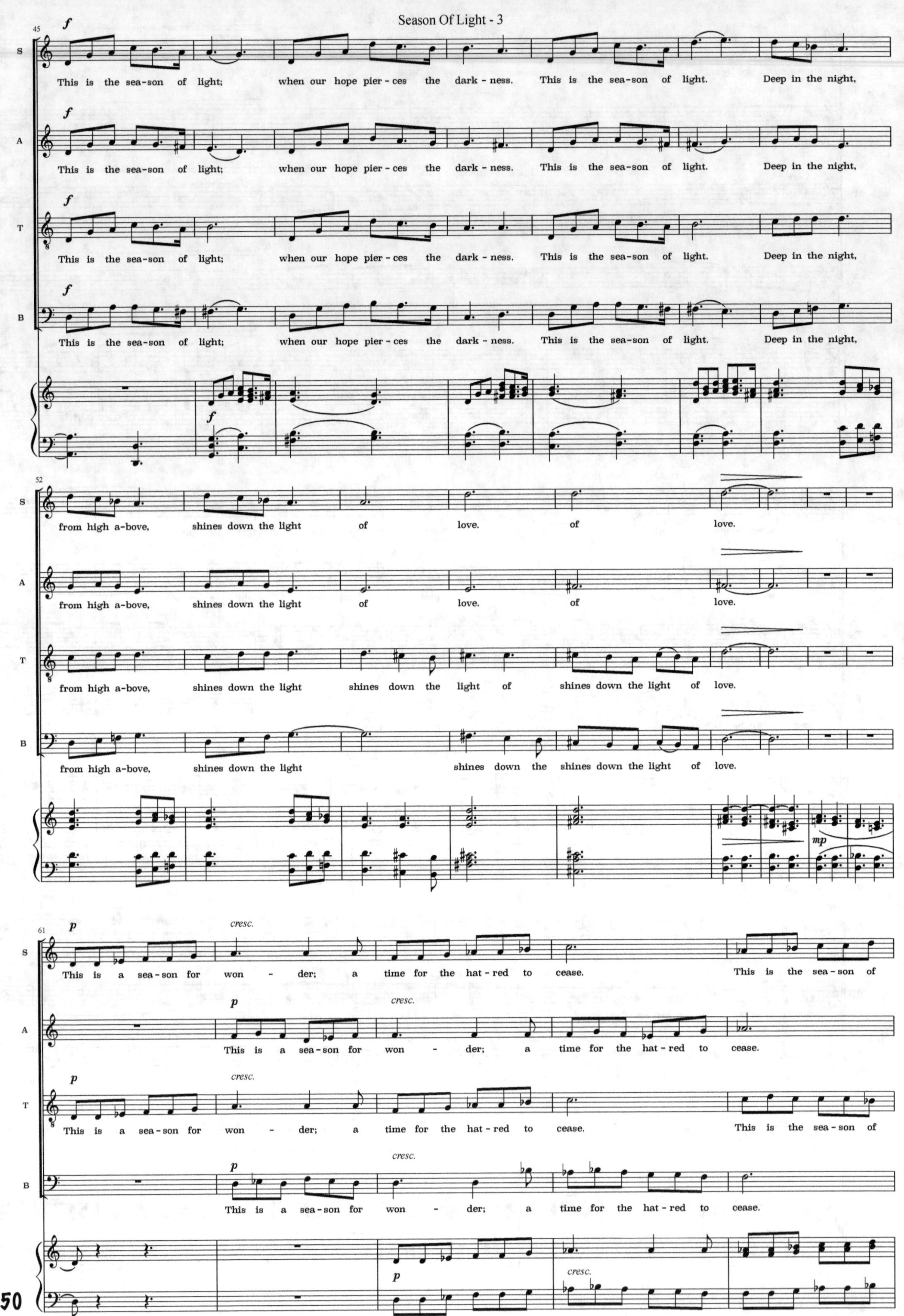
45
S
A
T
B
f
This is the sea-son of light; when our hope pier-ces the dark-ness. This is the sea-son of light. Deep in the night,
52
from high a-bove, shines down the light of love. of love.
from high a-bove, shines down the light shines down the light of shines down the light of love.
from high a-bove, shines down the light shines down the shines down the light of love.
mp
61
p
cresc.
This is a sea-son for won - der; a time for the hat-red to cease. This is the sea-son of
This is a sea-son for won - der; a time for the hat-red to cease.

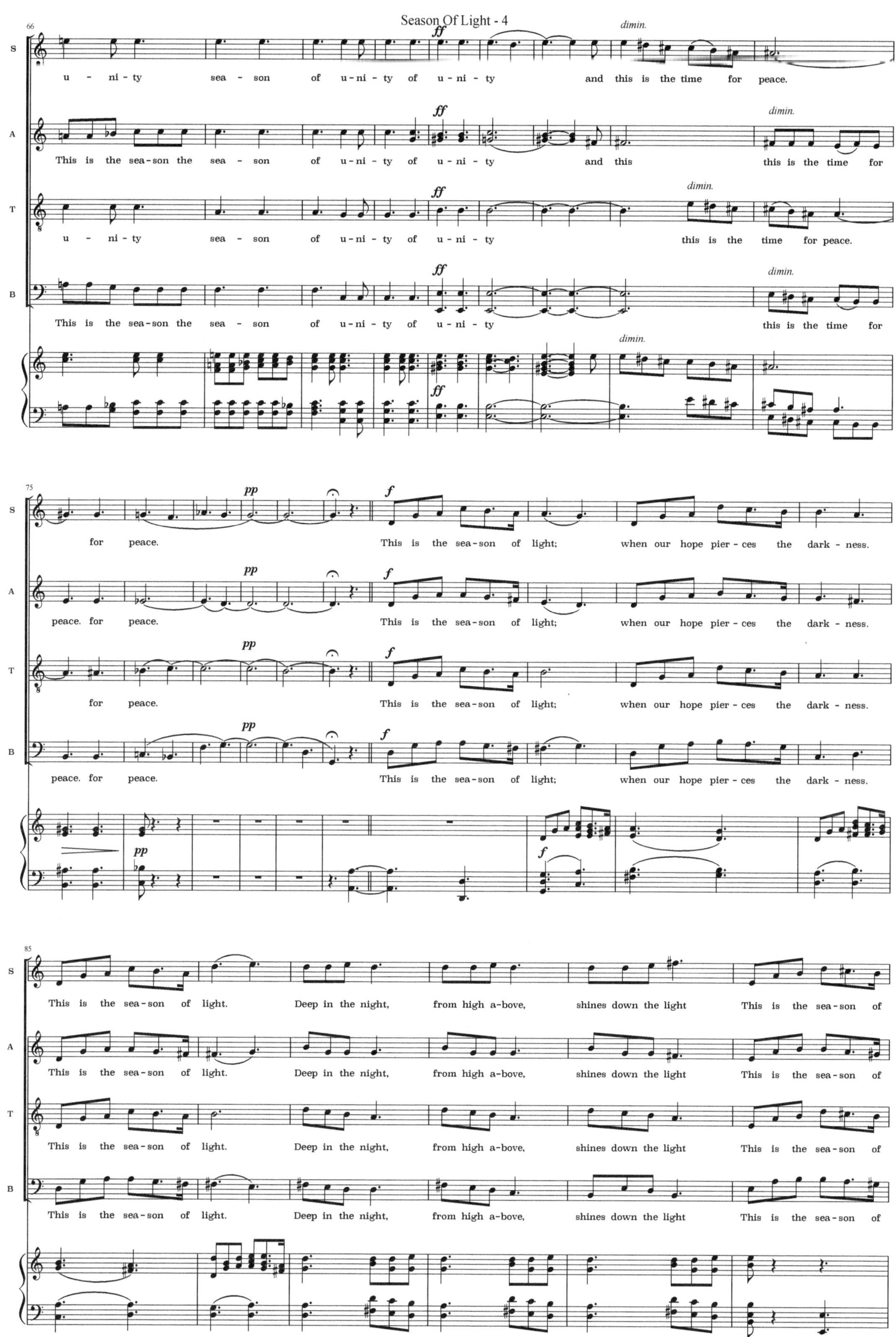
66
S
u - ni - ty sea - son of u - ni - ty of u - ni - ty and this is the time for peace.
A
This is the sea - son the sea - son of u - ni - ty of u - ni - ty and this this is the time for
T
u - ni - ty sea - son of u - ni - ty of u - ni - ty this is the time for peace.
B
This is the sea - son the sea - son of u - ni - ty of u - ni - ty this is the time for
ff
dimin.
75
for peace.
peace. for peace.
for peace.
peace. for peace.
This is the sea - son of light; when our hope pier - ces the dark - ness.
pp
f
85
This is the sea - son of light. Deep in the night, from high a - bove, shines down the light This is the sea - son of

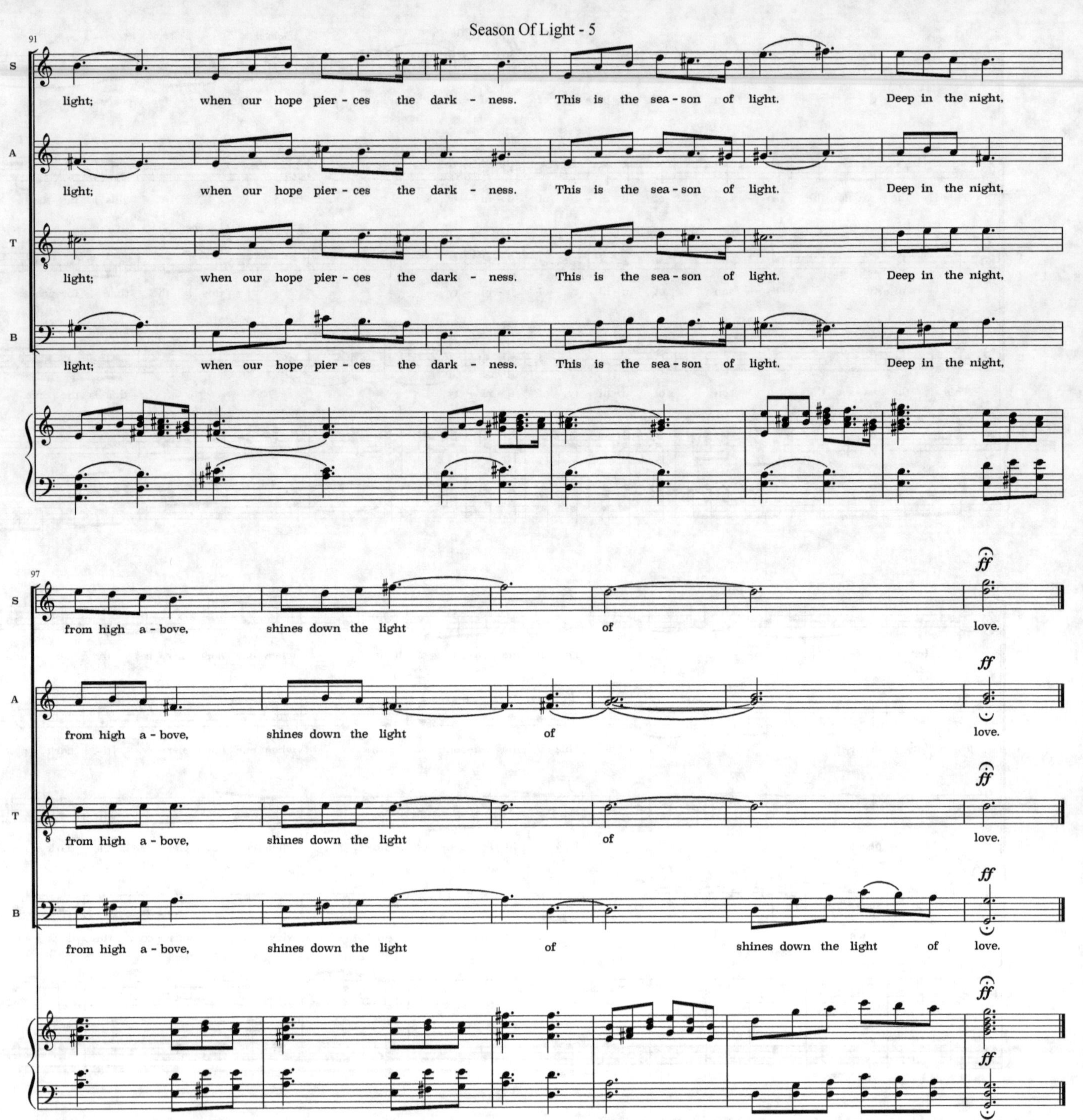
91
S
light; when our hope pier - ces the dark - ness. This is the sea - son of light. Deep in the night,
A
light; when our hope pier - ces the dark - ness. This is the sea - son of light. Deep in the night,
T
light; when our hope pier - ces the dark - ness. This is the sea - son of light. Deep in the night,
B
light; when our hope pier - ces the dark - ness. This is the sea - son of light. Deep in the night,
97
S
from high a - bove, shines down the light of love.
A
from high a - bove, shines down the light of love.
T
from high a - bove, shines down the light of love.
B
from high a - bove, shines down the light of shines down the light of love.
ff

Sound Over All Waters

adapted from John Greenleaf Whittier

Ken Langer

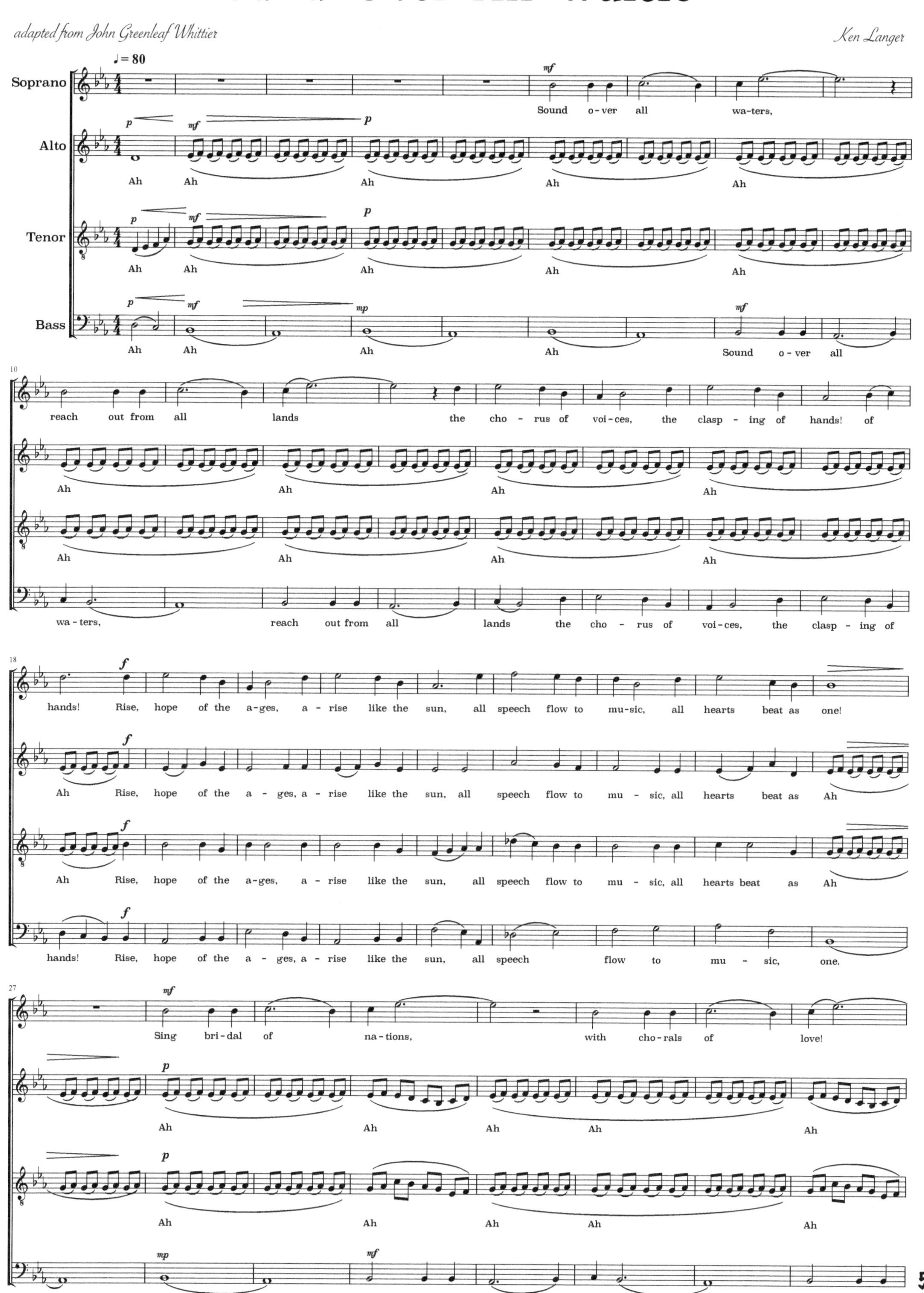

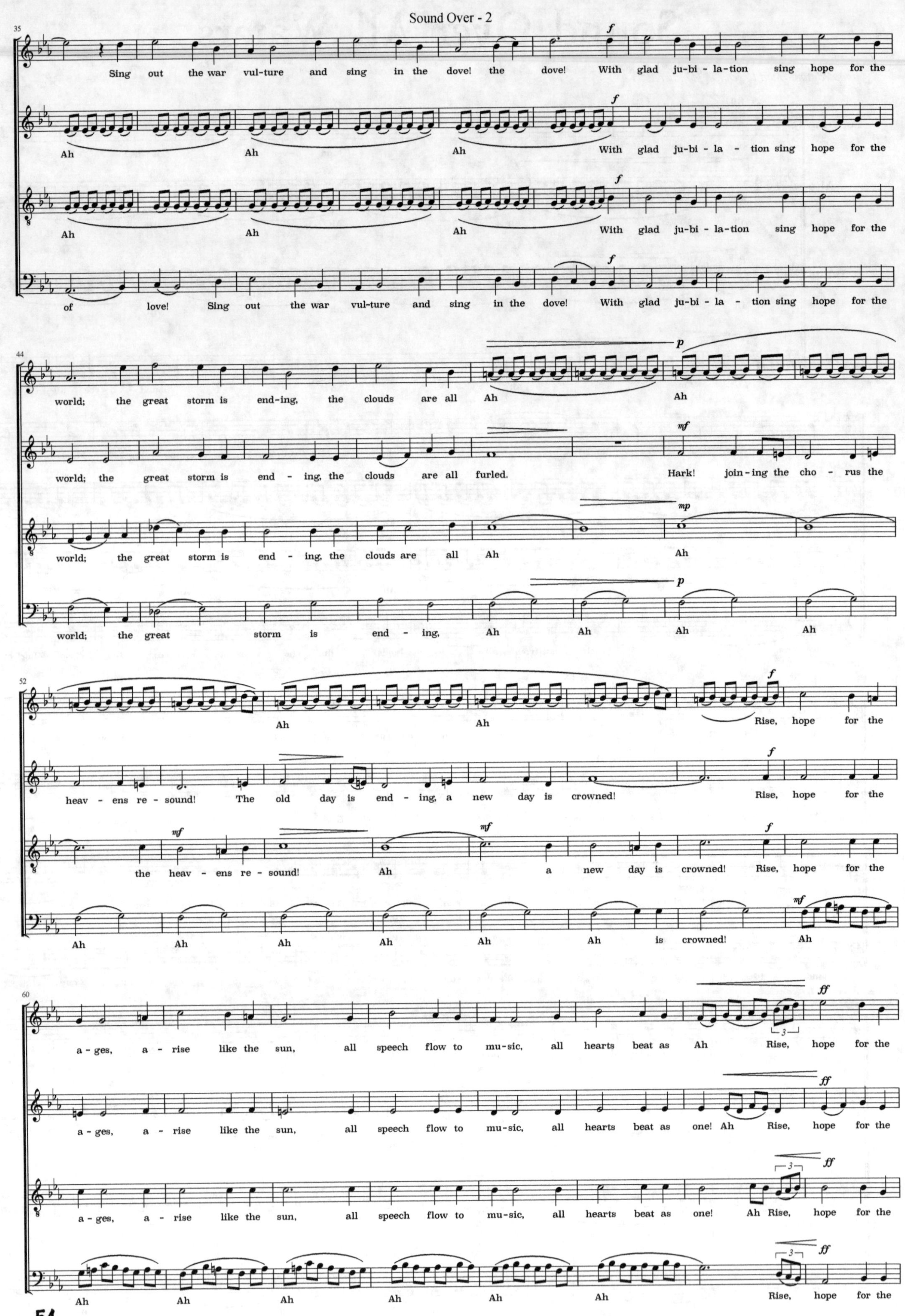
Sing out the war vul-ture and sing in the dove! the dove! With glad ju-bi-la-tion sing hope for the
Ah Ah Ah With glad ju-bi-la - tion sing hope for the
Ah Ah Ah With glad ju-bi-la-tion sing hope for the
of love! Sing out the war vul-ture and sing in the dove! With glad ju-bi-la - tion sing hope for the
world; the great storm is end-ing, the clouds are all Ah Ah
world; the great storm is end - ing, the clouds are all furled. Hark! join-ing the cho - rus the
world; the great storm is end - ing, the clouds are all Ah Ah
world; the great storm is end - ing, Ah Ah Ah Ah
Ah Ah Rise, hope for the
heav - ens re - sound! The old day is end - ing, a new day is crowned! Rise, hope for the
the heav - ens re - sound! Ah a new day is crowned! Rise, hope for the
Ah Ah Ah Ah Ah Ah is crowned! Ah
a - ges, a - rise like the sun, all speech flow to mu-sic, all hearts beat as Ah Rise, hope for the
a - ges, a - rise like the sun, all speech flow to mu-sic, all hearts beat as one! Ah Rise, hope for the
a - ges, a - rise like the sun, all speech flow to mu-sic, all hearts beat as one! Ah Rise, hope for the
Ah Ah Ah Ah Ah Ah Rise, hope for the

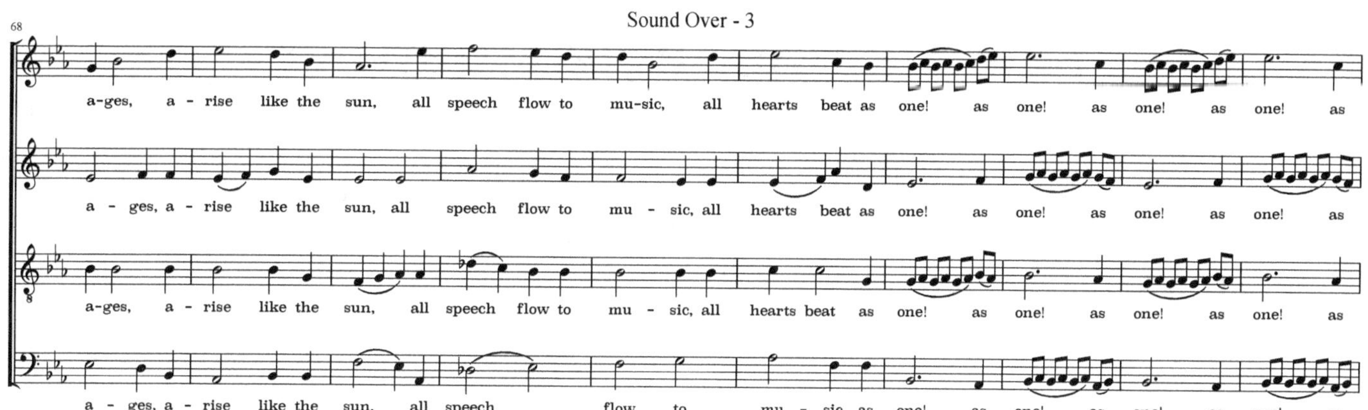
68
a-ges, a - rise like the sun, all speech flow to mu-sic, all hearts beat as one! as one! as one! as one! as
a - ges, a - rise like the sun, all speech flow to mu - sic, all hearts beat as one! as one! as one! as one! as
a-ges, a - rise like the sun, all speech flow to mu - sic, all hearts beat as one! as one! as one! as one! as
a - ges, a - rise like the sun, all speech flow to mu - sic, as one! as one! as one! as one! as

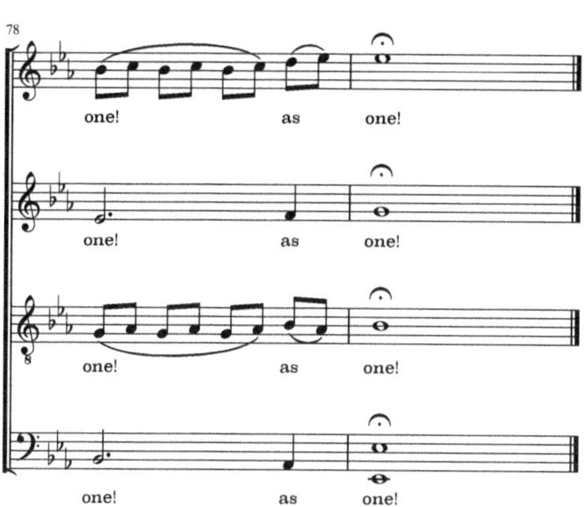
78
one! as one!
one! as one!
one! as one!
one! as one!

The Star Spangled Banner

"The Star Spangled Banner" by Francis Scott Key, "America The Beautiful" by Katherine Lee Bates, and "America" by Walt Whitman

arr. Ken Langer

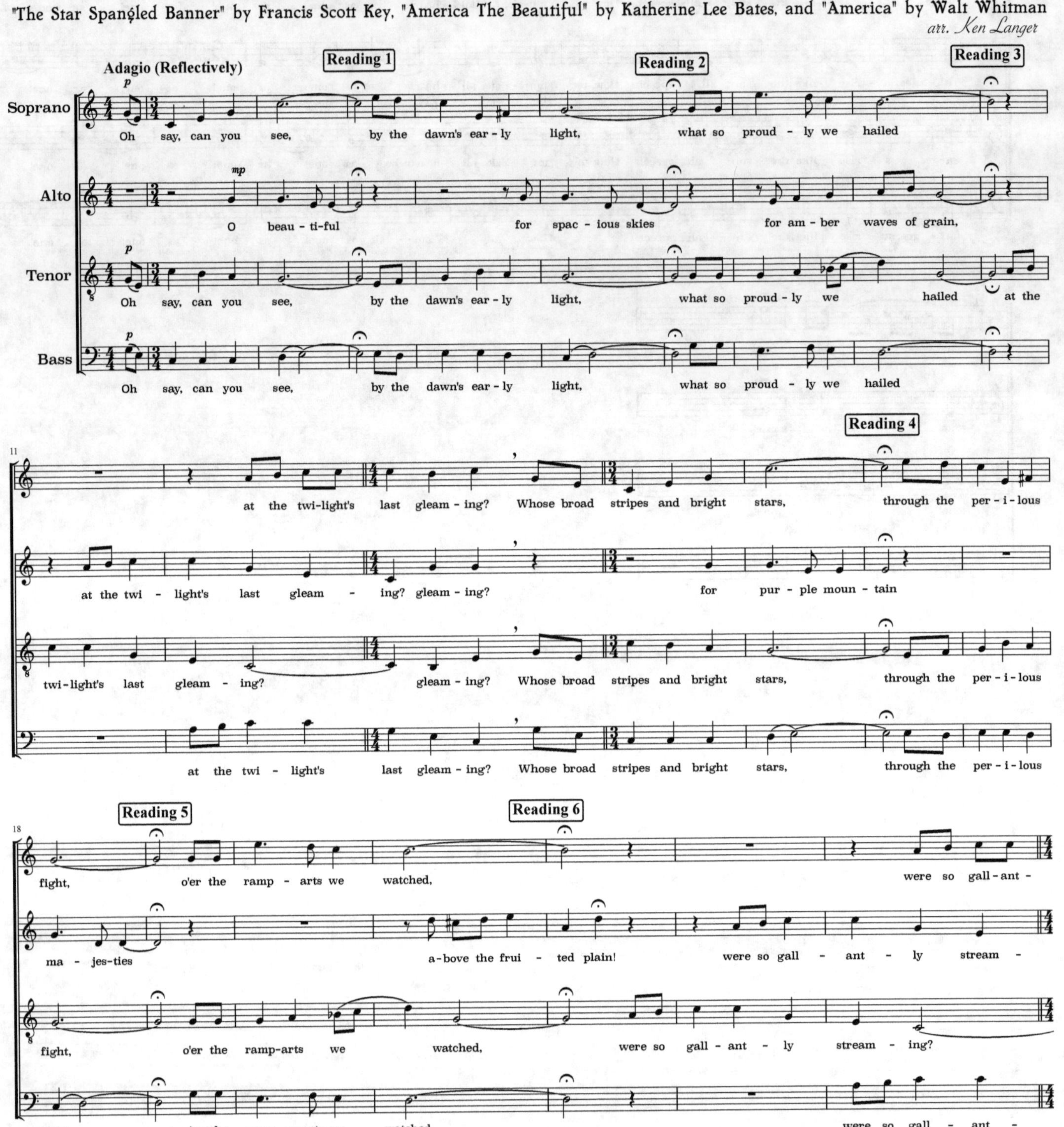

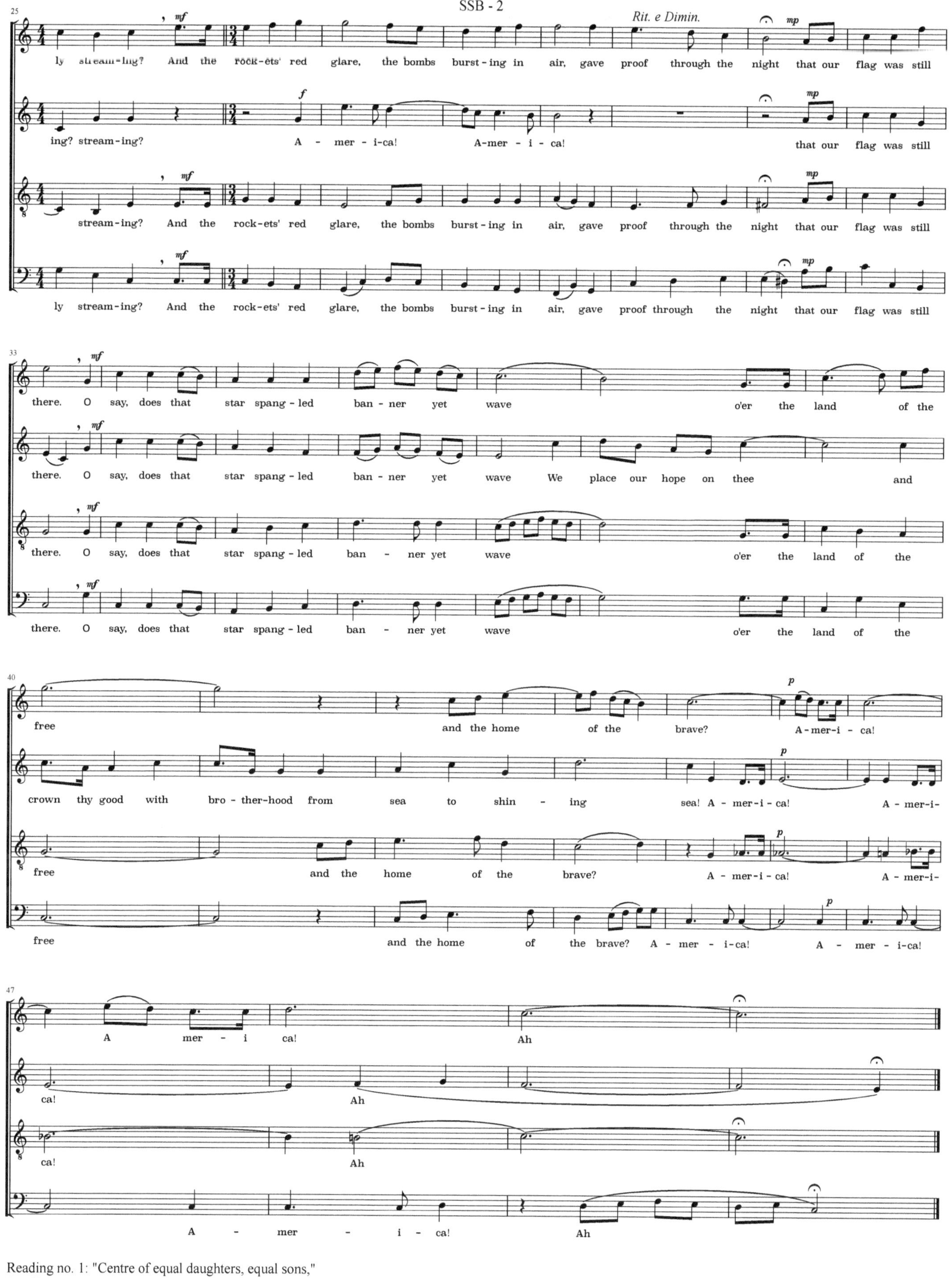

Reading no. 1: "Centre of equal daughters, equal sons,"
Reading no. 2: "All, all alike endear'd, grown, ungrown, young or old,"
Reading no. 3: "Strong, ample, fair, enduring, capable, rich,"
Reading no. 4: "Perennial with the Earth, with Freedom, Law and Love,
Reading no. 5: "A grand, sane, towering, seated Mother,"
Reading no. 6: "Chair'd in the adamant of Time".

Thanksgiving Round

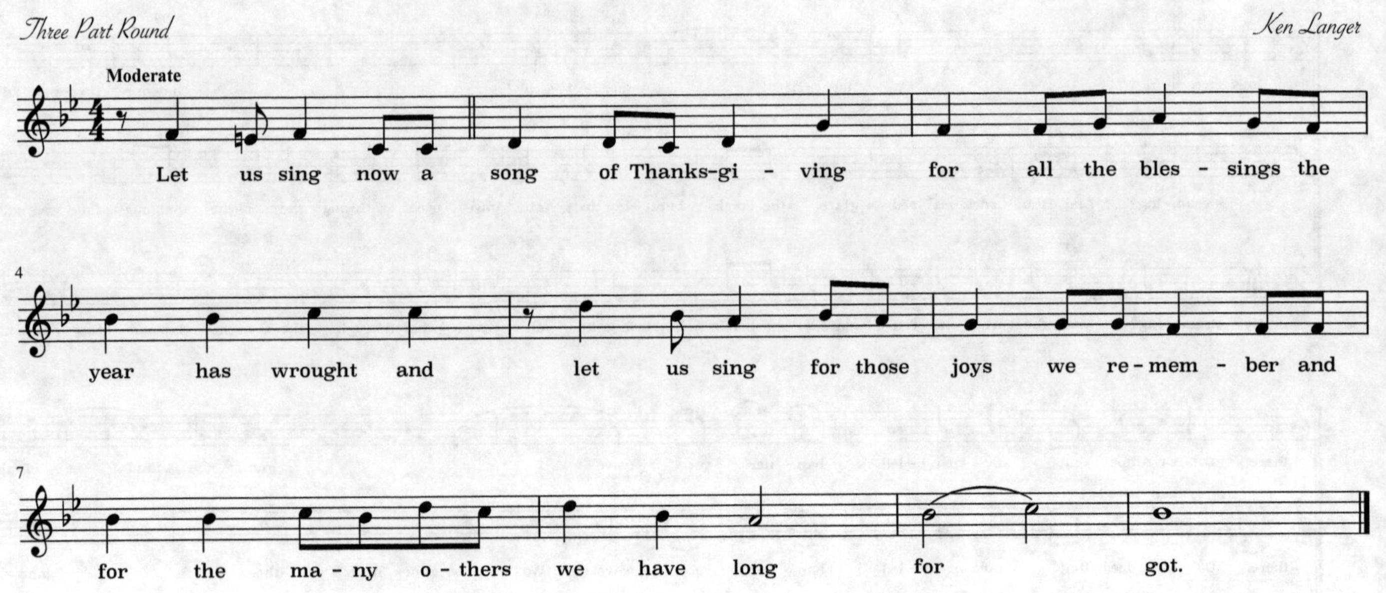

There Are Flowers

Ken Langer

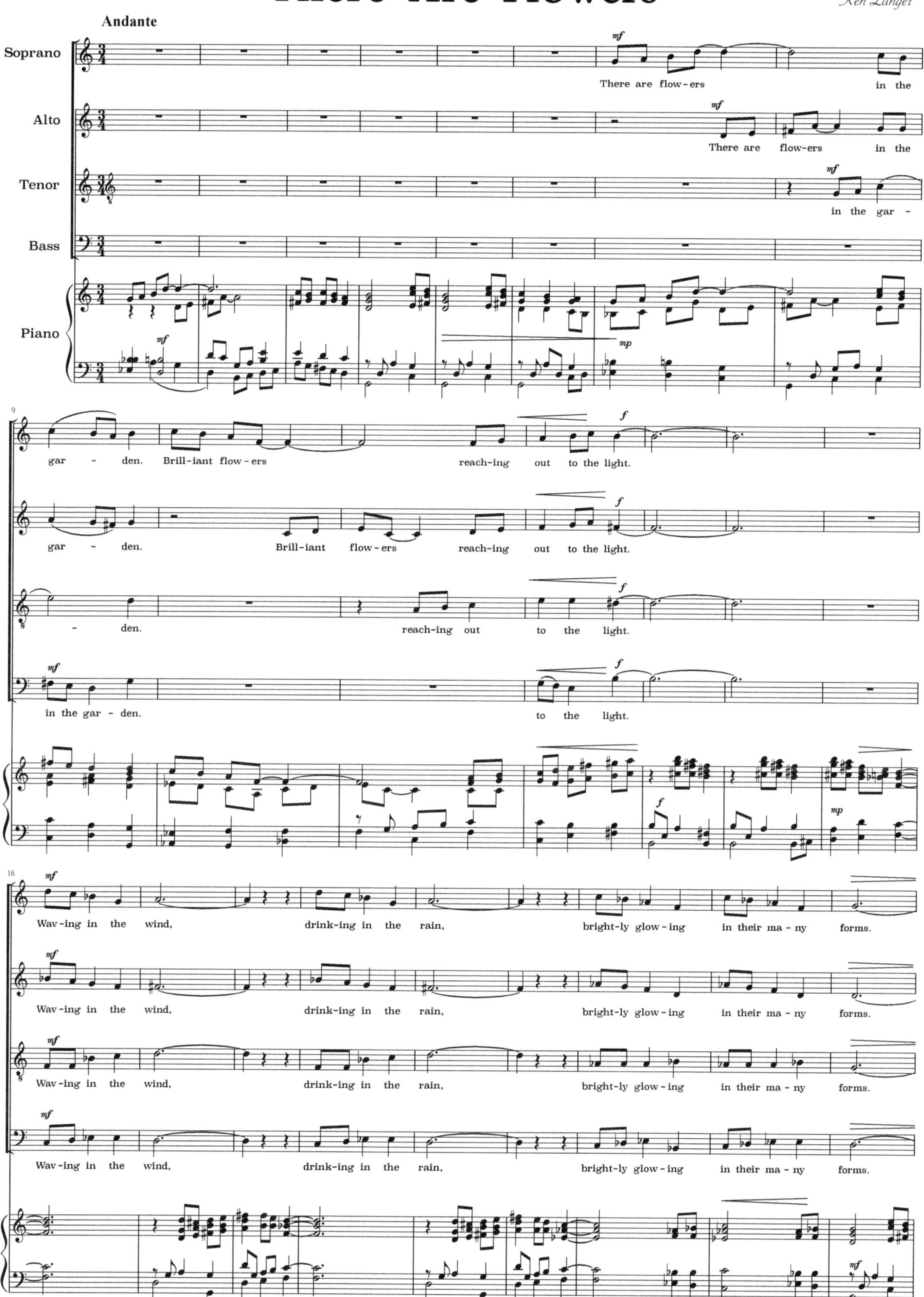

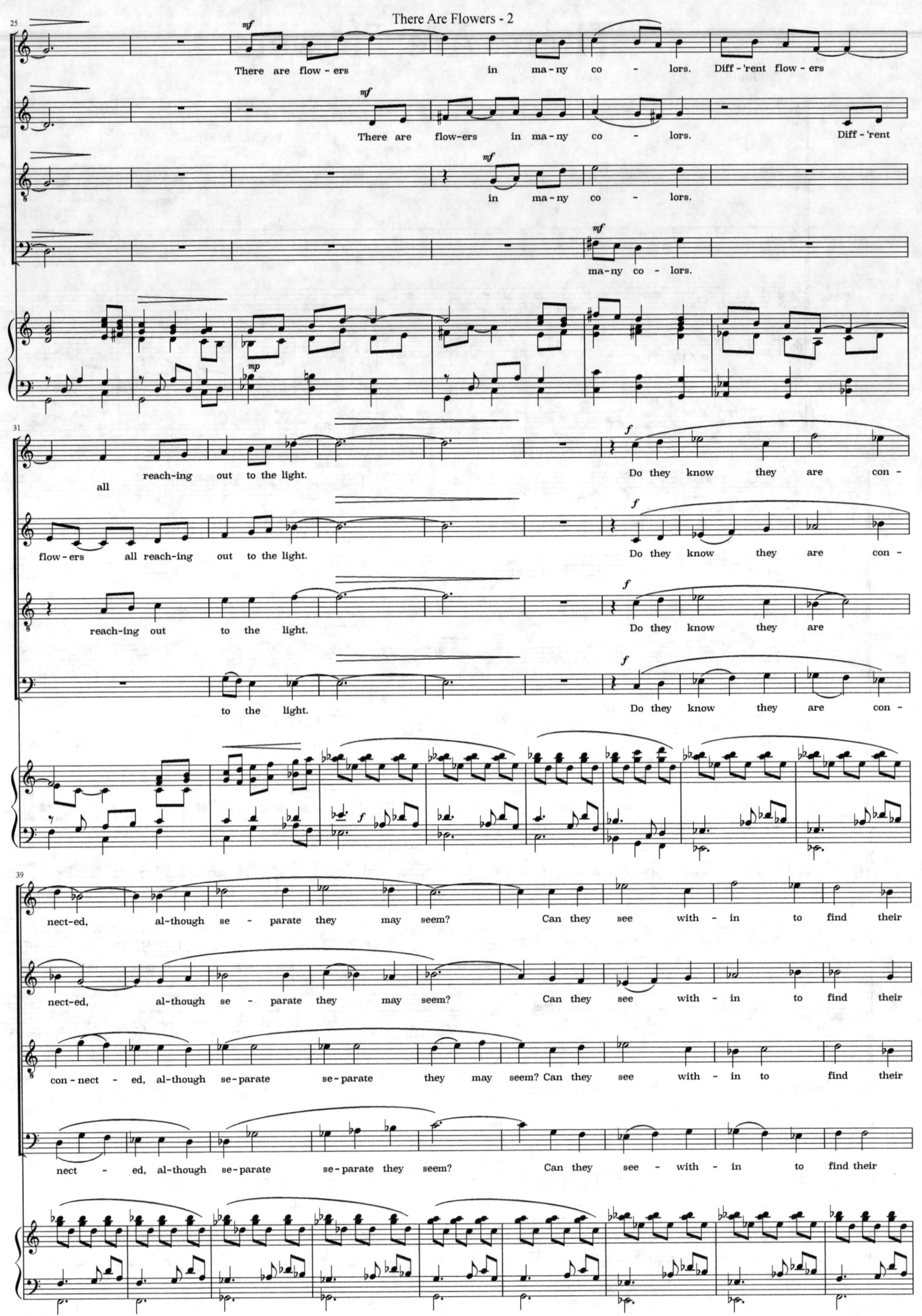
25
mf
There are flow - ers in ma - ny co - lors. Diff - 'rent flow - ers
There are flow-ers in ma - ny co - lors. Diff - 'rent
in ma - ny co - lors.
ma - ny co - lors.
mp
31
all reach-ing out to the light. Do they know they are con -
flow - ers all reach-ing out to the light. Do they know they are con -
reach-ing out to the light. Do they know they are
to the light. Do they know they are con -
f
39
nect-ed, al-though se - parate they may seem? Can they see with - in to find their
nect-ed, al-though se - parate they may seem? Can they see with - in to find their
con - nect - ed, al-though se-parate se-parate they may seem? Can they see with - in to find their
nect - ed, al-though se-parate se-parate they seem? Can they see - with - in to find their

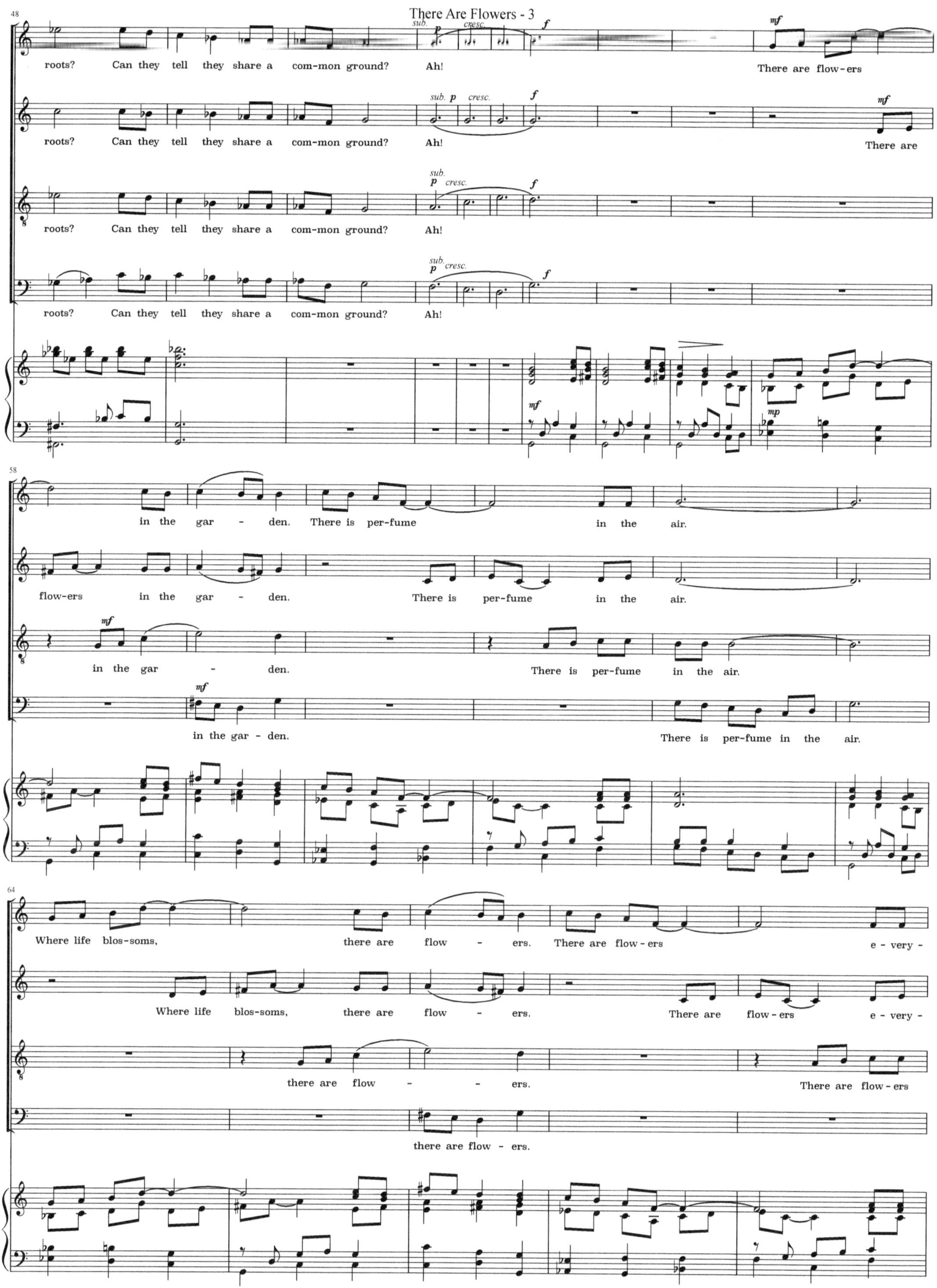
48
sub. p cresc. f
roots? Can they tell they share a com-mon ground? Ah!
mf
There are flow-ers
roots? Can they tell they share a com-mon ground? Ah!
There are
roots? Can they tell they share a com-mon ground? Ah!
roots? Can they tell they share a com-mon ground? Ah!
mp
58
in the gar - den. There is per-fume in the air.
flow-ers in the gar - den. There is per-fume in the air.
in the gar - den. There is per-fume in the air.
in the gar - den. There is per-fume in the air.
64
Where life blos-soms, there are flow - ers. There are flow-ers e - very -
Where life blos-soms, there are flow - ers. There are flow-ers e - very -
there are flow - - ers. There are flow-ers
there are flow - ers.

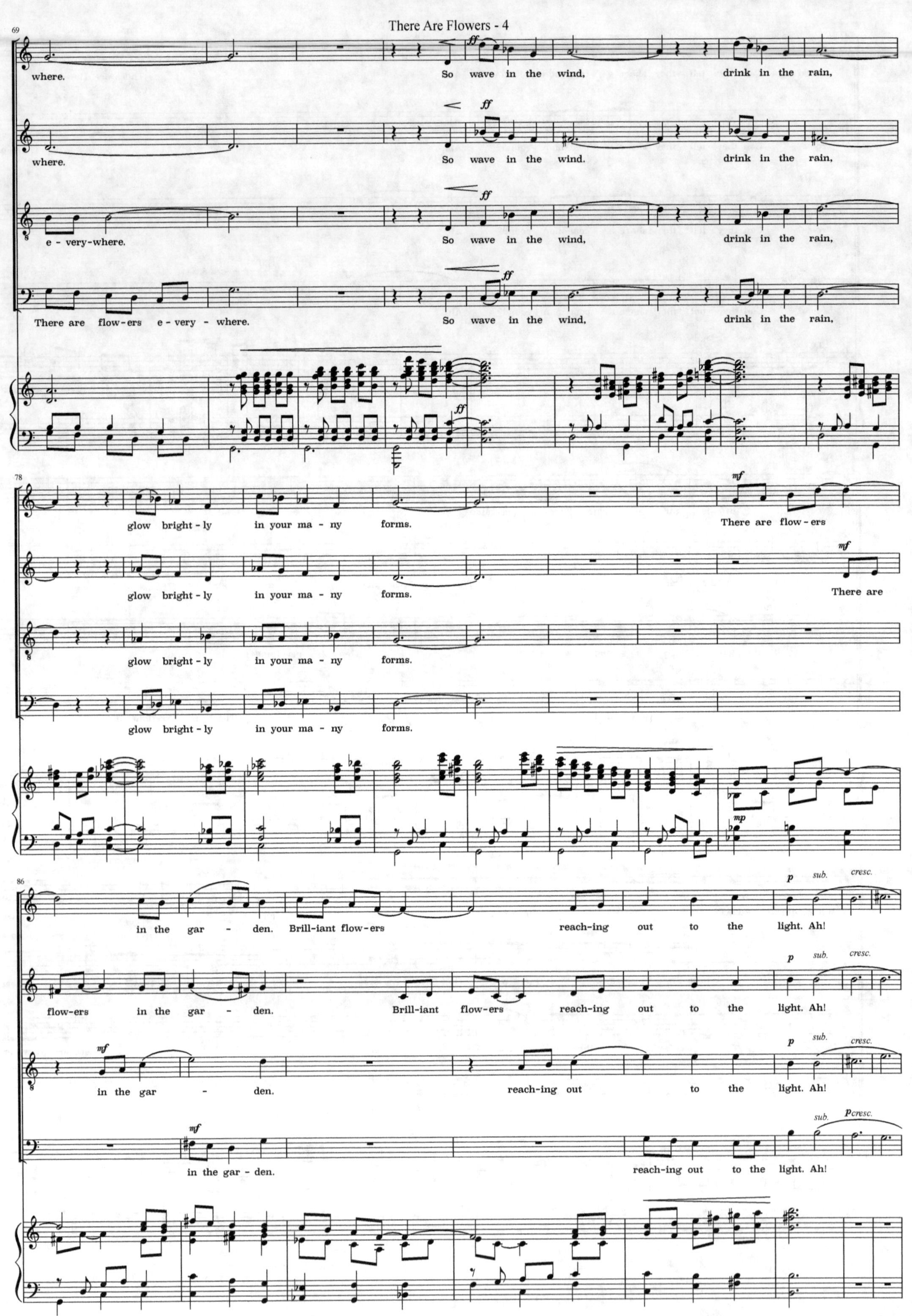
69
ff
where.
So wave in the wind,
drink in the rain,
ff
where.
So wave in the wind,
drink in the rain,
ff
e - very-where.
So wave in the wind,
drink in the rain,
ff
There are flow-ers e - very - where.
So wave in the wind,
drink in the rain,
ff
78
glow bright - ly in your ma - ny forms.
mf
There are flow - ers
glow bright - ly in your ma - ny forms.
mf
There are
glow bright - ly in your ma - ny forms.
glow bright - ly in your ma - ny forms.
mp
86
in the gar - den. Brill-iant flow-ers reach-ing out to the light. Ah!
p sub. cresc.
flow-ers in the gar - den. Brill-iant flow-ers reach-ing out to the light. Ah!
p sub. cresc.
mf
in the gar - den. reach-ing out to the light. Ah!
p sub. cresc.
mf
in the gar - den. reach-ing out to the light. Ah!
sub. p cresc.

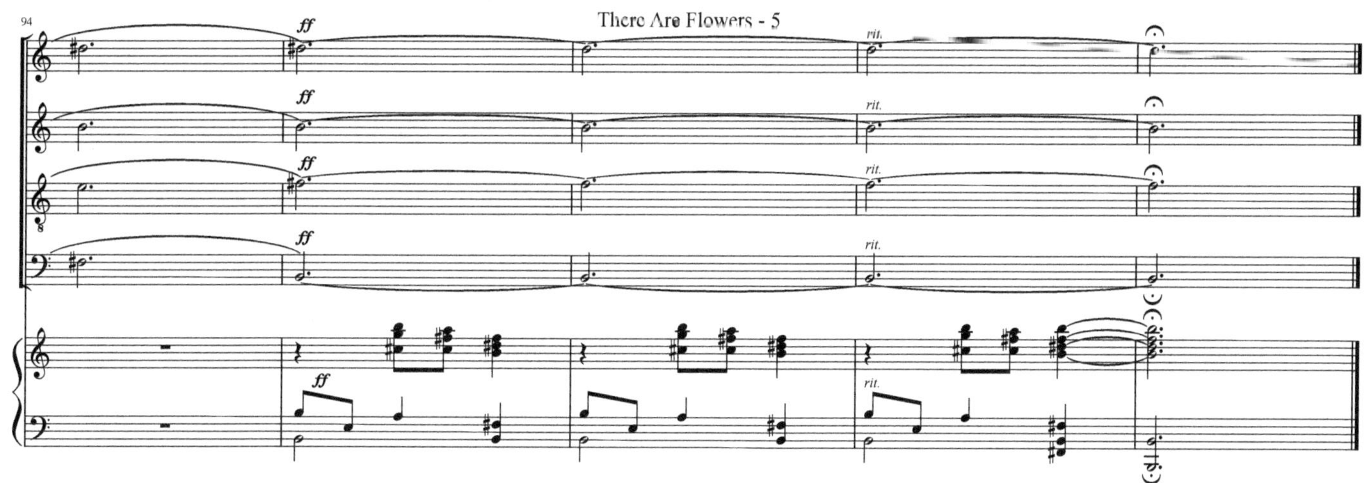
94
ff
rit.

There's A Way

Ken Langer

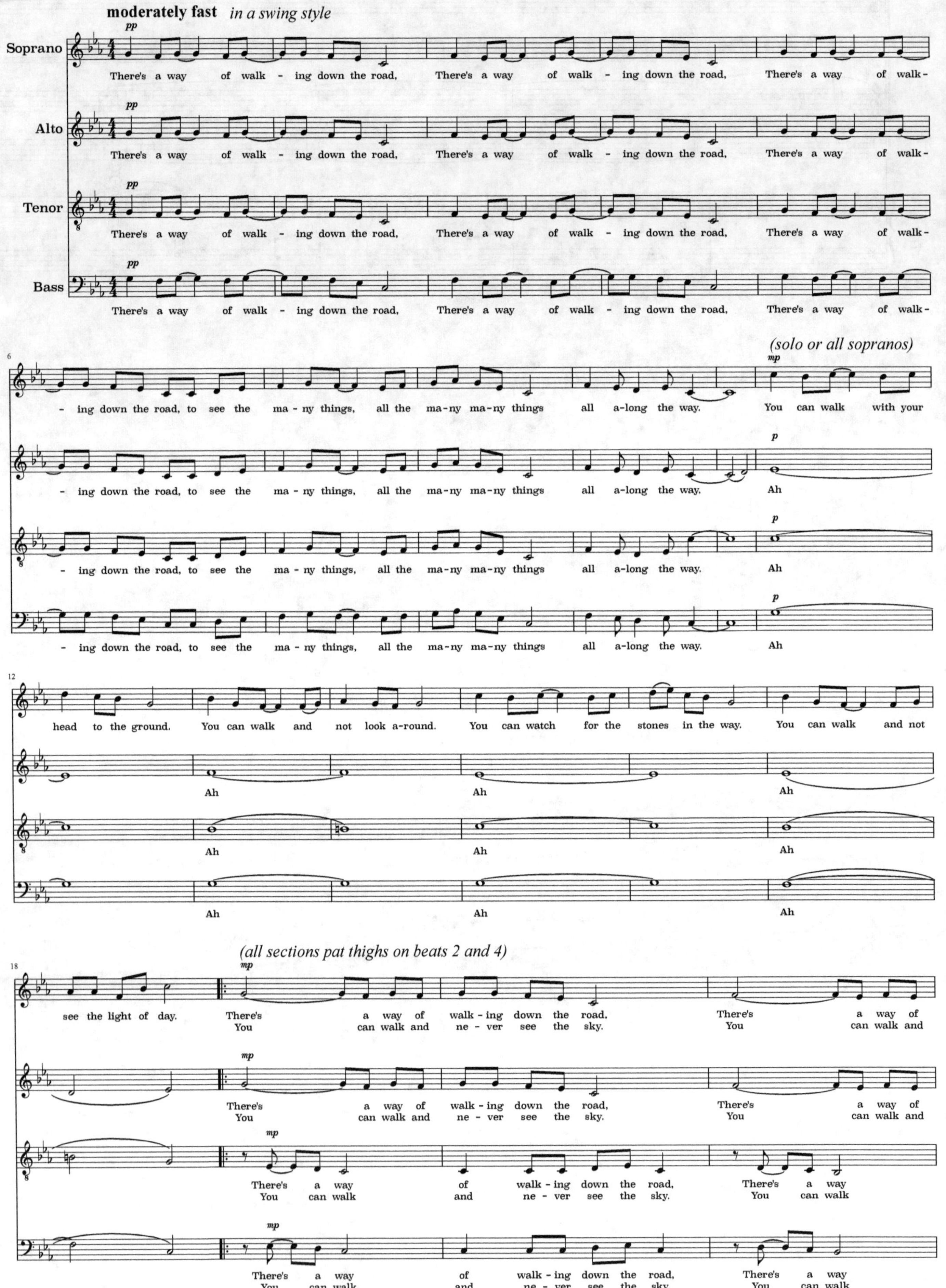

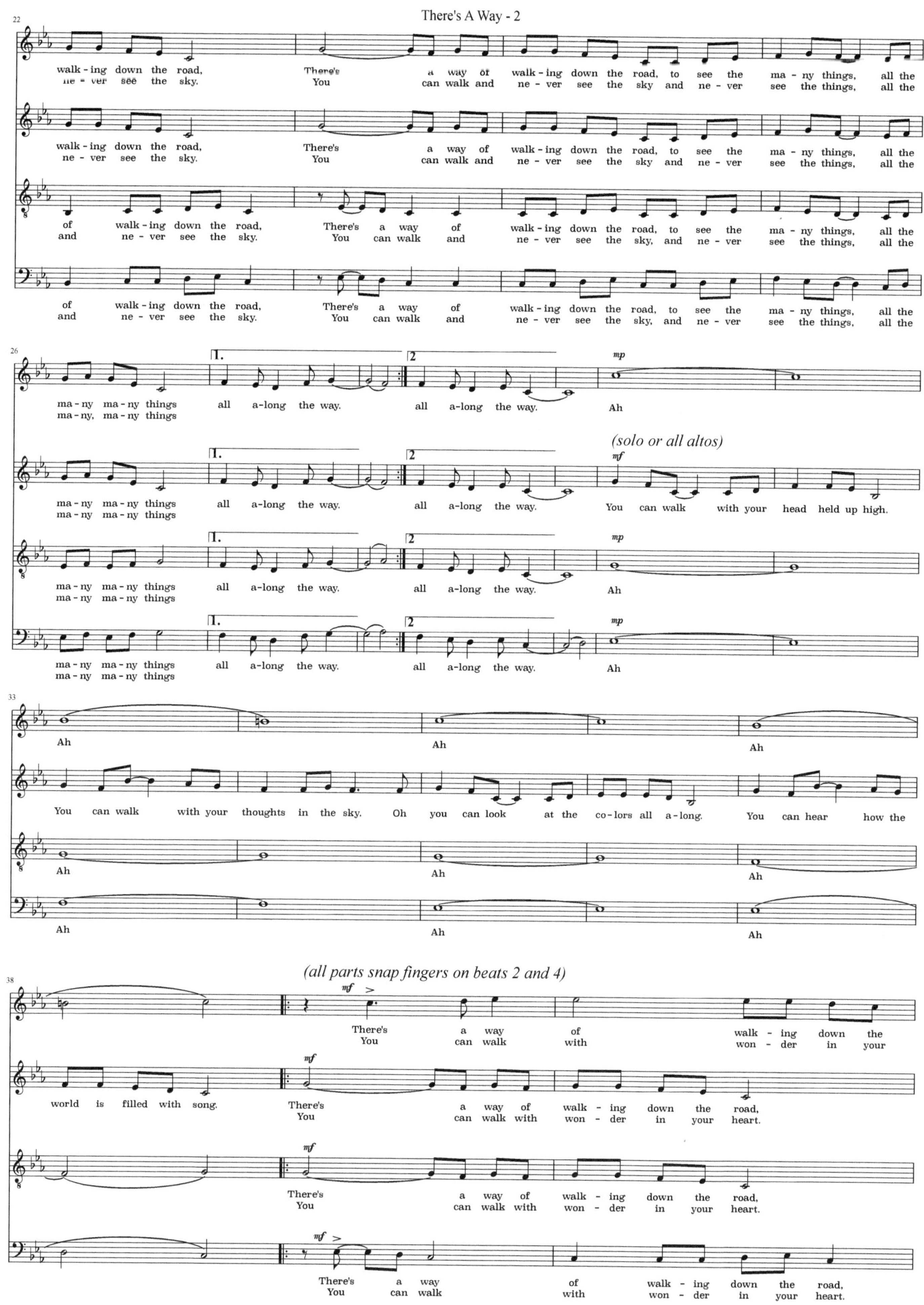
22
walk - ing down the road, There's a way of walk - ing down the road, to see the ma - ny things, all the
ne - ver see the sky. You can walk and ne - ver see the sky and ne - ver see the things, all the
walk - ing down the road, There's a way of walk - ing down the road, to see the ma - ny things, all the
ne - ver see the sky. You can walk and ne - ver see the sky and ne - ver see the things, all the
of walk - ing down the road, There's a way of walk - ing down the road, to see the ma - ny things, all the
and ne - ver see the sky. You can walk and ne - ver see the sky, and ne - ver see the things, all the
of walk - ing down the road, There's a way of walk - ing down the road, to see the ma - ny things, all the
and ne - ver see the sky. You can walk and ne - ver see the sky, and ne - ver see the things, all the
26
1. 2.
mp
ma - ny ma - ny things all a-long the way. all a-long the way. Ah
ma - ny, ma - ny things
(solo or all altos)
mf
ma - ny ma - ny things all a-long the way. all a-long the way. You can walk with your head held up high.
ma - ny ma - ny things
ma - ny ma - ny things all a-long the way. all a-long the way. Ah
ma - ny ma - ny things
ma - ny ma - ny things all a-long the way. all a-long the way. Ah
ma - ny ma - ny things
33
Ah Ah Ah
You can walk with your thoughts in the sky. Oh you can look at the co-lors all a-long. You can hear how the
Ah Ah Ah
Ah Ah Ah
38
(all parts snap fingers on beats 2 and 4)
mf
There's a way of walk - ing down the
You can walk with won - der in your
world is filled with song. There's a way of walk - ing down the road,
You can walk with won - der in your heart.
There's a way of walk - ing down the road,
You can walk with won - der in your heart.
There's a way of walk - ing down the road,
You can walk with won - der in your heart.

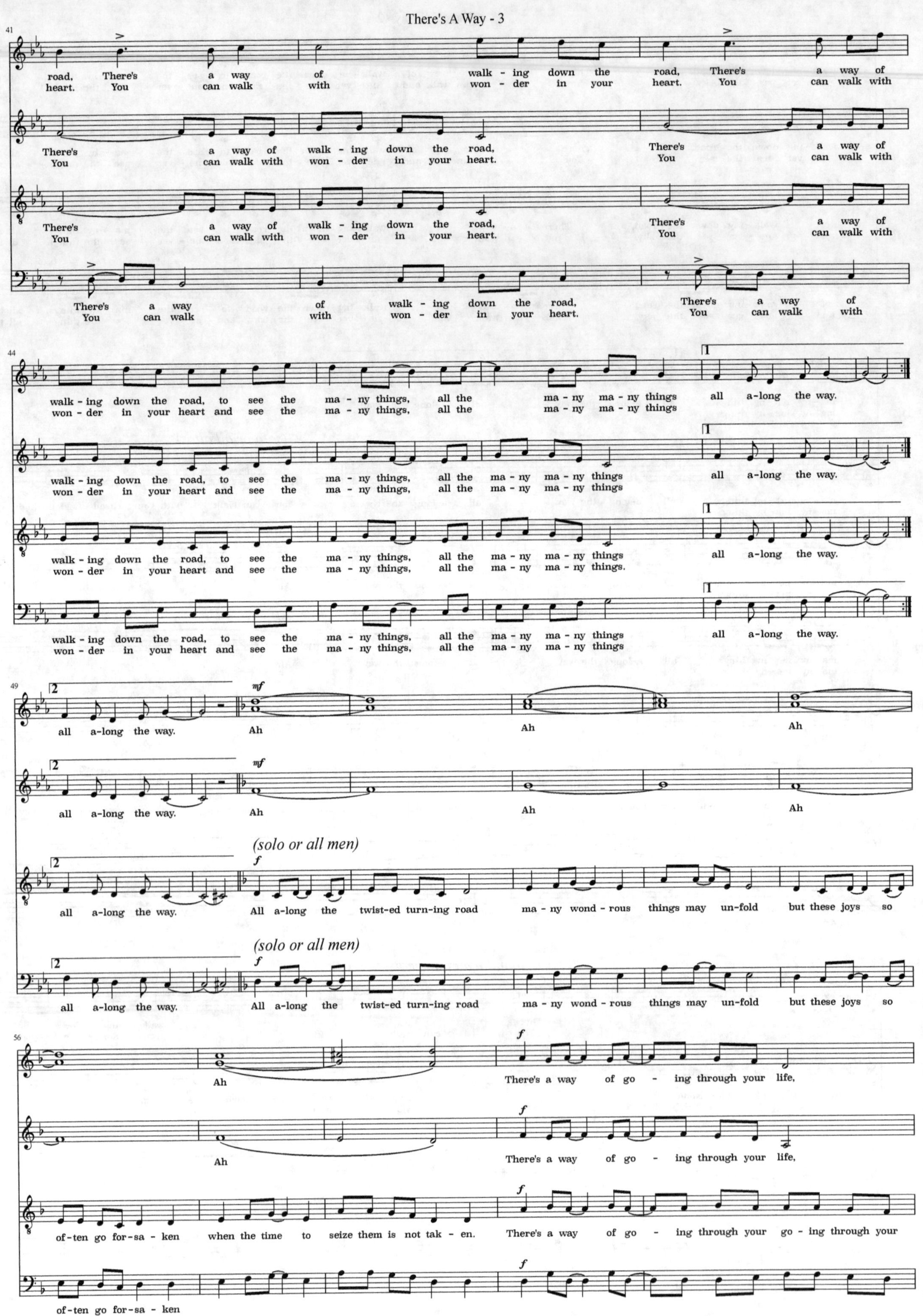
41
road, There's a way of walk - ing down the road, There's a way of
heart. You can walk with won - der in your heart. You can walk with
There's a way of walk - ing down the road, There's a way of
You can walk with won - der in your heart. You can walk with
There's a way of walk - ing down the road, There's a way of
You can walk with won - der in your heart. You can walk with
There's a way of walk - ing down the road, There's a way of
You can walk with won - der in your heart. You can walk with
44
walk - ing down the road, to see the ma - ny things, all the ma - ny ma - ny things all a-long the way.
won - der in your heart and see the ma - ny things, all the ma - ny ma - ny things
walk - ing down the road, to see the ma - ny things, all the ma - ny ma - ny things all a-long the way.
won - der in your heart and see the ma - ny things, all the ma - ny ma - ny things.
49
all a-long the way. Ah Ah Ah
(solo or all men)
All a-long the twist-ed turn-ing road ma - ny wond - rous things may un-fold but these joys so
56
Ah There's a way of go - ing through your life,
of-ten go for-sa - ken when the time to seize them is not tak - en. There's a way of go - ing through your go - ing through your
of-ten go for-sa - ken

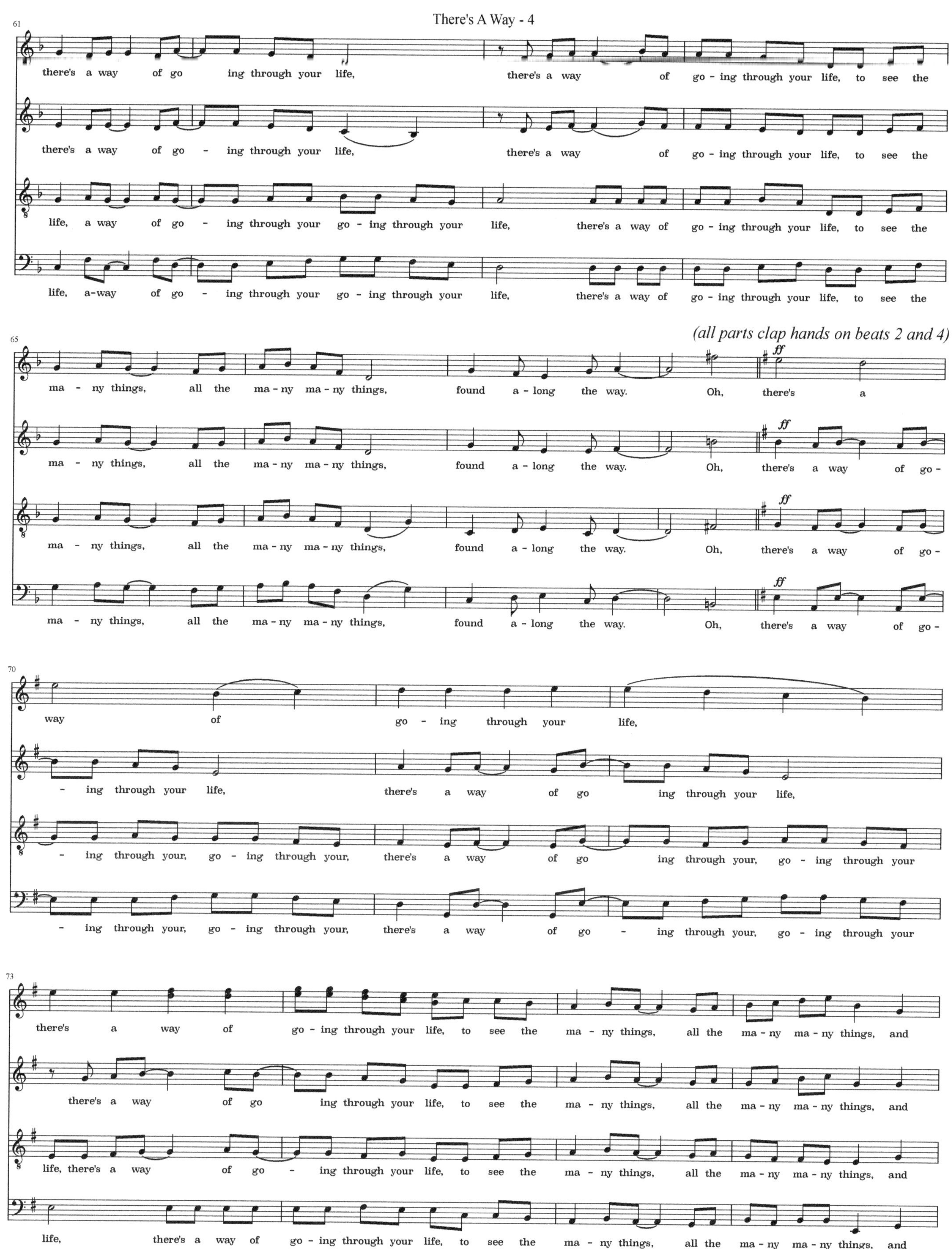
61
there's a way of go ing through your life, there's a way of go - ing through your life, to see the
there's a way of go - ing through your life, there's a way of go - ing through your life, to see the
life, a way of go - ing through your go - ing through your life, there's a way of go - ing through your life, to see the
life, a-way of go - ing through your go - ing through your life, there's a way of go - ing through your life, to see the
65
(all parts clap hands on beats 2 and 4)
ff
ma - ny things, all the ma - ny ma - ny things, found a - long the way. Oh, there's a
ma - ny things, all the ma - ny ma - ny things, found a - long the way. Oh, there's a way of go -
ma - ny things, all the ma - ny ma - ny things, found a - long the way. Oh, there's a way of go -
ma - ny things, all the ma - ny ma - ny things, found a - long the way. Oh, there's a way of go -
70
way of go - ing through your life,
- ing through your life, there's a way of go ing through your life,
- ing through your, go - ing through your, there's a way of go ing through your, go - ing through your
- ing through your, go - ing through your, there's a way of go - ing through your, go - ing through your
73
there's a way of go - ing through your life, to see the ma - ny things, all the ma - ny ma - ny things, and
there's a way of go ing through your life, to see the ma - ny things, all the ma - ny ma - ny things, and
life, there's a way of go - ing through your life, to see the ma - ny things, all the ma - ny ma - ny things, and
life, there's a way of go - ing through your life, to see the ma - ny things, all the ma - ny ma - ny things, and

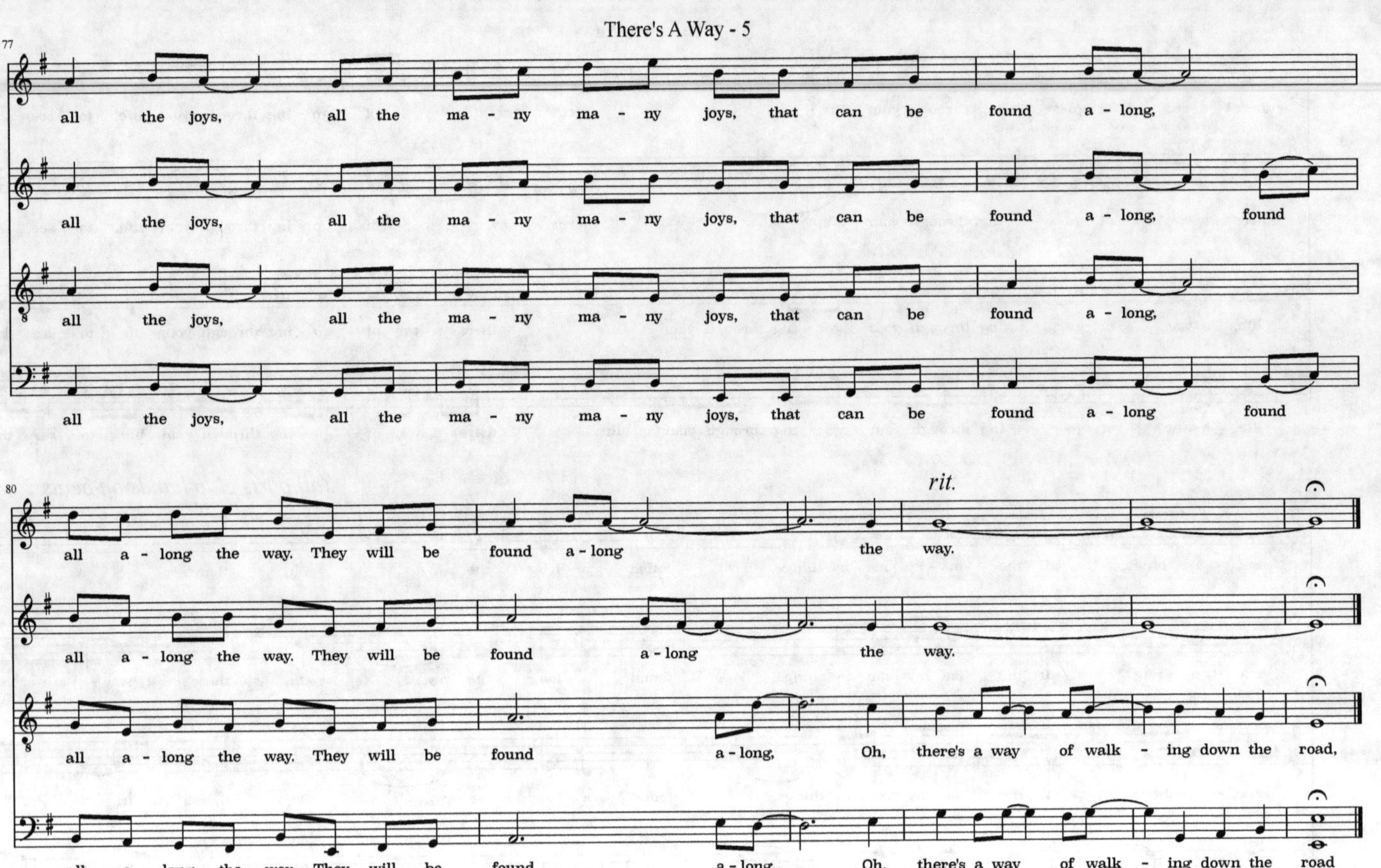
77
all the joys, all the ma - ny ma - ny joys, that can be found a - long,
all the joys, all the ma - ny ma - ny joys, that can be found a - long, found
all the joys, all the ma - ny ma - ny joys, that can be found a - long,
all the joys, all the ma - ny ma - ny joys, that can be found a - long found
80
rit.
all a - long the way. They will be found a - long the way.
all a - long the way. They will be found a - long the way.
all a - long the way. They will be found a - long, Oh, there's a way of walk - ing down the road,
all a - long the way. They will be found a - long, Oh, there's a way of walk - ing down the road

This Is The Night

Ken Langer

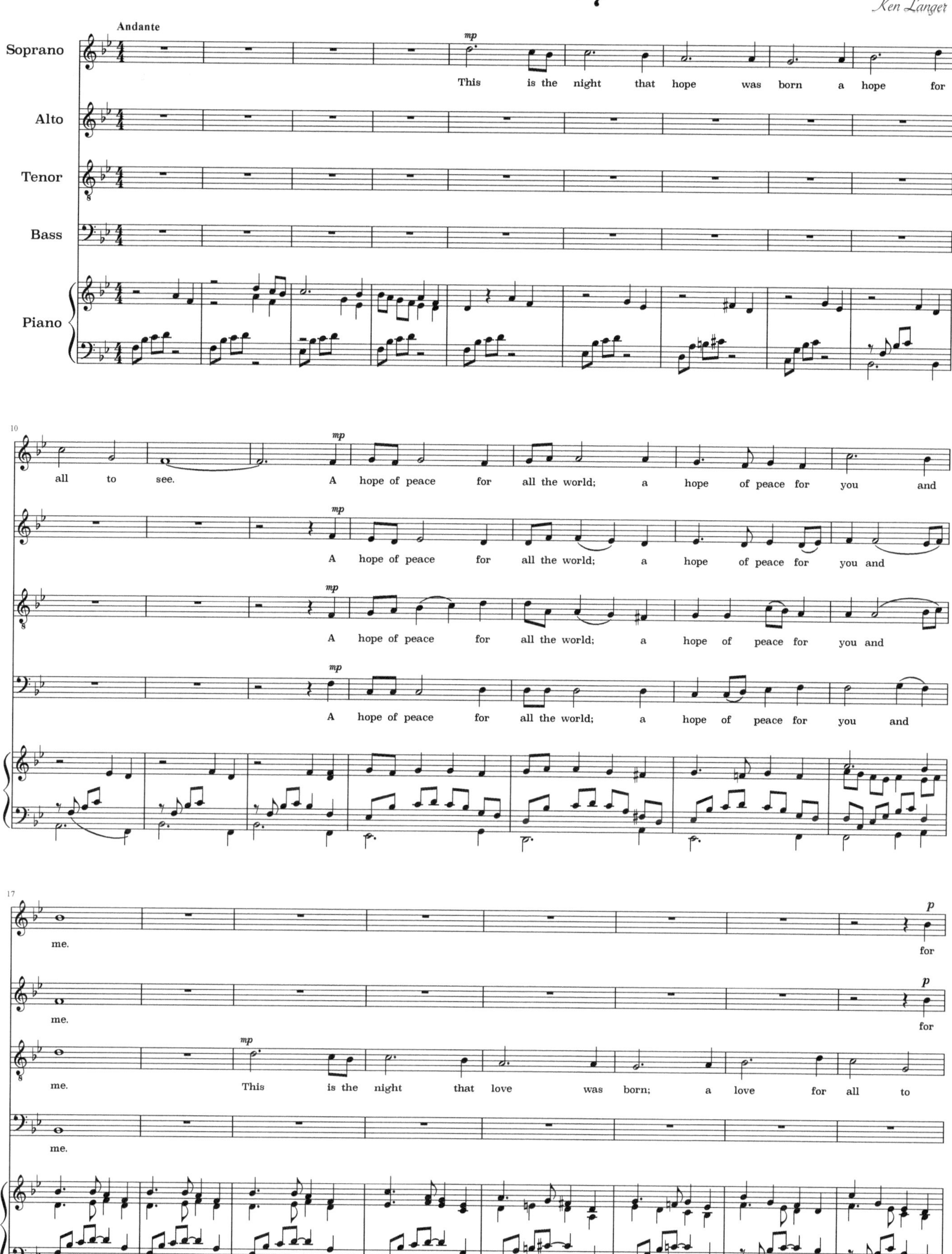

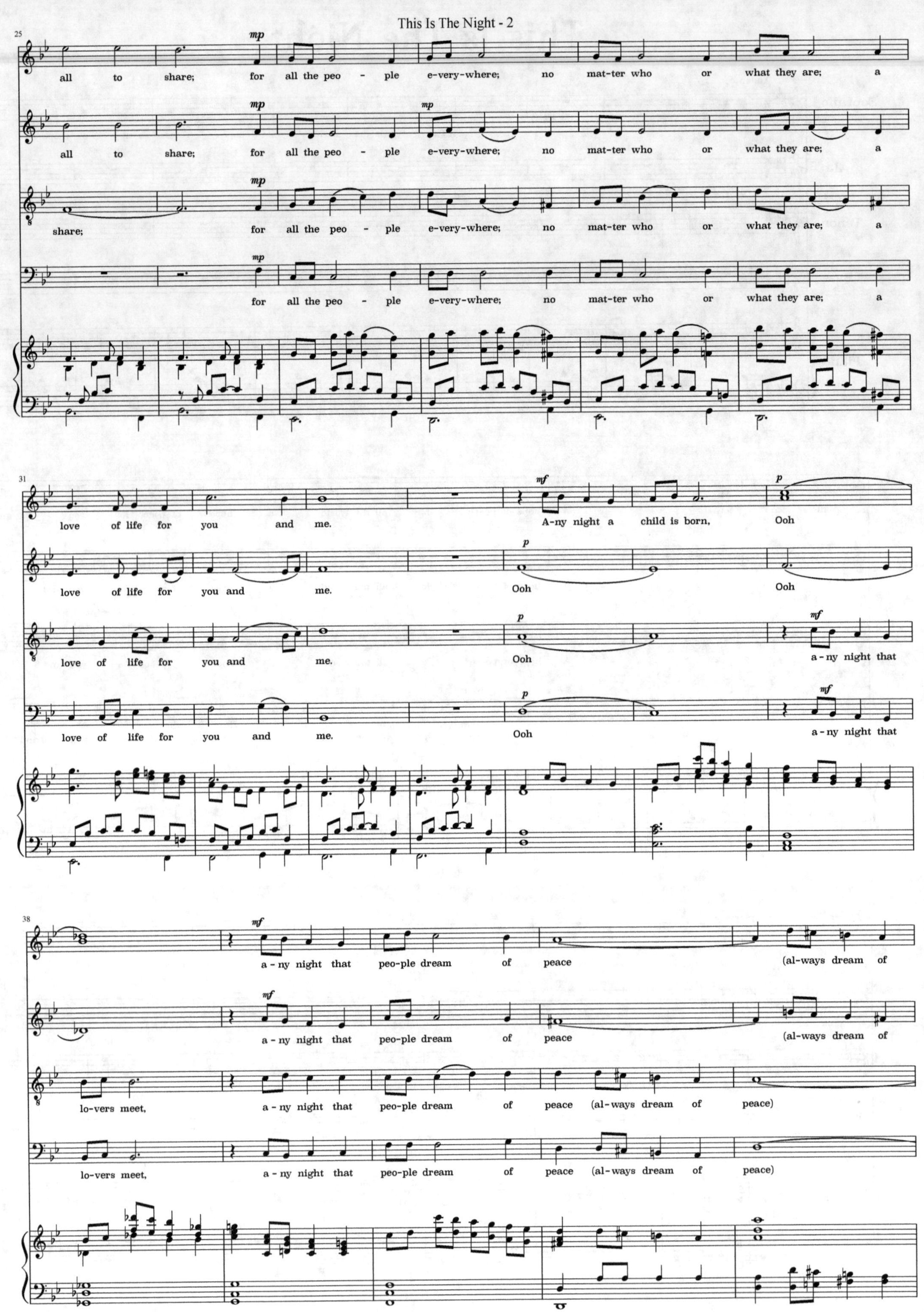
This Is The Night - 2
25
mp
all to share; for all the peo - ple e-very-where; no mat-ter who or what they are; a
share; for all the peo - ple e-very-where; no mat-ter who or what they are; a
31
love of life for you and me.
mf
A-ny night a child is born,
p
Ooh
a-ny night that
38
lo-vers meet,
a-ny night that peo-ple dream of peace
(al-ways dream of
(al-ways dream of peace)

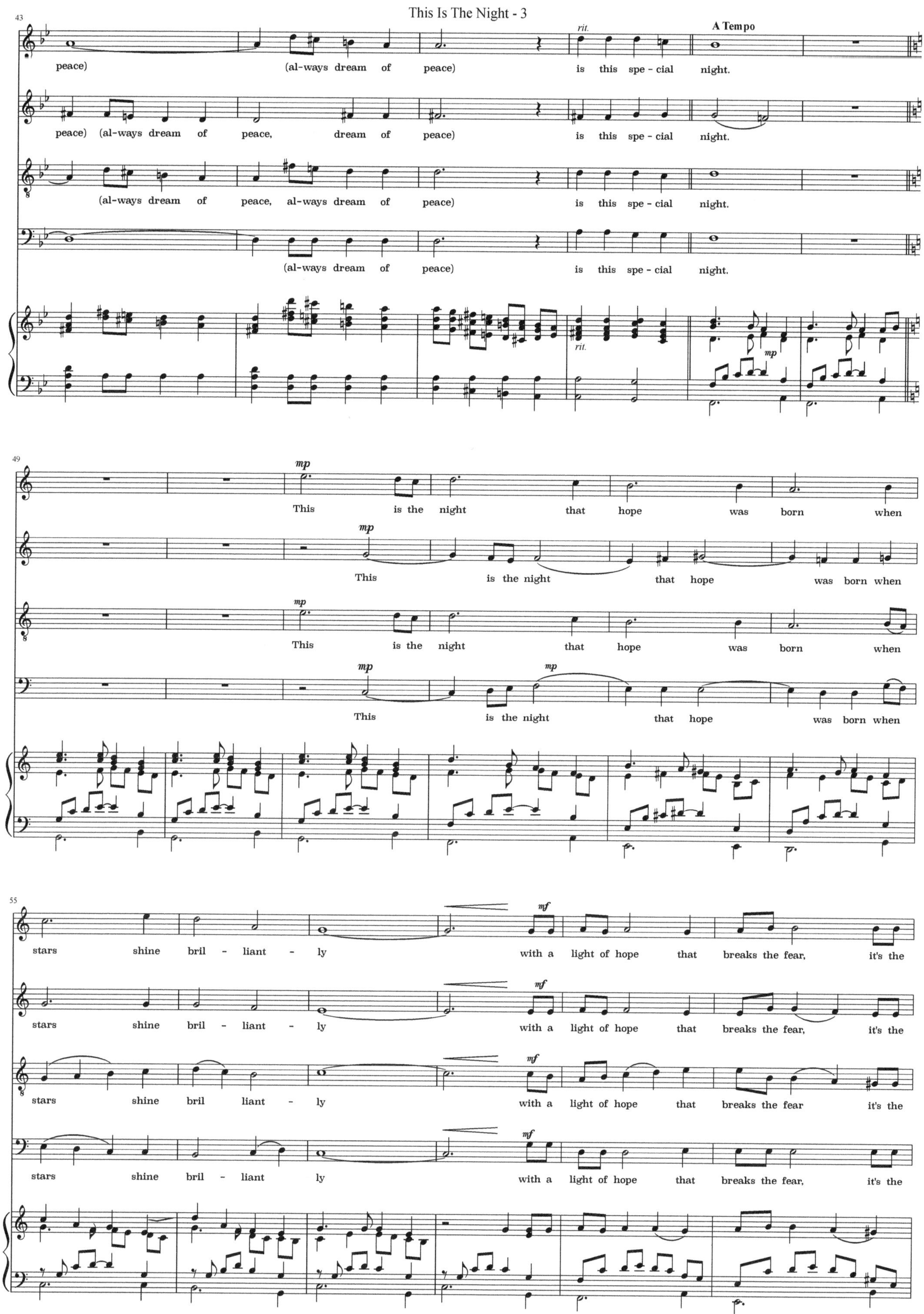
43
rit.
A Tempo
peace) (al-ways dream of peace) is this spe - cial night.
peace) (al-ways dream of peace, dream of peace) is this spe - cial night.
(al-ways dream of peace, al-ways dream of peace) is this spe - cial night.
(al-ways dream of peace) is this spe - cial night.
rit.
mp
49
mp
This is the night that hope was born when
This is the night that hope was born when
This is the night that hope was born when
This is the night that hope was born when
55
mf
stars shine bril - liant - ly with a light of hope that breaks the fear, it's the
stars shine bril - liant - ly with a light of hope that breaks the fear, it's the
stars shine bril liant - ly with a light of hope that breaks the fear it's the
stars shine bril - liant ly with a light of hope that breaks the fear, it's the

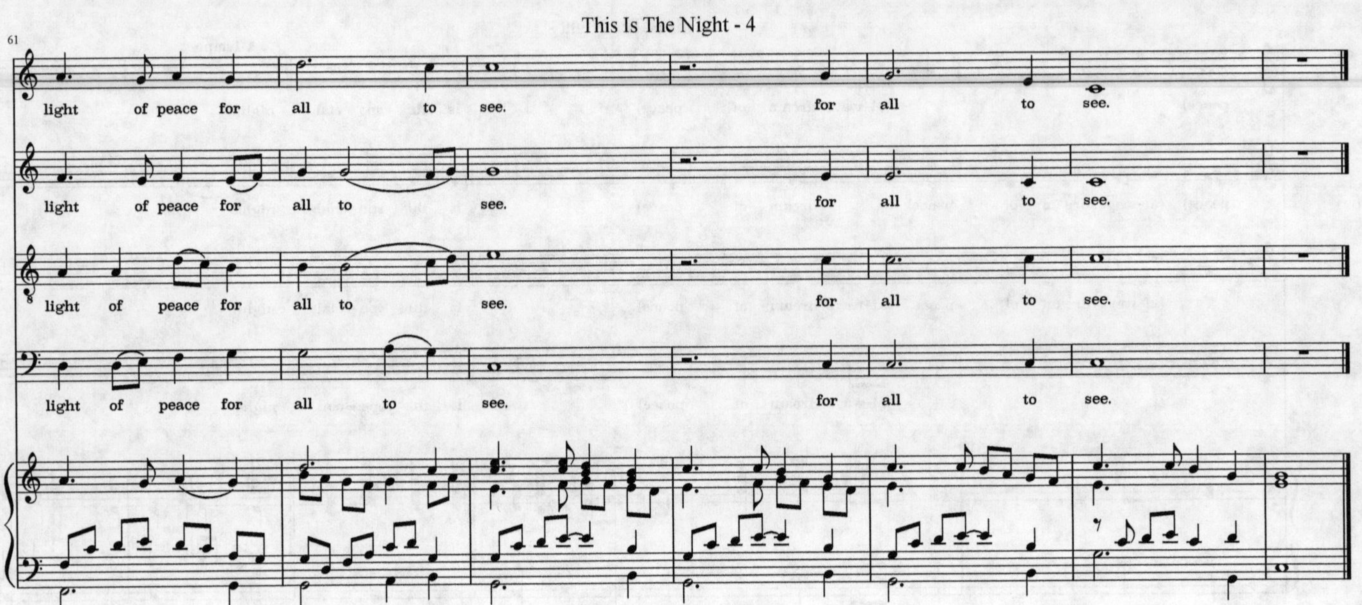
61
light of peace for all to see. for all to see.
light of peace for all to see. for all to see.
light of peace for all to see. for all to see.
light of peace for all to see. for all to see.

Walk In Freedom

a spiritual

arr. Ken Langer

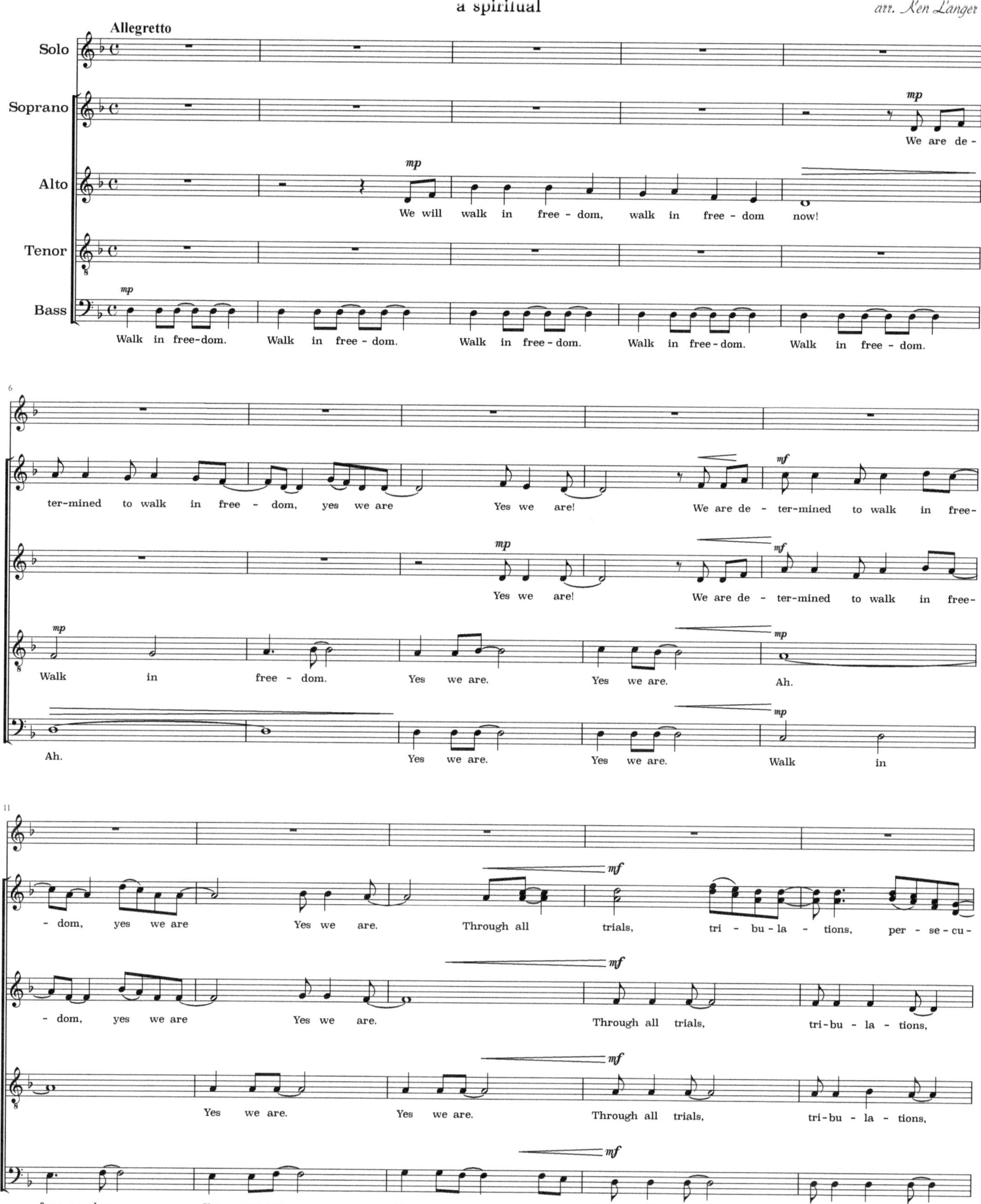

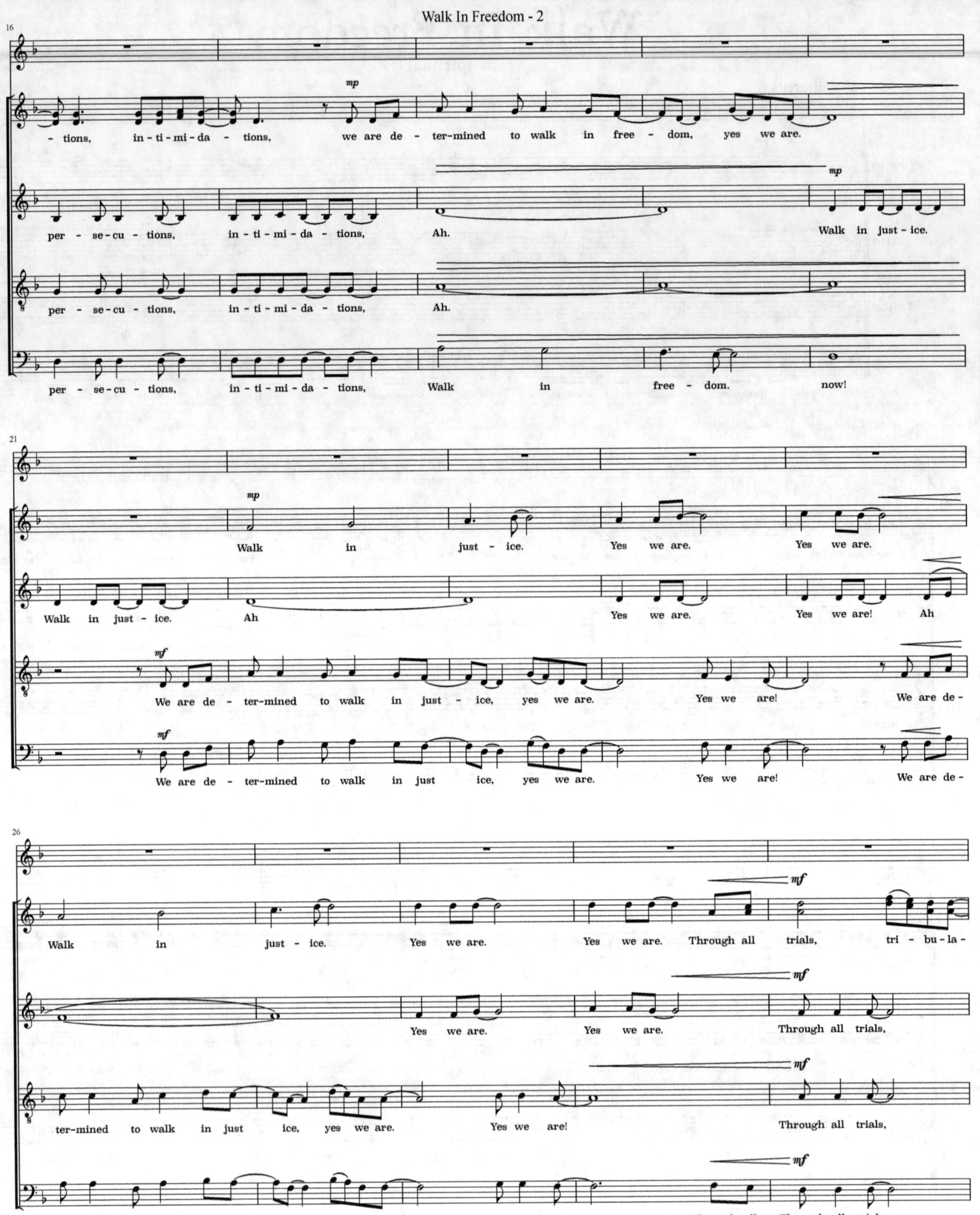
16
mp
- tions, in - ti - mi - da - tions, we are de - ter-mined to walk in free - dom, yes we are.
per - se - cu - tions, in - ti - mi - da - tions, Ah. Walk in just - ice.
per - se - cu - tions, in - ti - mi - da - tions, Ah.
per - se - cu - tions, in - ti - mi - da - tions, Walk in free - dom. now!
21
Walk in just - ice. Yes we are. Yes we are.
Walk in just - ice. Ah Yes we are. Yes we are! Ah
mf
We are de - ter-mined to walk in just - ice, yes we are. Yes we are! We are de -
We are de - ter-mined to walk in just ice, yes we are. Yes we are! We are de -
26
Walk in just - ice. Yes we are. Yes we are. Through all trials, tri - bu - la -
Yes we are. Yes we are. Through all trials,
ter-mined to walk in just ice, yes we are. Yes we are! Through all trials,
ter-mined to walk in just - ice, yes we are. Yes we are! Through all Through all trials,

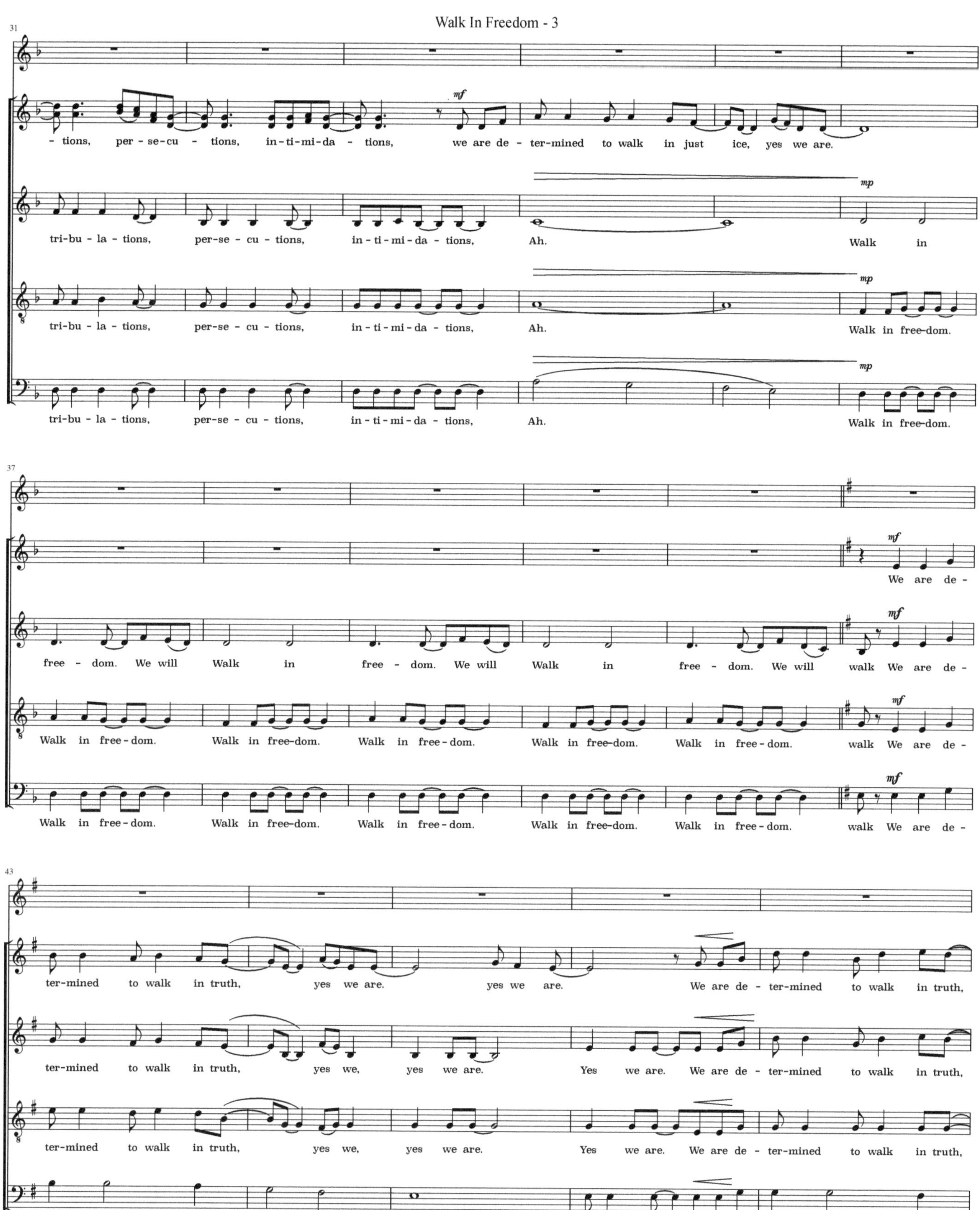
31
mf
- tions, per - se - cu - tions, in - ti - mi - da - tions, we are de - ter - mined to walk in just ice, yes we are.
tri - bu - la - tions, per - se - cu - tions, in - ti - mi - da - tions, Ah.
mp
Walk in
tri - bu - la - tions, per - se - cu - tions, in - ti - mi - da - tions, Ah.
Walk in free - dom.
37
We are de -
free - dom. We will Walk in free - dom. We will Walk in free - dom. We will walk We are de -
Walk in free - dom. Walk in free - dom. Walk in free - dom. Walk in free - dom. Walk in free - dom. walk We are de -
43
ter - mined to walk in truth, yes we are. yes we are. We are de - ter - mined to walk in truth,
ter - mined to walk in truth, yes we, yes we are. Yes we are. We are de - ter - mined to walk in truth,
ter - mined to walk in truth, yes we are. We are de - ter - mined to

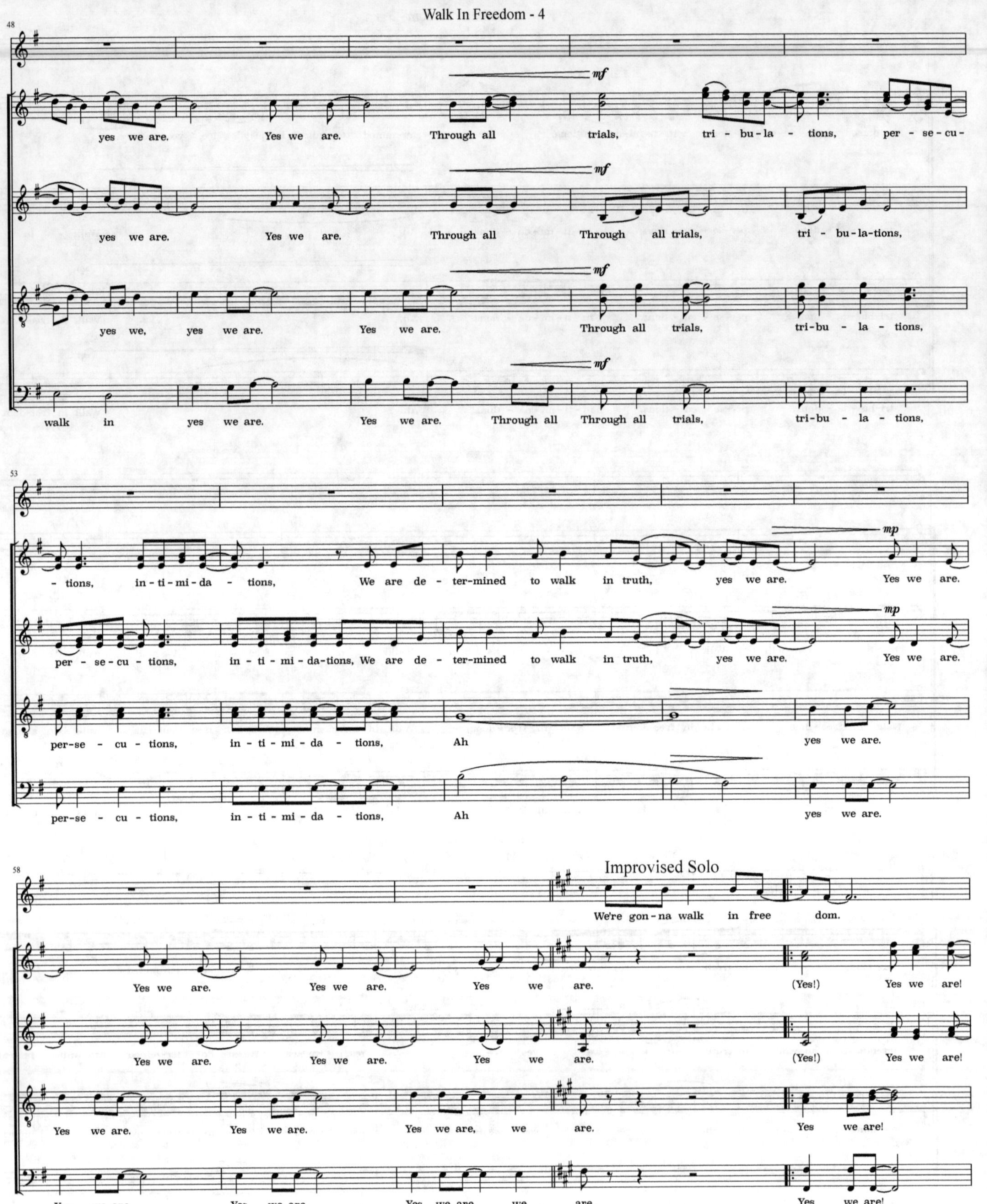
48
yes we are. Yes we are. Through all trials, tri - bu - la - tions, per - se - cu-
yes we are. Yes we are. Through all Through all trials, tri - bu - la - tions,
yes we, yes we are. Yes we are. Through all trials, tri-bu - la - tions,
walk in yes we are. Yes we are. Through all Through all trials, tri-bu - la - tions,
53
- tions, in - ti - mi - da - tions, We are de - ter-mined to walk in truth, yes we are. Yes we are.
per - se - cu - tions, in - ti - mi - da - tions, We are de - ter-mined to walk in truth, yes we are. Yes we are.
per-se - cu - tions, in - ti - mi - da - tions, Ah yes we are.
per-se - cu - tions, in - ti - mi - da - tions, Ah yes we are.
58
Improvised Solo
We're gon - na walk in free dom.
Yes we are. Yes we are. Yes we are. (Yes!) Yes we are!
Yes we are. Yes we are. Yes we are. (Yes!) Yes we are!
Yes we are. Yes we are. Yes we are, we are. Yes we are!
Yes we are. Yes we are. Yes we are, we are. Yes we are!

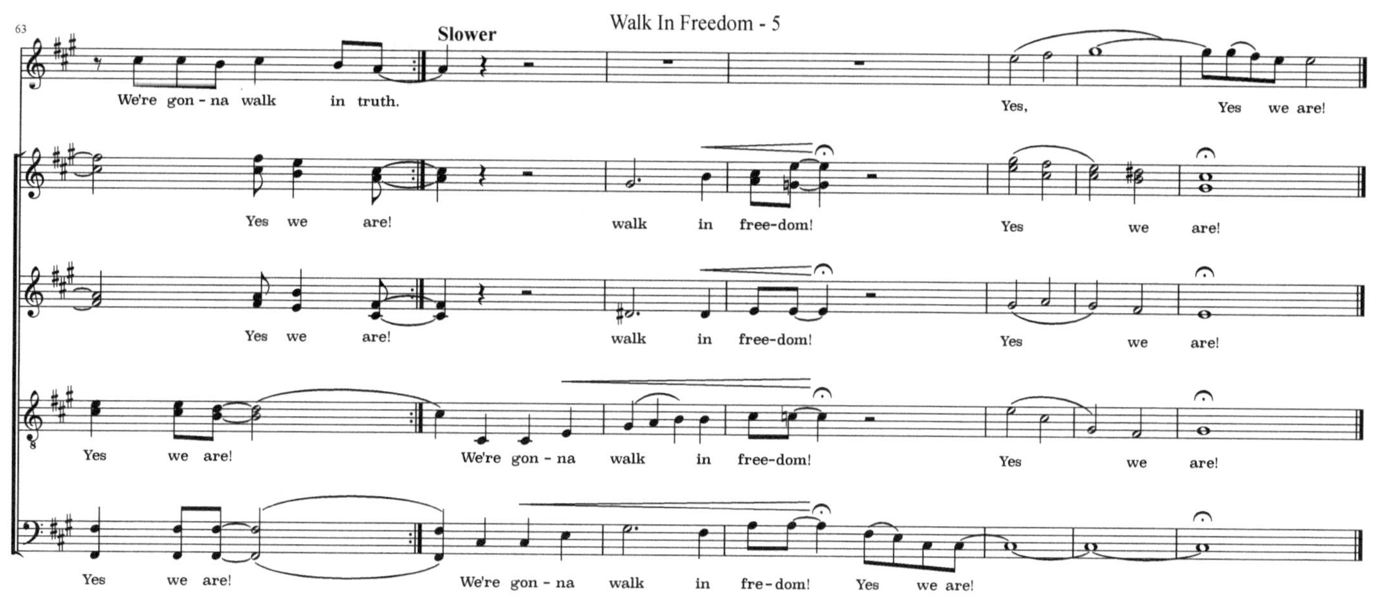
63
Slower
We're gon - na walk in truth.
Yes, Yes we are!
Yes we are!
walk in free-dom!
Yes we are!
Yes we are!
walk in free-dom!
Yes we are!
Yes we are!
We're gon - na walk in free-dom!
Yes we are!
Yes we are!
We're gon - na walk in fre-dom! Yes we are!

Waters of the World

Ken Langer

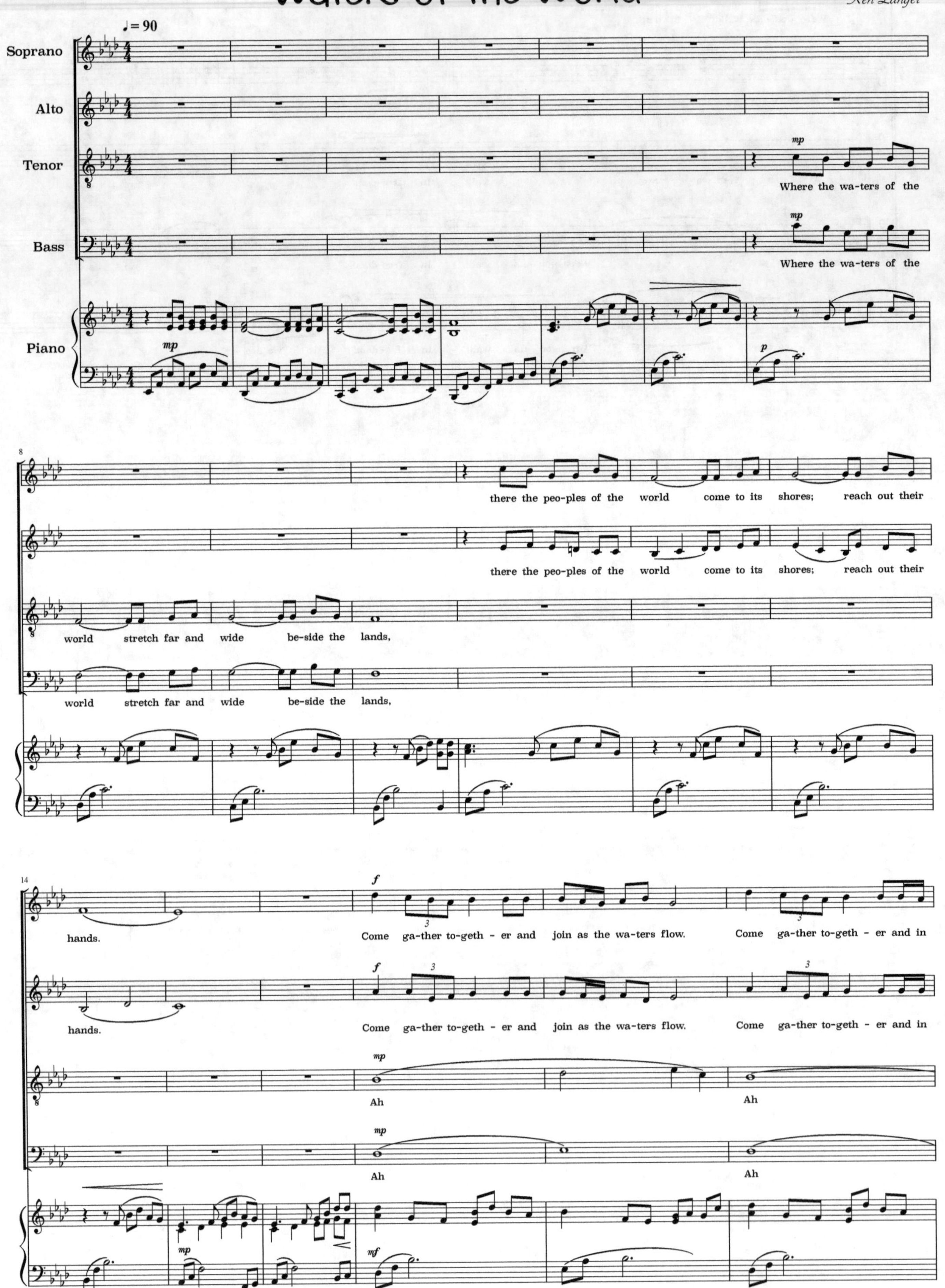

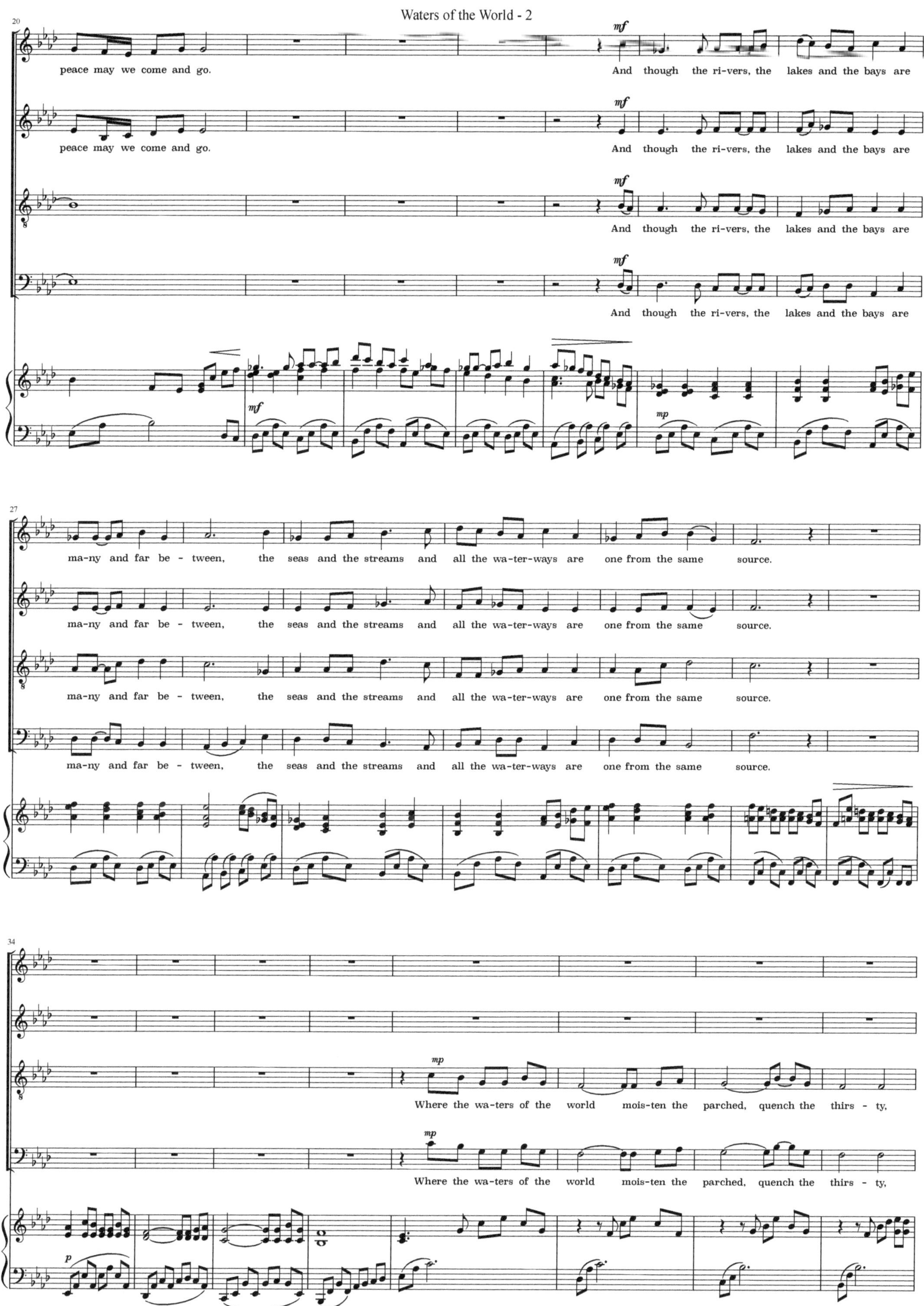
20
peace may we come and go.
mf
And though the ri-vers, the lakes and the bays are
27
ma-ny and far be - tween, the seas and the streams and all the wa-ter-ways are one from the same source.
34
mp
Where the wa-ters of the world mois-ten the parched, quench the thirs - ty,
p

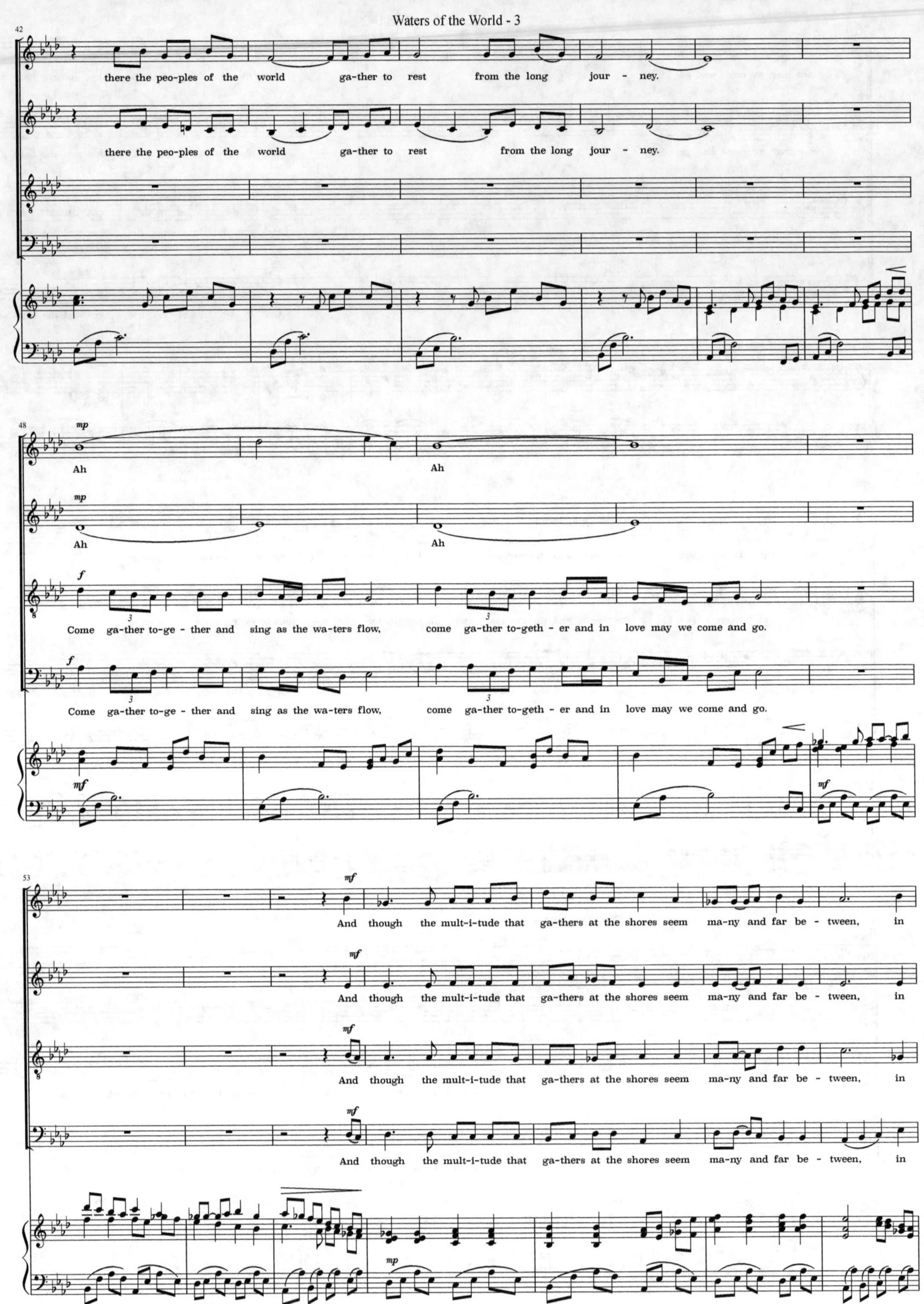
42
there the peo-ples of the world ga-ther to rest from the long jour - ney.
there the peo-ples of the world ga-ther to rest from the long jour - ney.
48
mp
Ah
Ah
mp
Ah
Ah
f
Come ga-ther to-ge - ther and sing as the wa-ters flow, come ga-ther to-geth - er and in love may we come and go.
f
Come ga-ther to-ge - ther and sing as the wa-ters flow, come ga-ther to-geth - er and in love may we come and go.
mf
mf
53
mf
And though the mult-i-tude that ga-thers at the shores seem ma-ny and far be - tween, in
mf
And though the mult-i-tude that ga-thers at the shores seem ma-ny and far be - tween, in
mf
And though the mult-i-tude that ga-thers at the shores seem ma-ny and far be - tween, in
mf
And though the mult-i-tude that ga-thers at the shores seem ma-ny and far be - tween, in
mp

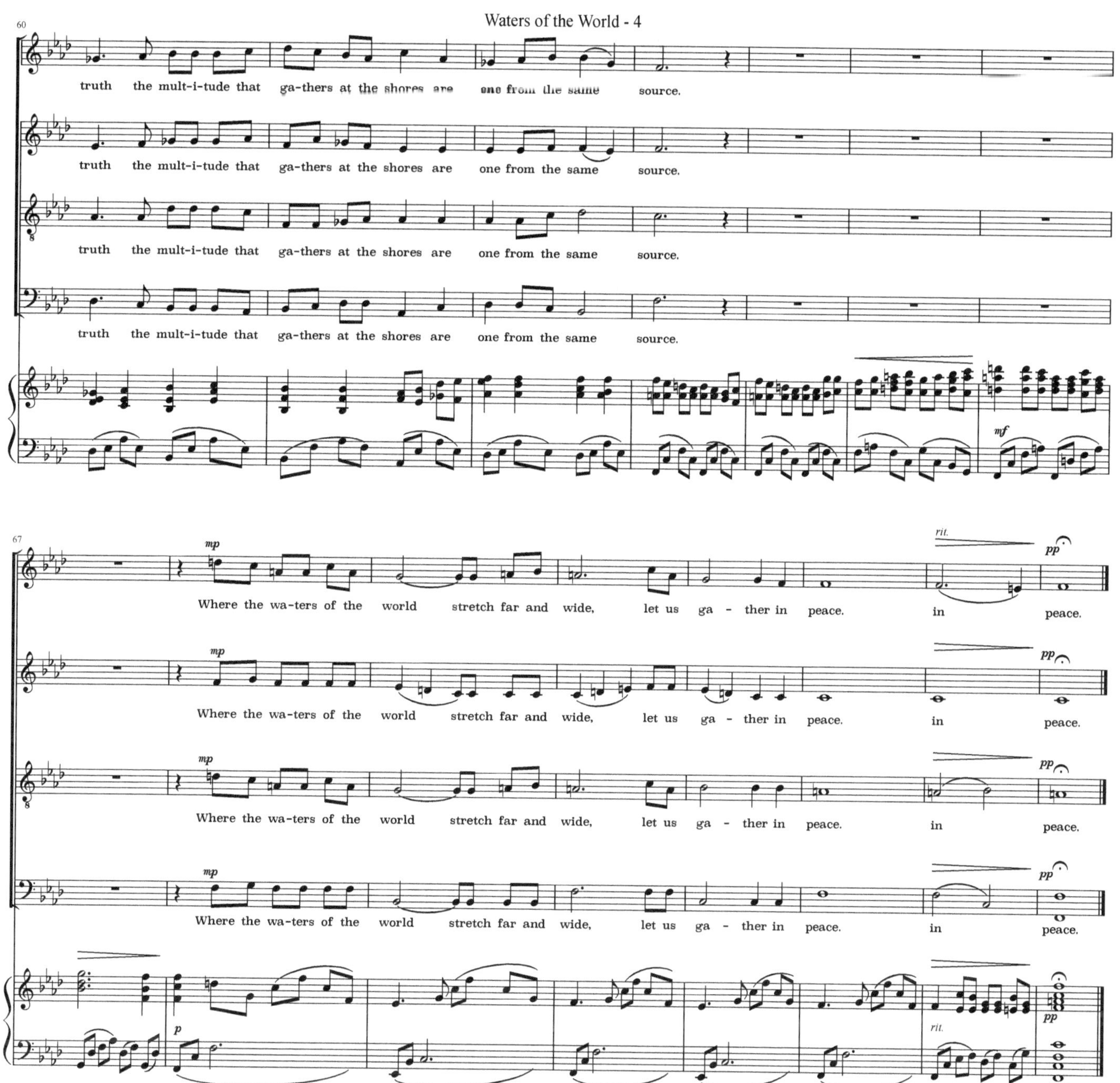
60
truth the mult-i-tude that ga-thers at the shores are one from the same source.
truth the mult-i-tude that ga-thers at the shores are one from the same source.
truth the mult-i-tude that ga-thers at the shores are one from the same source.
truth the mult-i-tude that ga-thers at the shores are one from the same source.
mf
67
mp
Where the wa-ters of the world stretch far and wide, let us ga - ther in peace. in peace.
rit.
pp
mp
Where the wa-ters of the world stretch far and wide, let us ga - ther in peace. in peace.
pp
mp
Where the wa-ters of the world stretch far and wide, let us ga - ther in peace. in peace.
pp
mp
Where the wa-ters of the world stretch far and wide, let us ga - ther in peace. in peace.
pp
p
rit.
pp

We Are One

inspired by the words of Mahmud Shabistari

Ken Langer

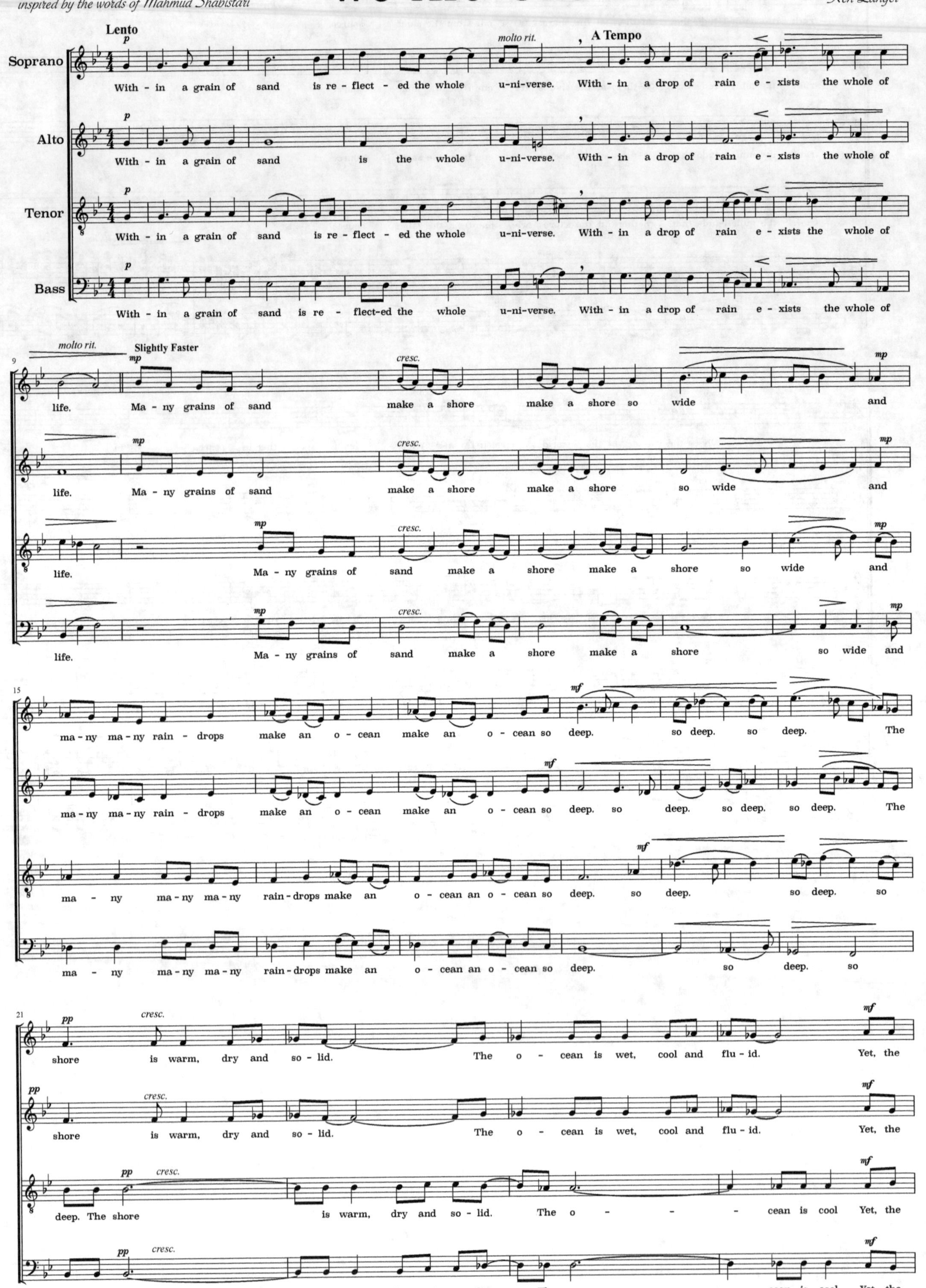

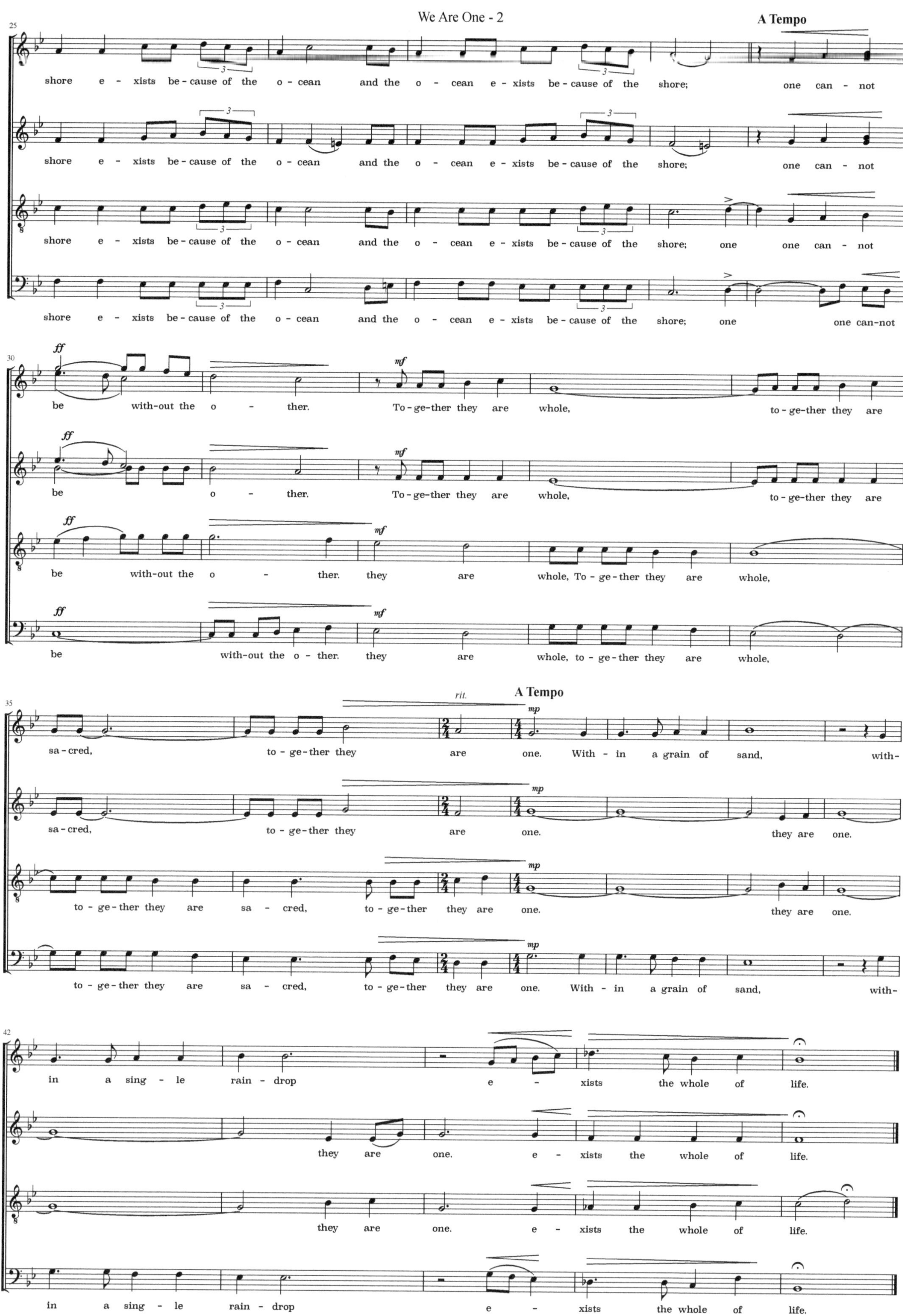
A Tempo
25
shore e - xists be - cause of the o - cean and the o - cean e - xists be - cause of the shore; one can - not
shore e - xists be - cause of the o - cean and the o - cean e - xists be - cause of the shore; one can - not
shore e - xists be - cause of the o - cean and the o - cean e - xists be - cause of the shore; one one can - not
shore e - xists be - cause of the o - cean and the o - cean e - xists be - cause of the shore; one one can-not
30
ff
mf
be with-out the o - ther. To - ge - ther they are whole, to - ge - ther they are
be o - ther. To - ge - ther they are whole, to - ge - ther they are
be with-out the o - ther. they are whole, To - ge - ther they are whole,
be with-out the o - ther. they are whole, to - ge - ther they are whole,
35
rit.
A Tempo
mp
sa - cred, to - ge - ther they are one. With - in a grain of sand, with-
sa - cred, to - ge - ther they are one. they are one.
to - ge - ther they are sa - cred, to - ge - ther they are one. they are one.
to - ge - ther they are sa - cred, to - ge - ther they are one. With - in a grain of sand, with-
42
in a sing - le rain - drop e - xists the whole of life.
they are one. e - xists the whole of life.
they are one. e - xists the whole of life.
in a sing - le rain - drop e - xists the whole of life.

We Welcome You

Ken Langer

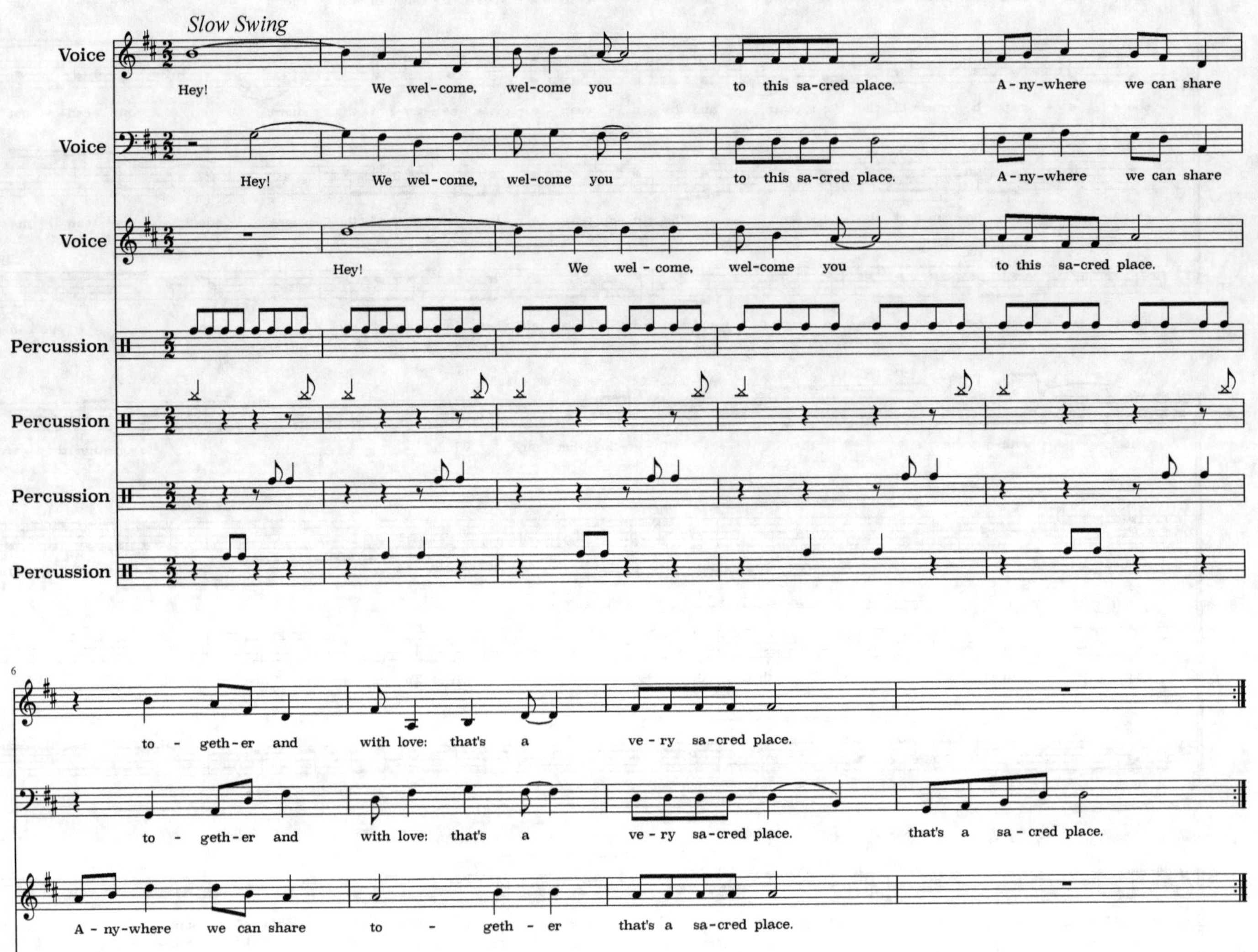

Performance Notes: Begin with percussion then add voices one line at a time. The rhythmic parts were originally written for musical tubes but any unpitched percussion instruments will do.

Seven Hymns

1. Let Us Come Now All Together

Ken Langer

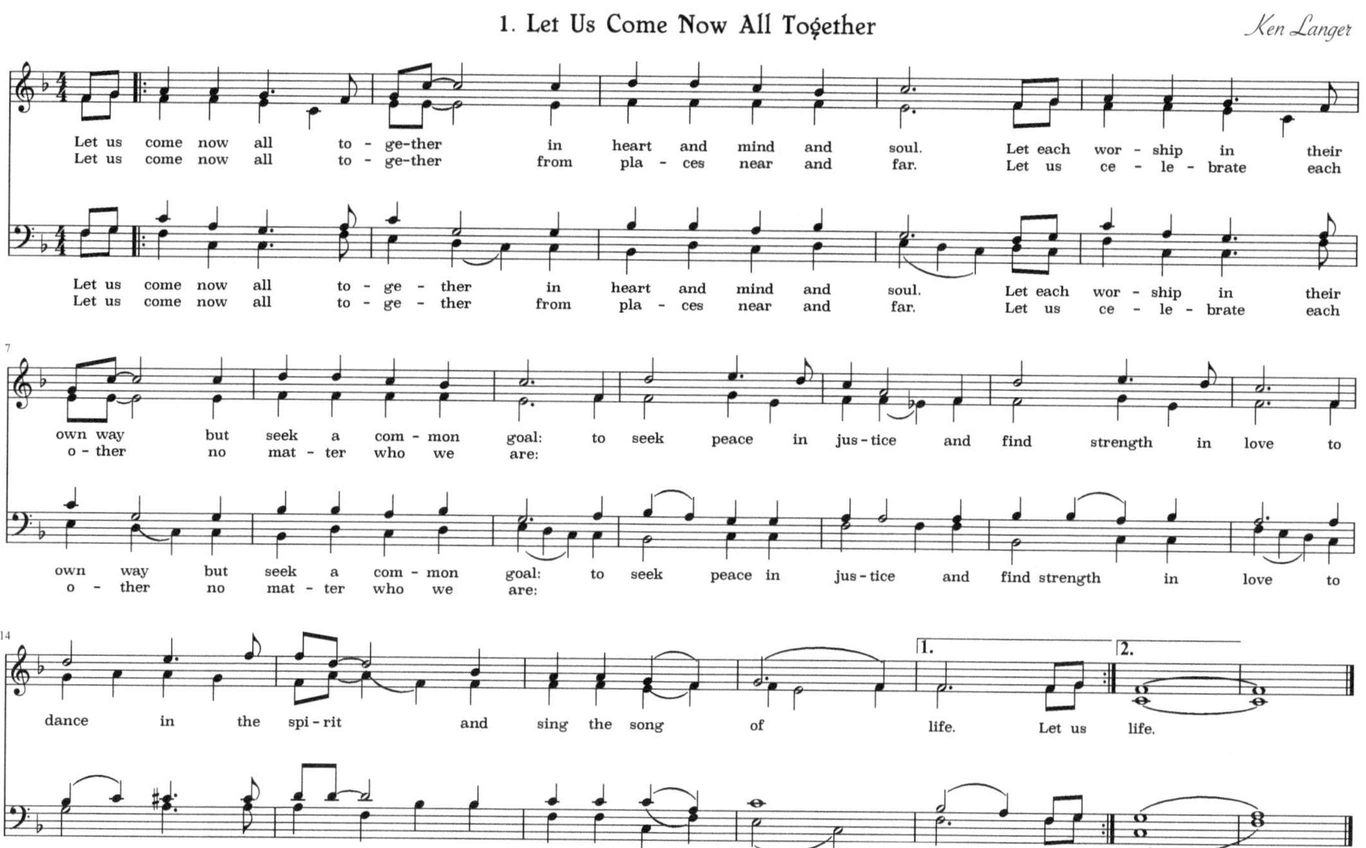

Seven Hymns

Samuel Longfellow

2. The Growing Light

Ken Langer

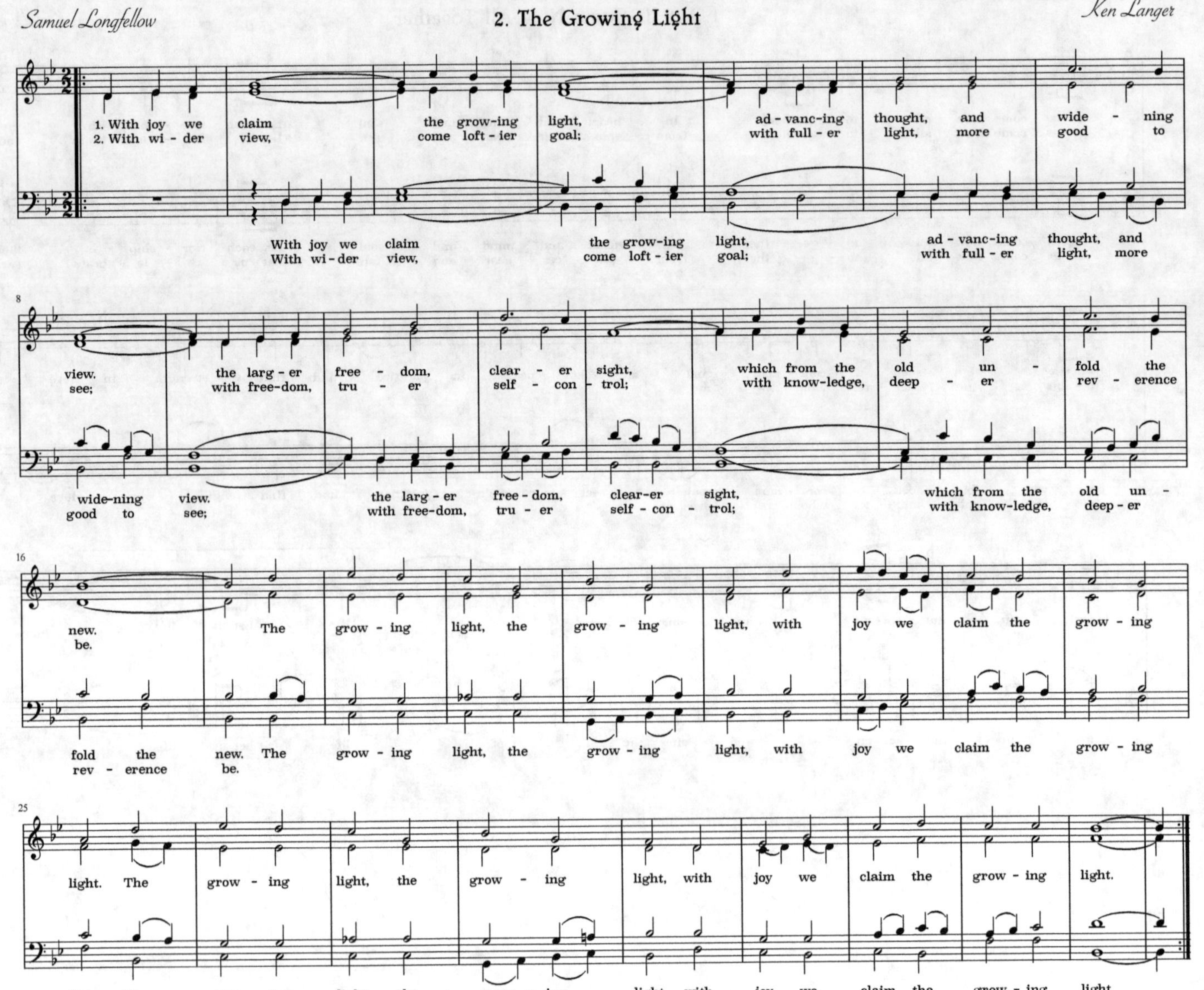

Seven Hymns

John Whittier

3. Immortal Love

Ken Langer

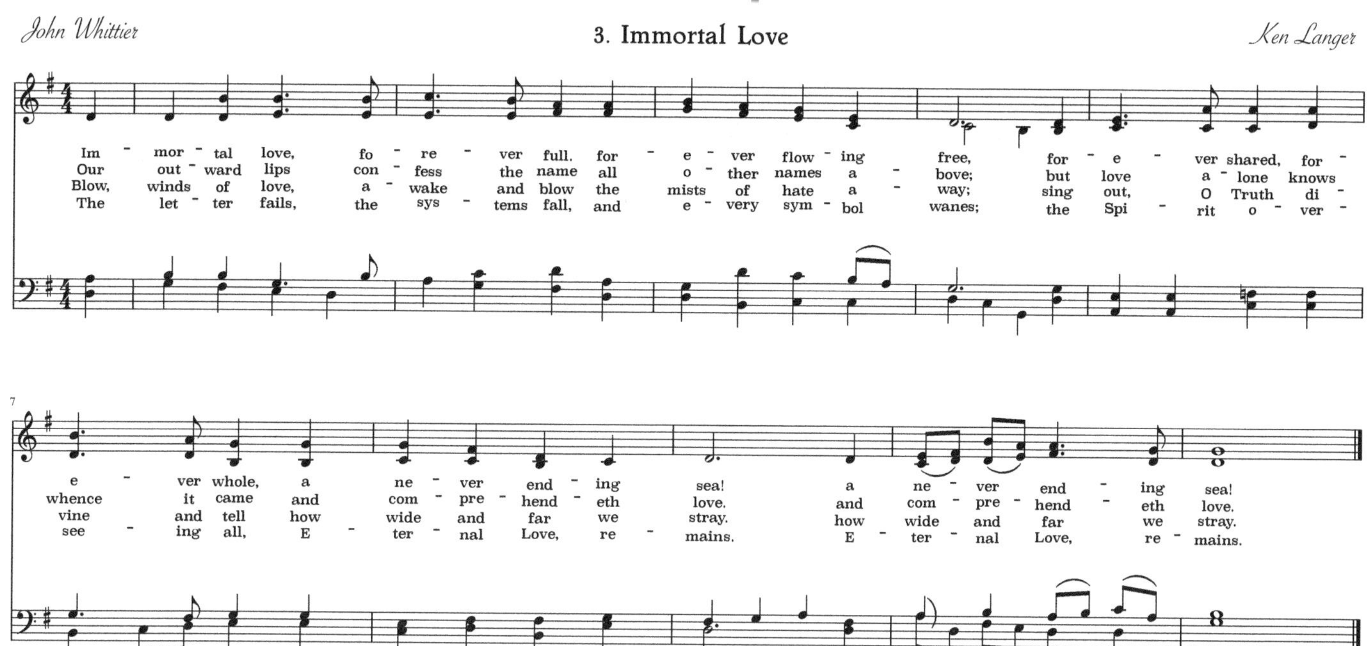

Seven Hymns

inspired by the words of R.W. Emerson

4. Revealed In Us

Ken Langer

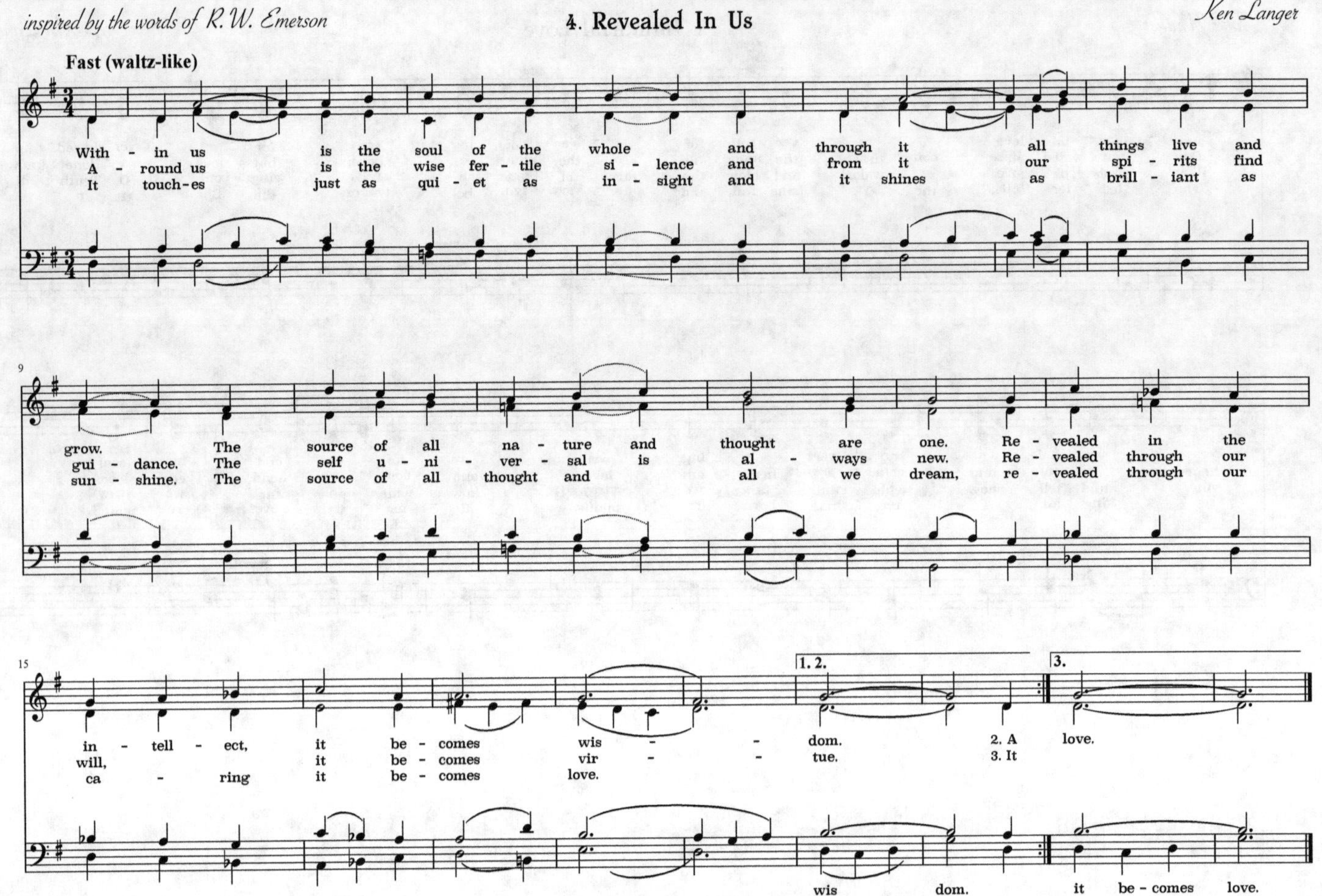

Seven Hymns

5. Sacred Space

Ken Langer

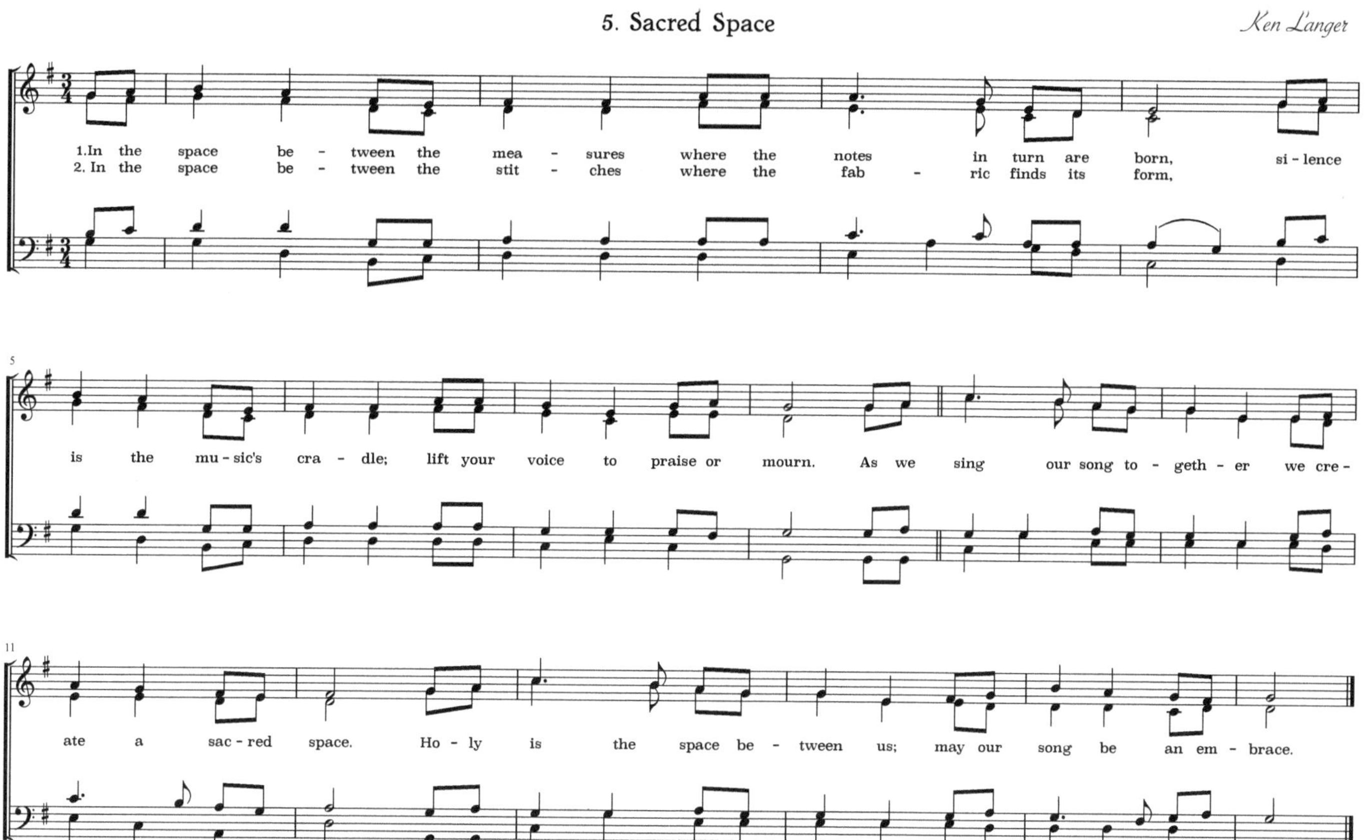

Seven Hymns

6. That Great and Fiery Force

Hildegard of Bingen — *Ken Langer*

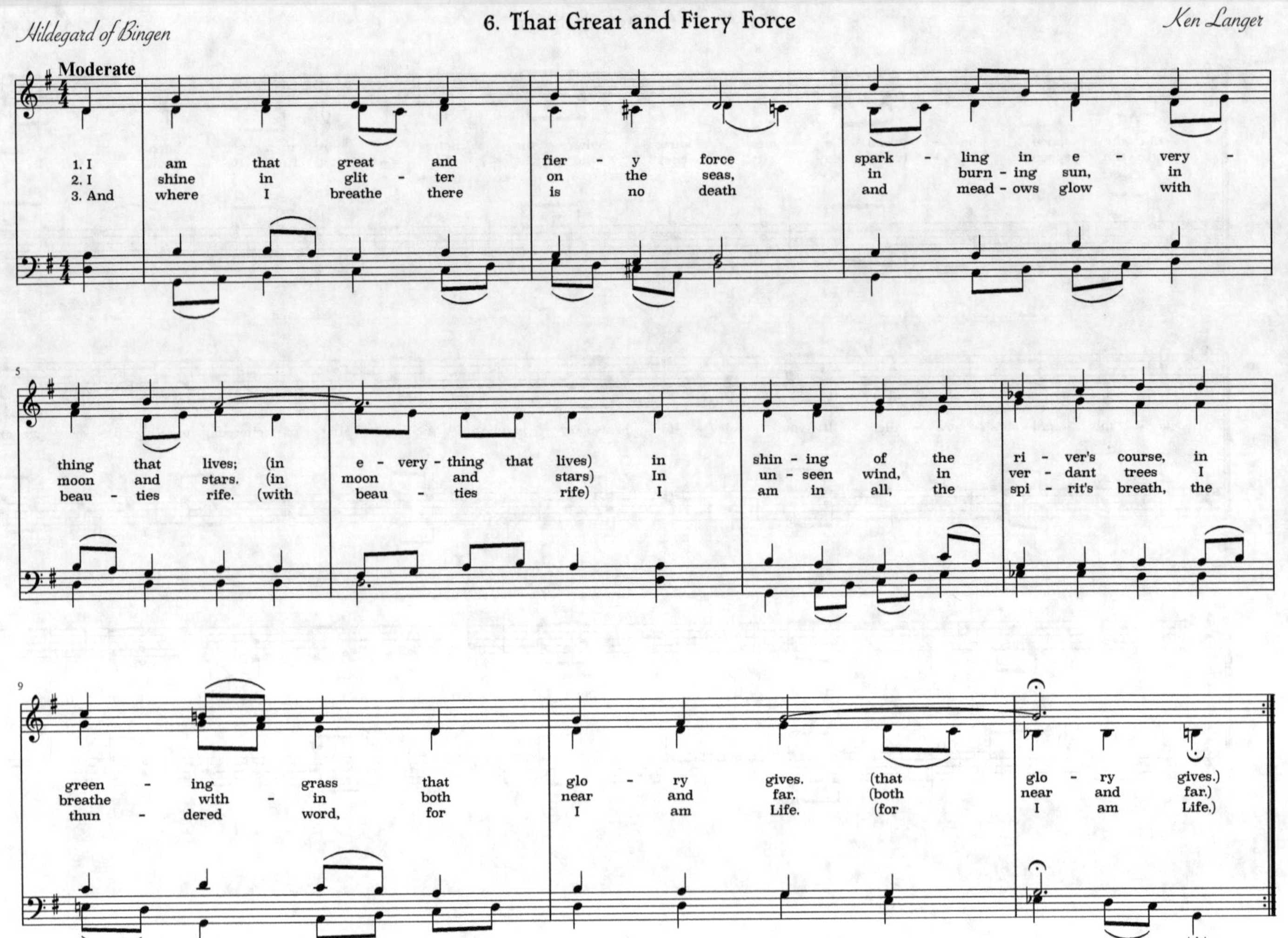

Seven Hymns

7. We Are All Sacred

Ken Langer

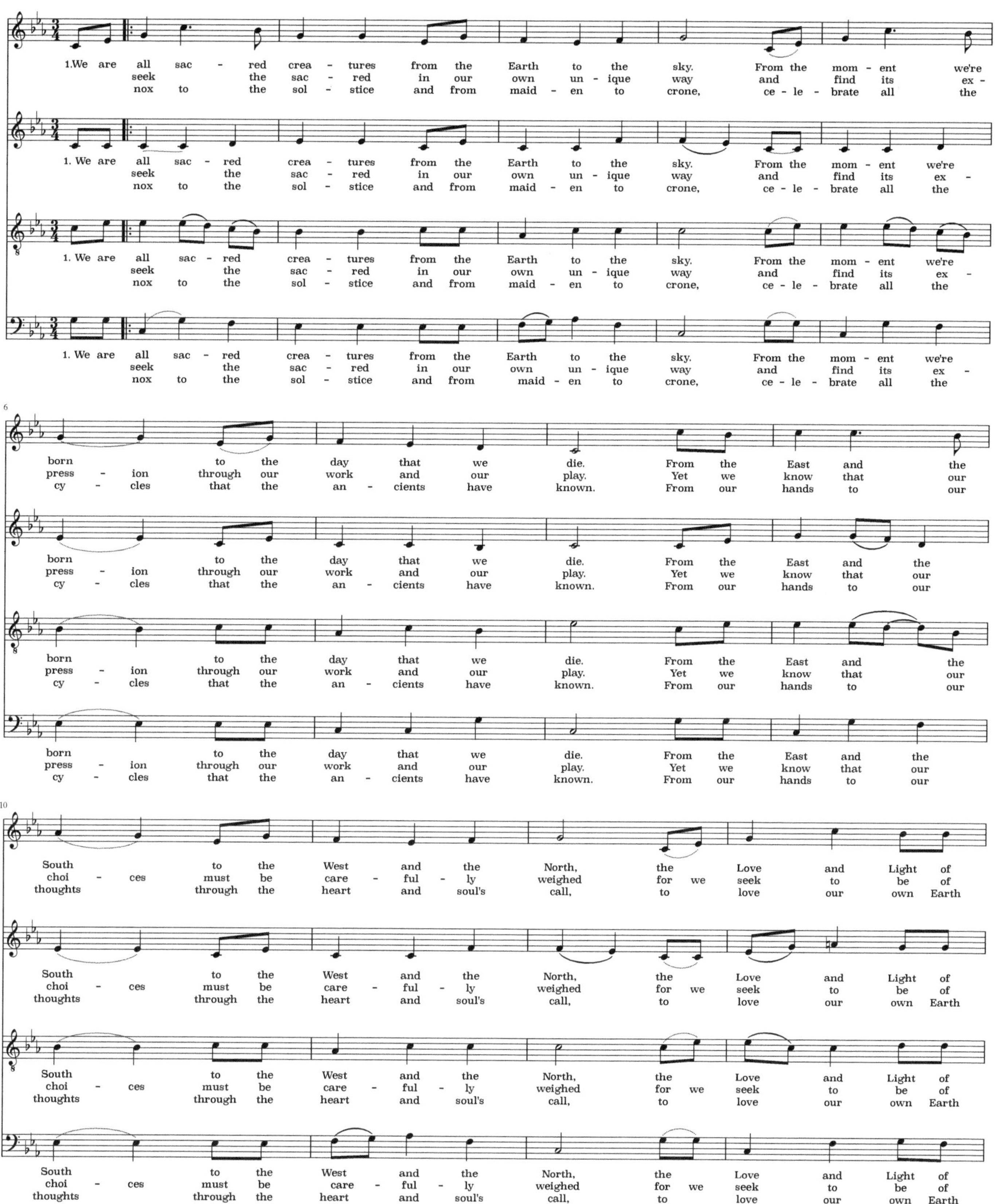

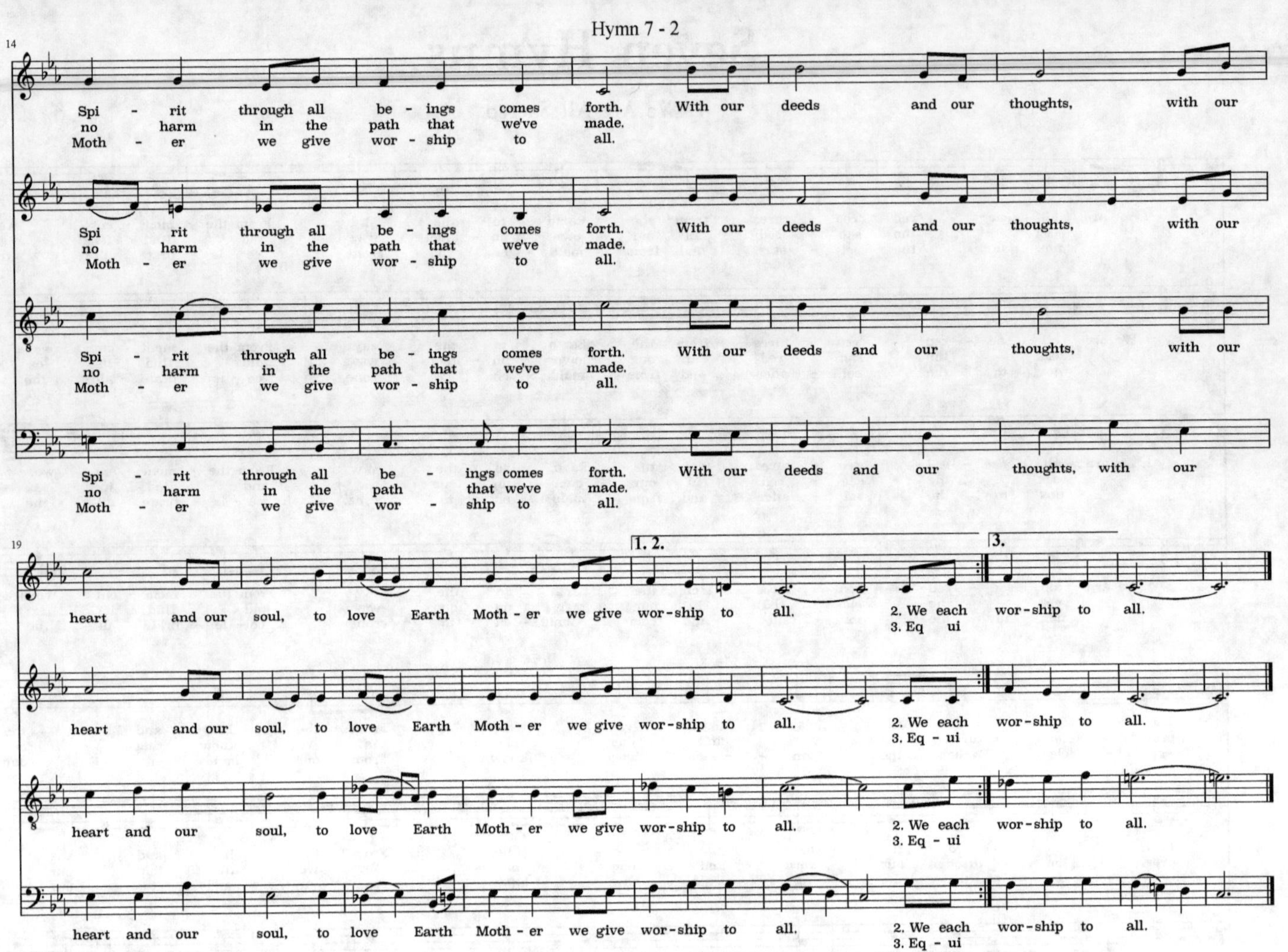
14
Spi - rit through all be - ings comes forth. With our deeds and our thoughts, with our
no harm in the path that we've made.
Moth - er we give wor - ship to all.
Spi rit through all be - ings comes forth. With our deeds and our thoughts, with our
no harm in the path that we've made.
Moth - er we give wor - ship to all.
Spi - rit through all be - ings comes forth. With our deeds and our thoughts, with our
no harm in the path that we've made.
Moth - er we give wor - ship to all.
Spi - rit through all be - ings comes forth. With our deeds and our thoughts, with our
no harm in the path that we've made.
Moth - er we give wor - ship to all.
19
1. 2.
3.
heart and our soul, to love Earth Moth - er we give wor-ship to all.
2. We each wor-ship to all.
3. Eq ui
heart and our soul, to love Earth Moth - er we give wor-ship to all.
2. We each wor-ship to all.
3. Eq - ui
heart and our soul, to love Earth Moth - er we give wor-ship to all.
2. We each wor-ship to all.
3. Eq - ui
heart and our soul, to love Earth Moth - er we give wor-ship to all.
2. We each wor-ship to all.
3. Eq - ui

12 Rounds and Canons

Four Part Round — **1. Around The Circle** — *Ken Langer*

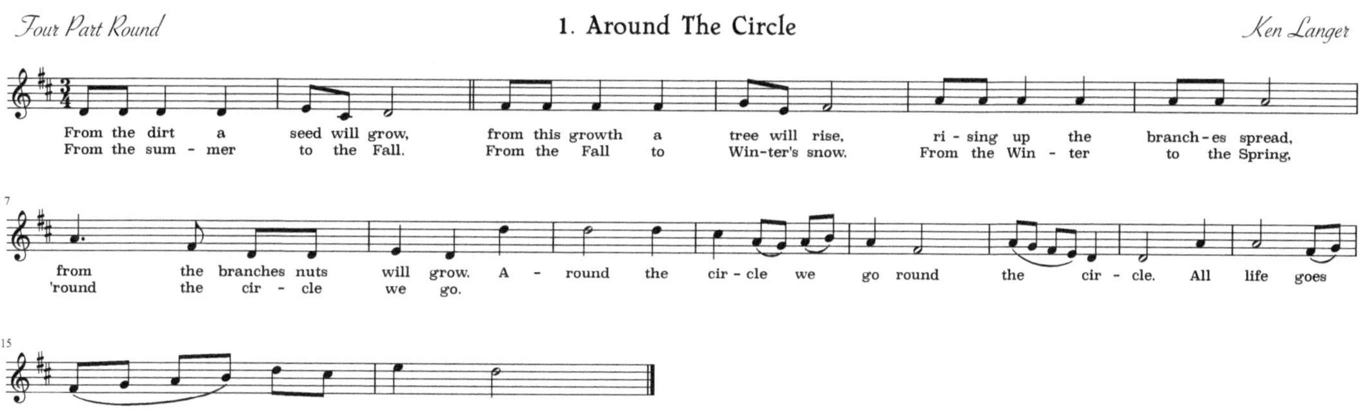

12 Rounds and Canons

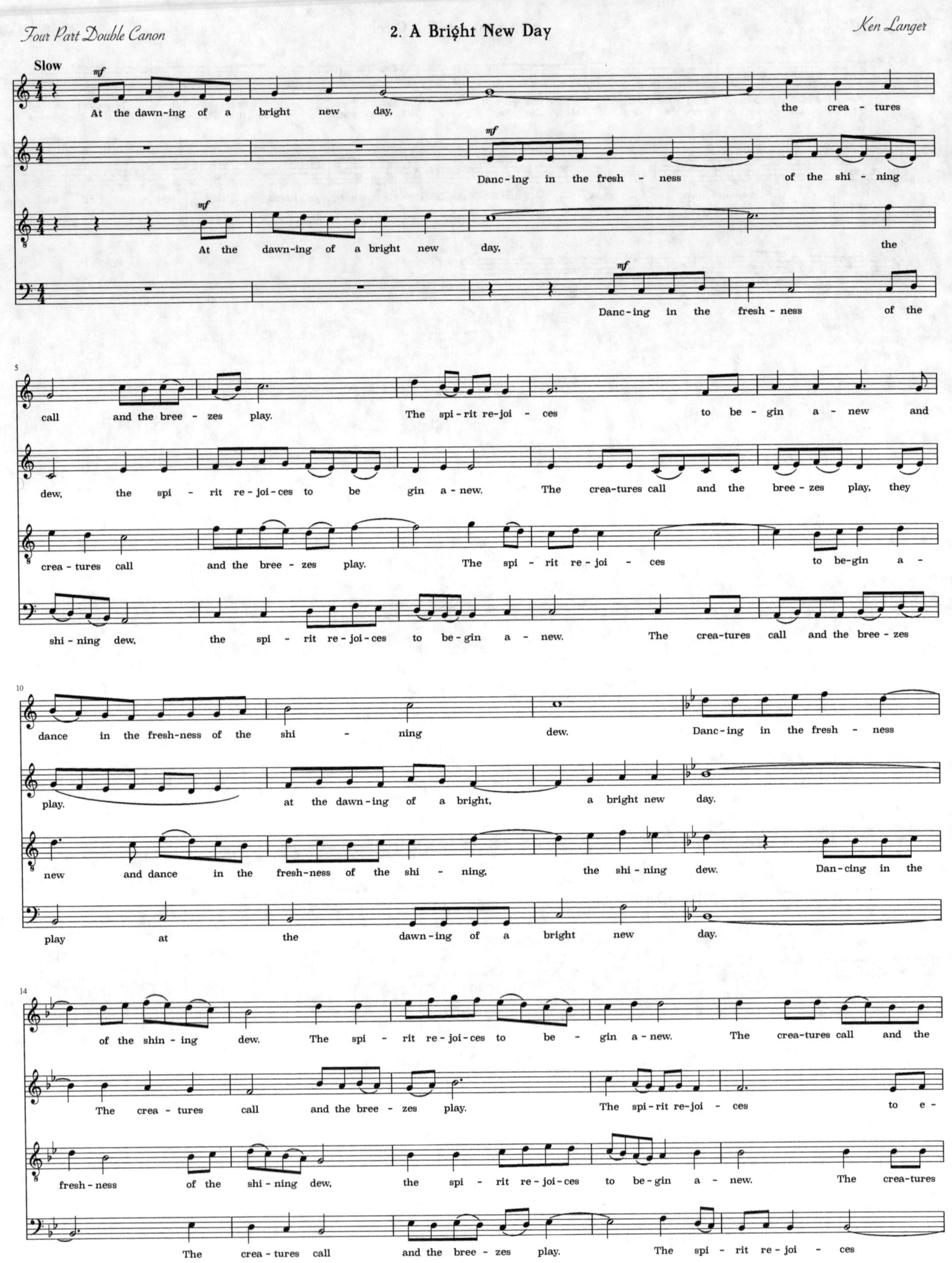

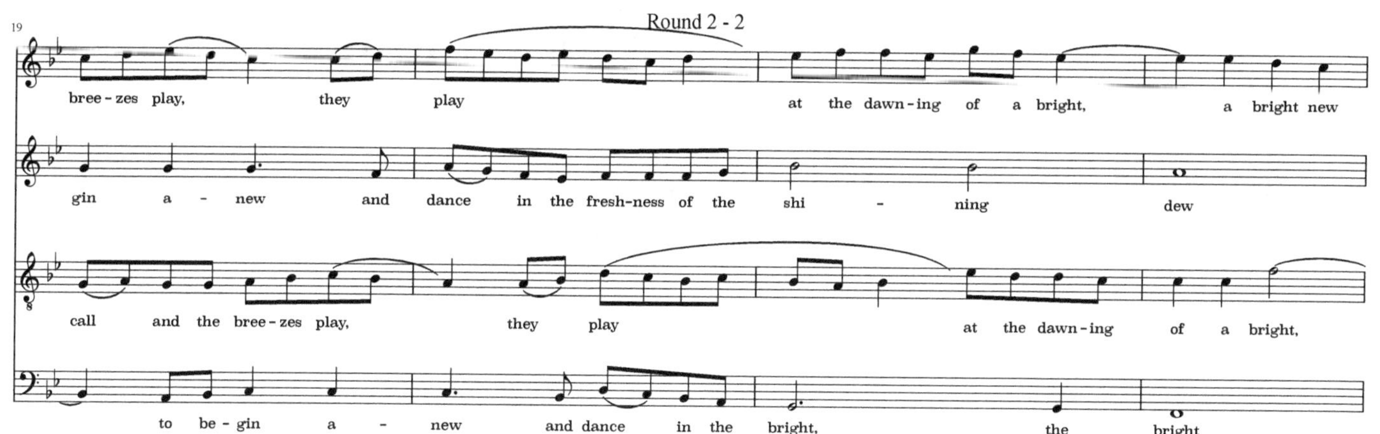
19
bree - zes play, they play at the dawn - ing of a bright, a bright new
gin a - new and dance in the fresh - ness of the shi - ning dew
call and the bree - zes play, they play at the dawn - ing of a bright,
to be - gin a - new and dance in the bright, the bright

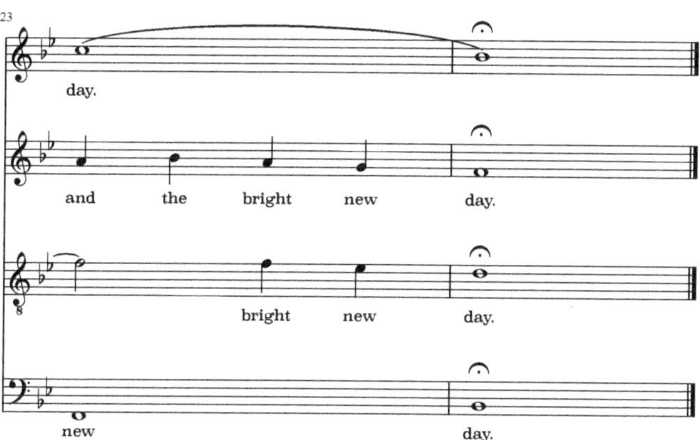
23
day.
and the bright new day.
bright new day.
new day.

12 Rounds and Canons

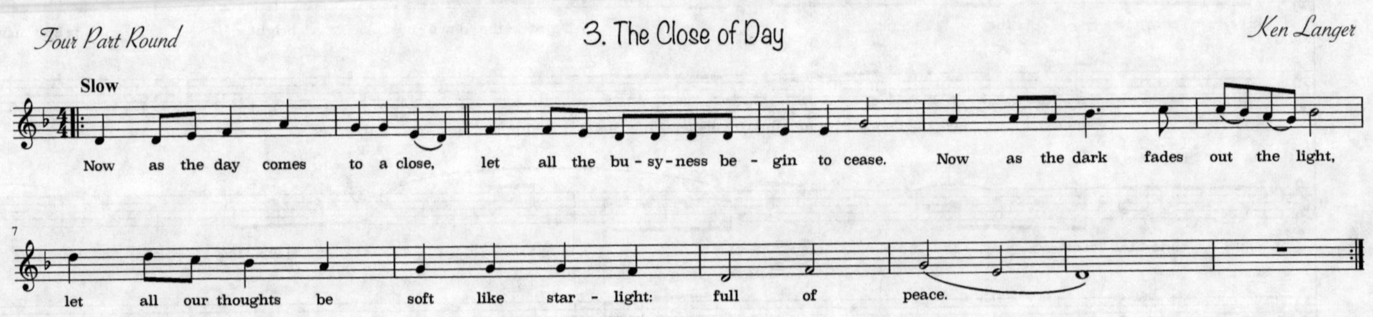

12 Rounds and Canons

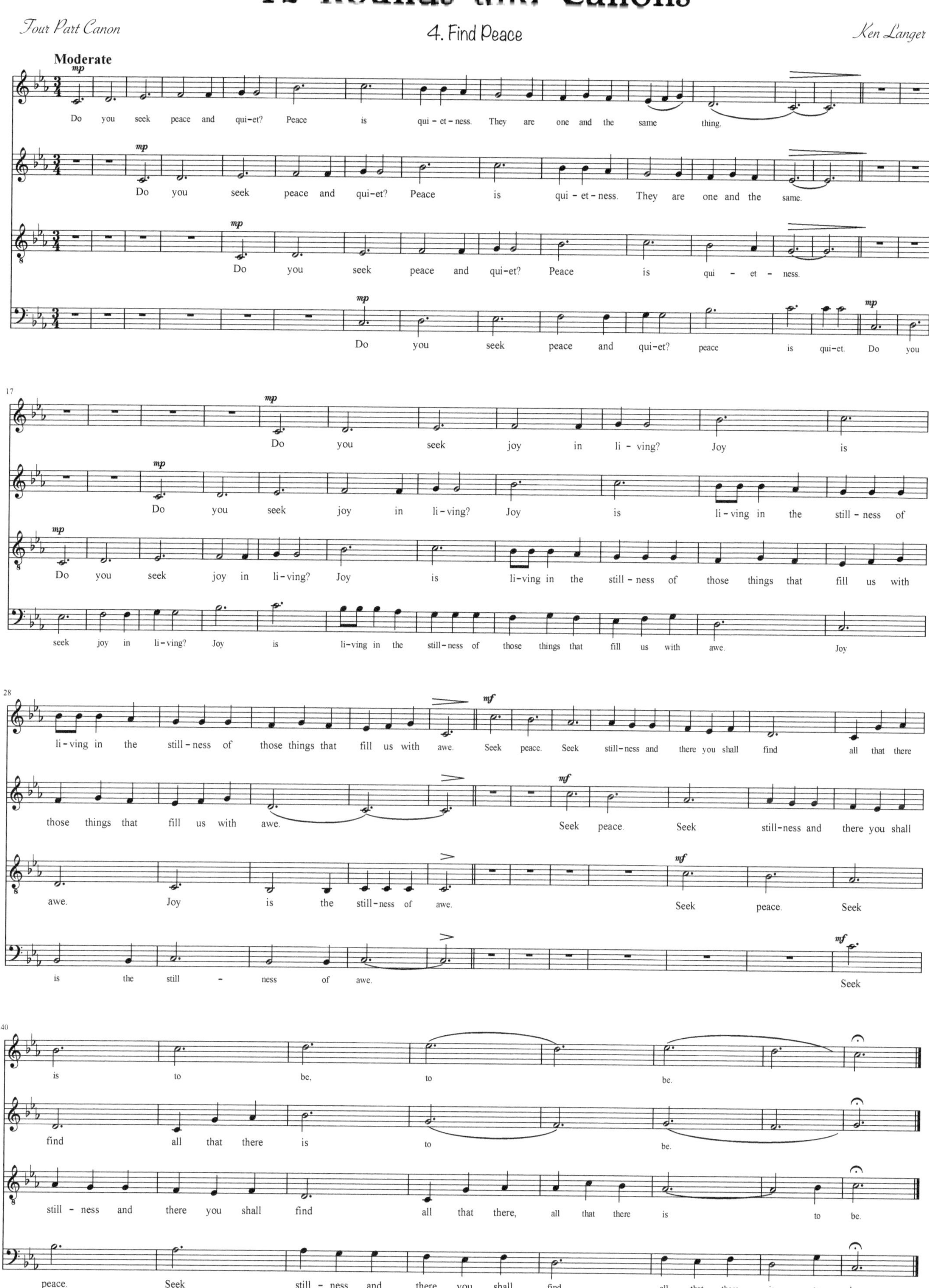

12 Rounds and Canons

Three part round

5. Find Yourself

Ken Langer

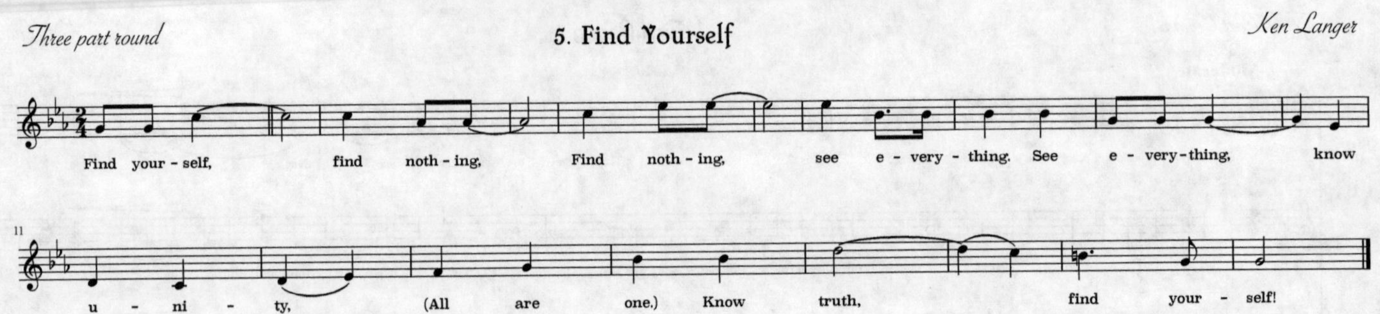

12 Rounds and Canons

Three Part Round

6. Go Now In Peace

Ken Langer

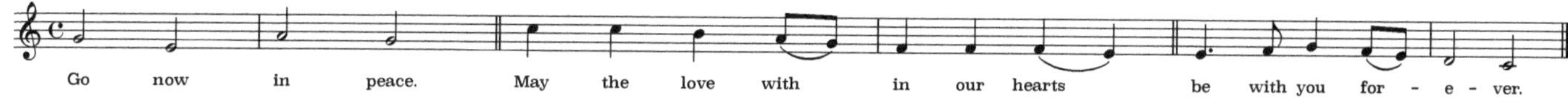

12 Rounds and Canons

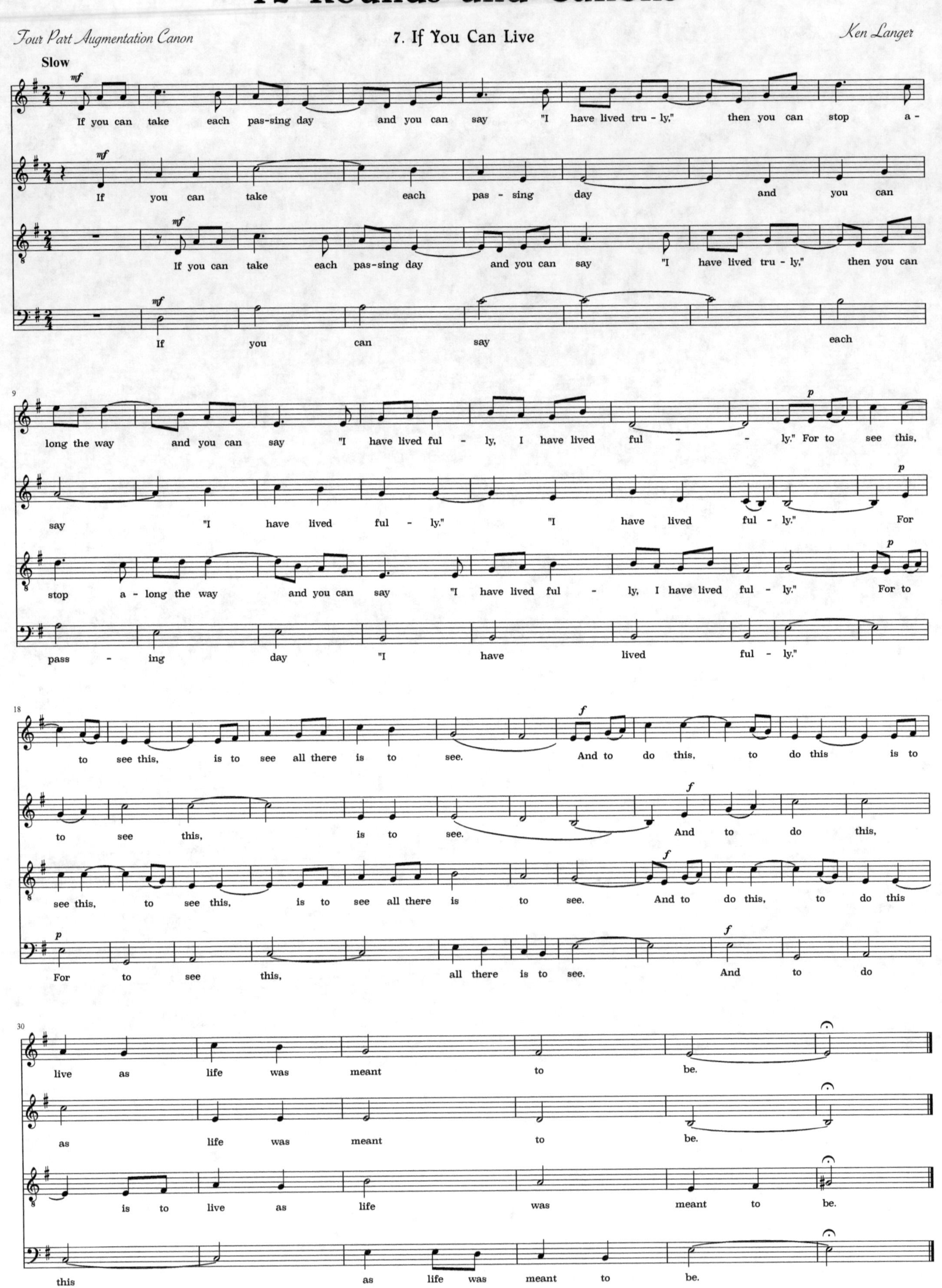

12 Rounds and Canons

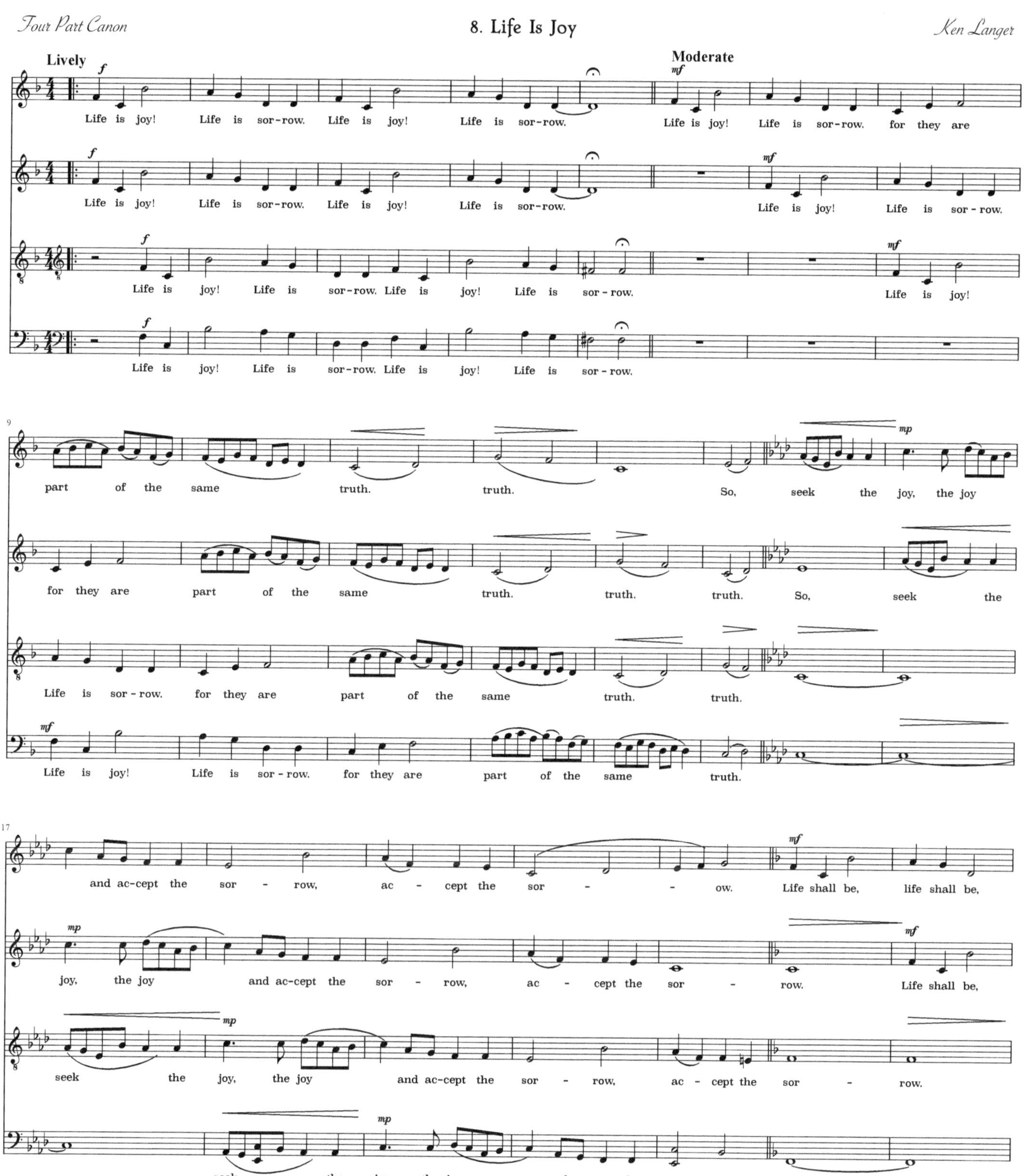

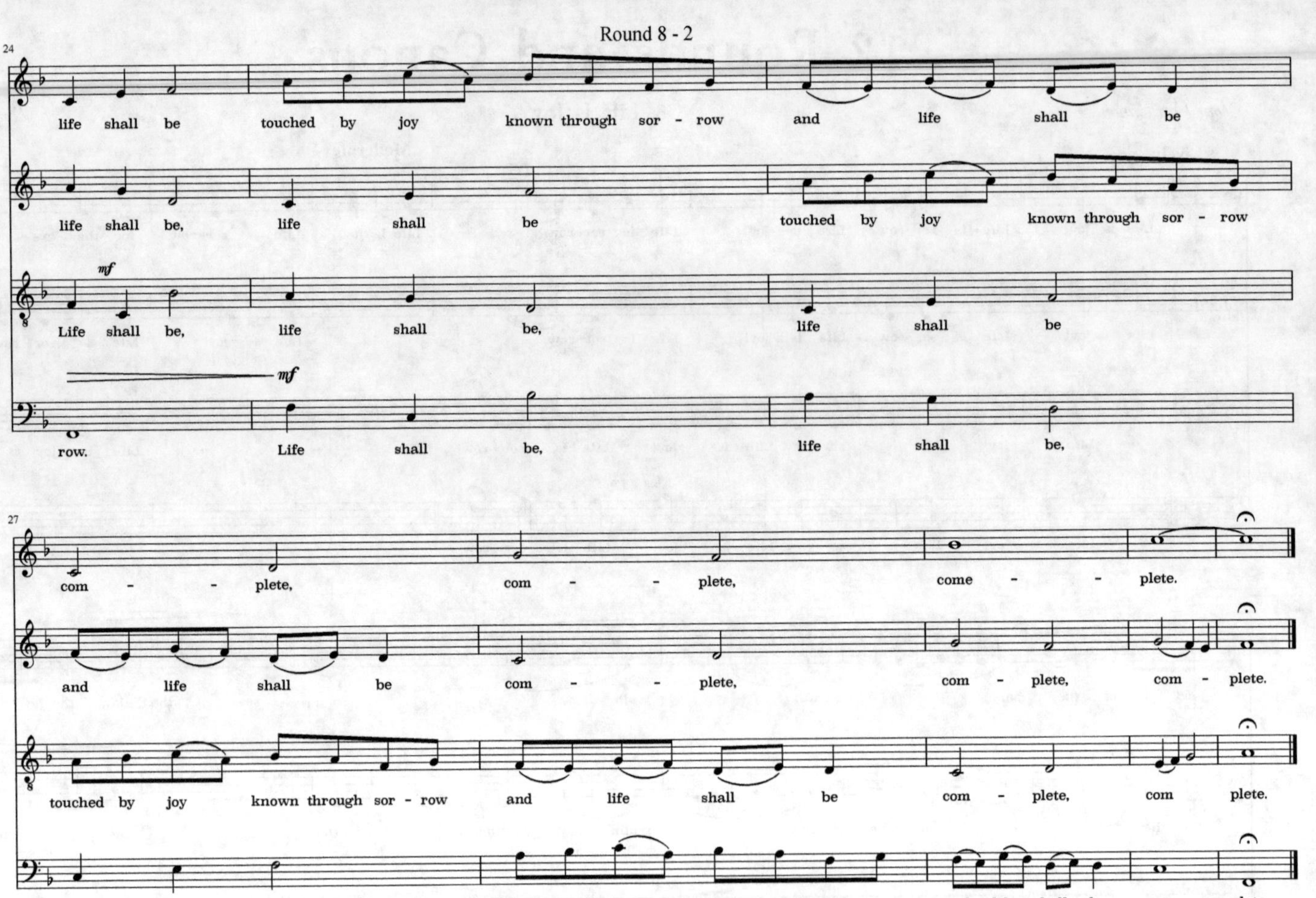
24
life shall be touched by joy known through sor - row and life shall be
life shall be, life shall be touched by joy known through sor - row
mf
Life shall be, life shall be, life shall be
mf
row. Life shall be, life shall be,
27
com - - plete, com - - plete, come - - plete.
and life shall be com - - plete, com - plete, com - plete.
touched by joy known through sor - row and life shall be com - plete, com plete.
life shall be touched by joy known through sor - row and life shall be com - plete.

12 Rounds and Canons

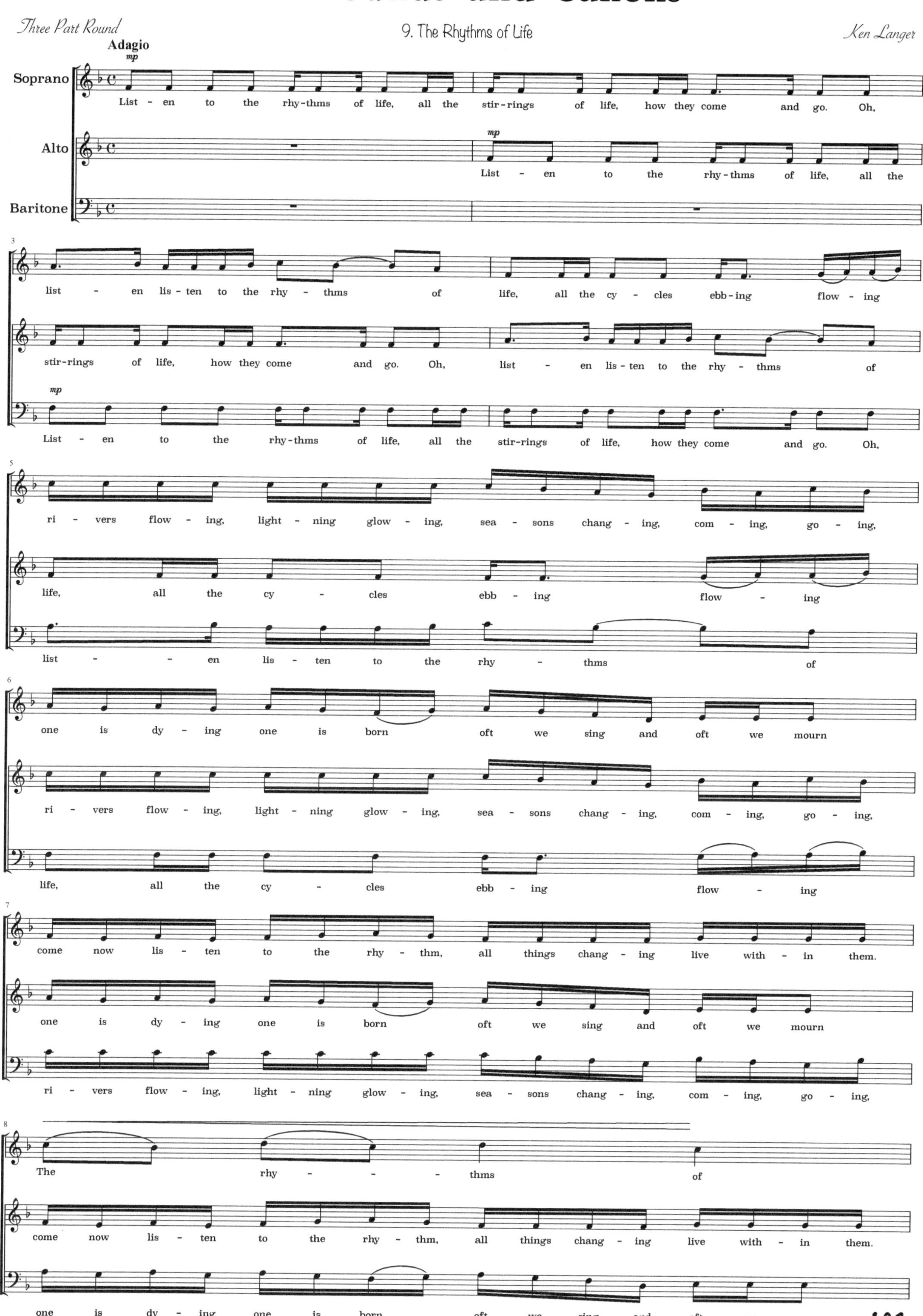

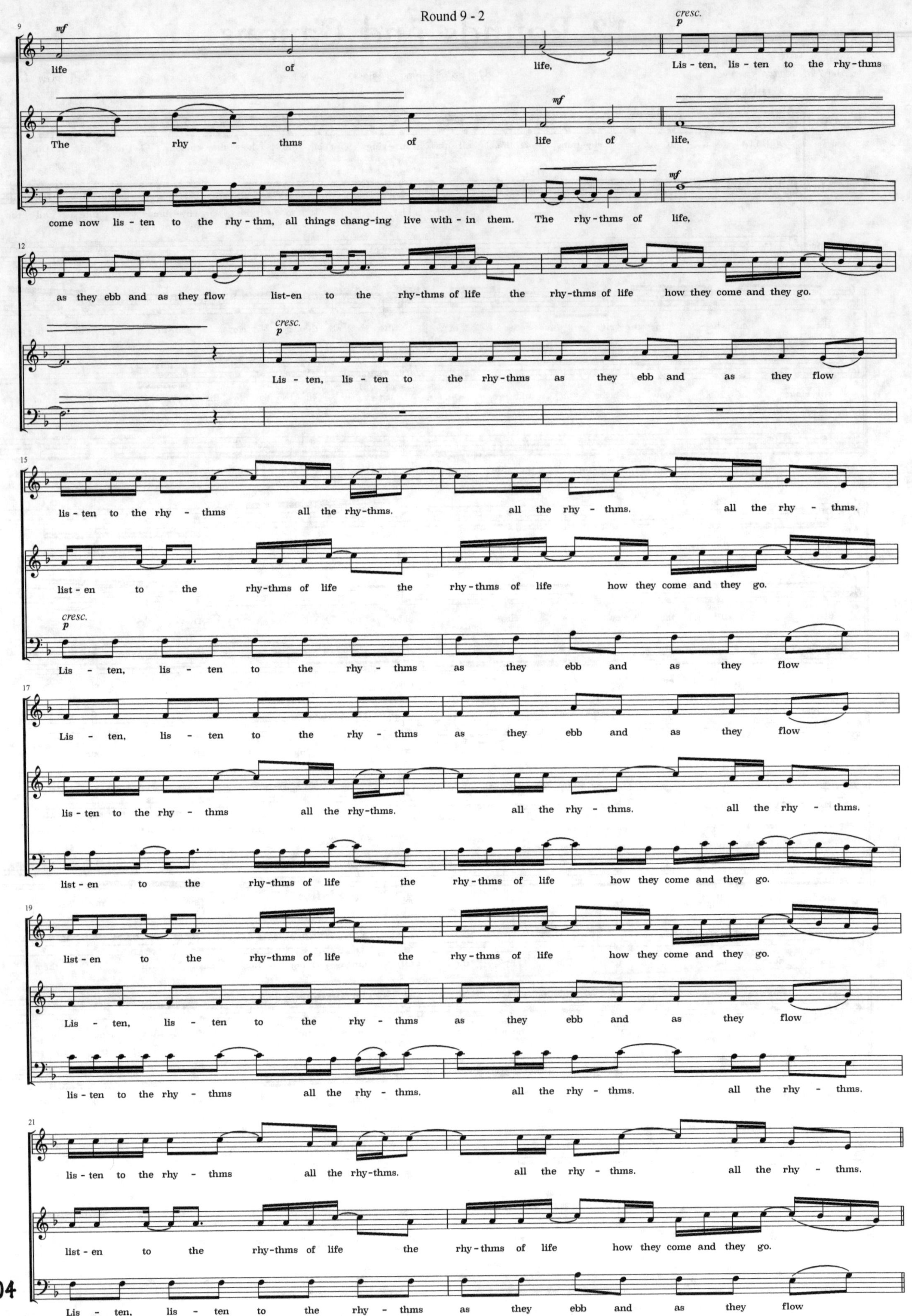
9
mf
life of life,
cresc.
p
Lis - ten, lis - ten to the rhy - thms
The rhy - thms of
mf
life of life,
come now lis - ten to the rhy - thm, all things chang - ing live with - in them. The rhy - thms of
mf
life,
12
as they ebb and as they flow
list - en to the rhy - thms of life the rhy - thms of life how they come and they go.
cresc.
p
Lis - ten, lis - ten to the rhy - thms as they ebb and as they flow
15
lis - ten to the rhy - thms all the rhy - thms. all the rhy - thms. all the rhy - thms.
list - en to the rhy - thms of life the rhy - thms of life how they come and they go.
cresc.
p
Lis - ten, lis - ten to the rhy - thms as they ebb and as they flow
17
Lis - ten, lis - ten to the rhy - thms as they ebb and as they flow
lis - ten to the rhy - thms all the rhy - thms. all the rhy - thms. all the rhy - thms.
list - en to the rhy - thms of life the rhy - thms of life how they come and they go.
19
list - en to the rhy - thms of life the rhy - thms of life how they come and they go.
Lis - ten, lis - ten to the rhy - thms as they ebb and as they flow
lis - ten to the rhy - thms all the rhy - thms. all the rhy - thms. all the rhy - thms.
21
lis - ten to the rhy - thms all the rhy - thms. all the rhy - thms. all the rhy - thms.
list - en to the rhy - thms of life the rhy - thms of life how they come and they go.
Lis - ten, lis - ten to the rhy - thms as they ebb and as they flow

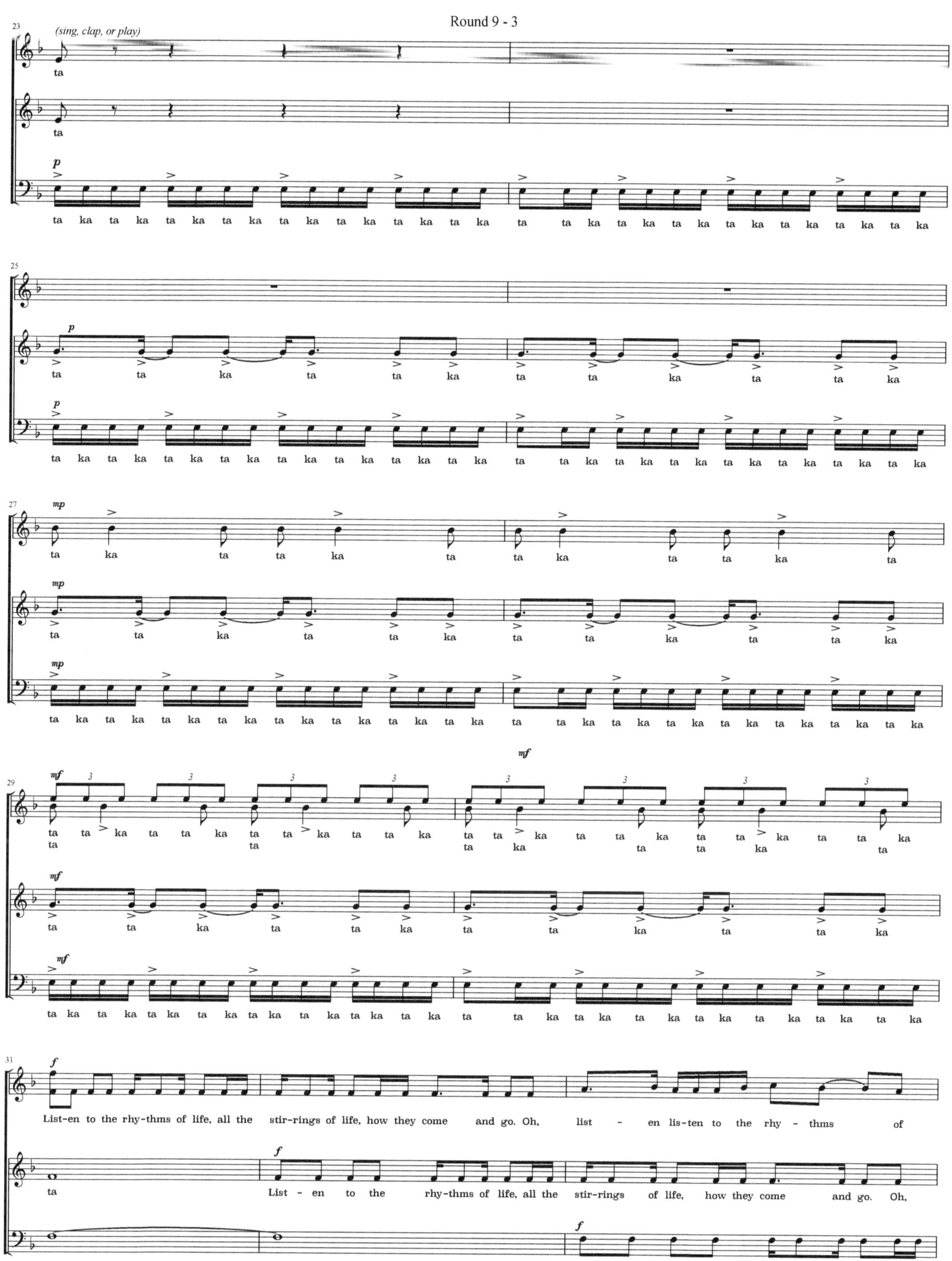
(sing, clap, or play)
ta
ta
ta ka ta ka ta ka ta ka ta ka ta ka ta ka ta ka
ta ta ka ta ka ta ka ta ka ta ka ta ka ta ka
ta ta ka ta ta ka
ta ta ka ta ta ka
ta ka ta ka ta ka ta ka ta ka ta ka ta ka ta ka
ta ta ka ta ka ta ka ta ka ta ka ta ka ta ka
ta ka ta ta ka ta
ta ka ta ta ka ta
ta ta ka ta ta ka
ta ta ka ta ta ka
ta ka ta ka ta ka ta ka ta ka ta ka ta ka ta ka
ta ta ka ta ka ta ka ta ka ta ka ta ka ta ka
ta ta ka ta ta ka ta ta ka ta ta ka
ta ta
ta ta ka ta ta ka ta ta ka ta ta ka
ta ka ta ta ka ta
ta ta ka ta ta ka
ta ta ka ta ta ka
ta ka ta ka ta ka ta ka ta ka ta ka ta ka ta ka
ta ta ka ta ka ta ka ta ka ta ka ta ka ta ka
List-en to the rhy-thms of life, all the stir-rings of life, how they come and go. Oh, list - en lis-ten to the rhy - thms of
ta
List - en to the rhy-thms of life, all the stir-rings of life, how they come and go. Oh,
ta
List - en to the rhy-thms of life, all the

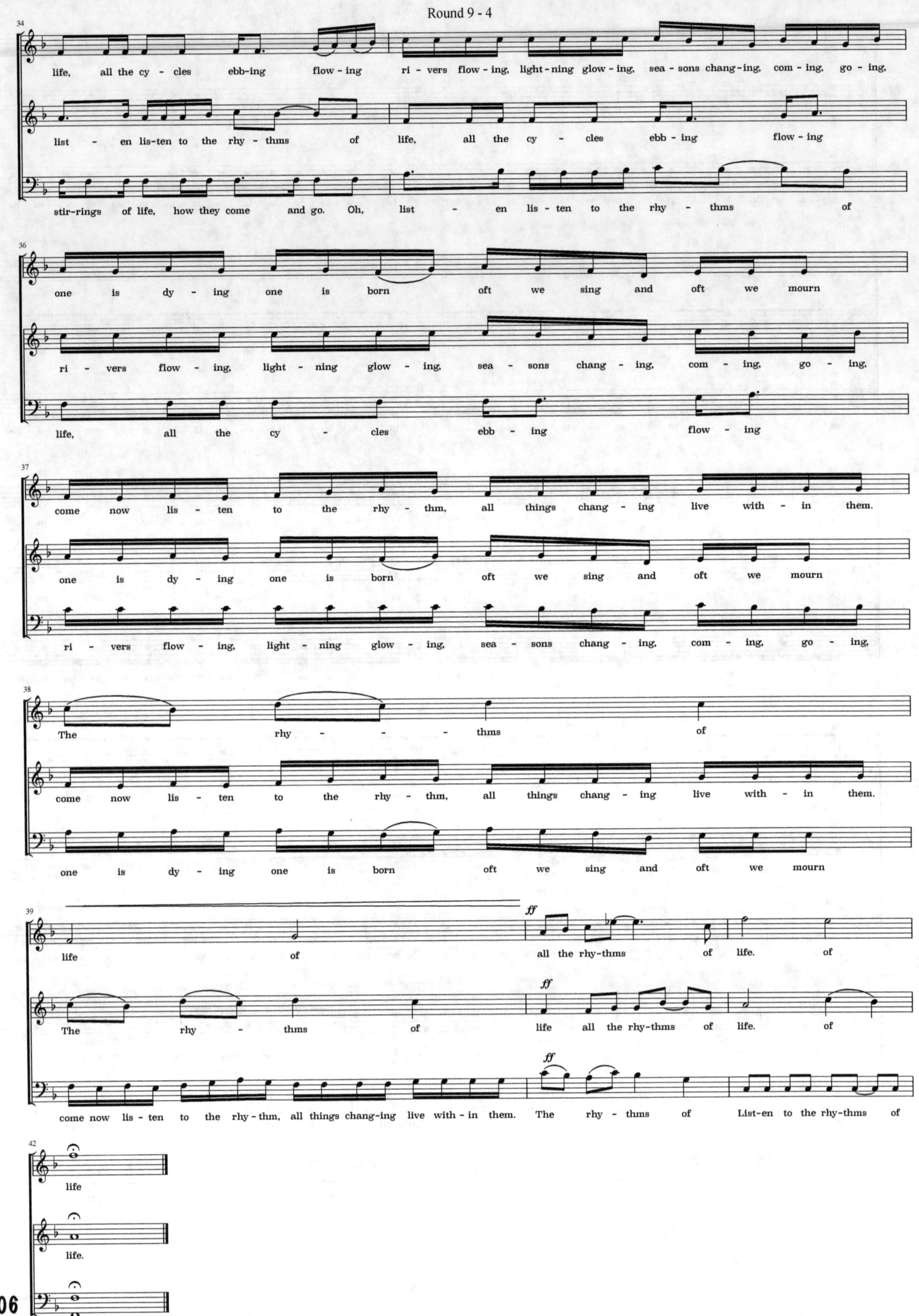
34
life, all the cy - cles ebb-ing flow - ing ri - vers flow - ing, light - ning glow - ing, sea - sons chang - ing, com - ing, go - ing,
list - en lis-ten to the rhy - thms of life, all the cy - cles ebb - ing flow - ing
stir-rings of life, how they come and go. Oh, list - en lis - ten to the rhy - thms of
36
one is dy - ing one is born oft we sing and oft we mourn
ri - vers flow - ing, light - ning glow - ing, sea - sons chang - ing, com - ing, go - ing,
life, all the cy - cles ebb - ing flow - ing
37
come now lis - ten to the rhy - thm, all things chang - ing live with - in them.
one is dy - ing one is born oft we sing and oft we mourn
ri - vers flow - ing, light - ning glow - ing, sea - sons chang - ing, com - ing, go - ing,
38
The rhy - - - thms of
come now lis - ten to the rhy - thm, all things chang - ing live with - in them.
one is dy - ing one is born oft we sing and oft we mourn
39
ff
life of all the rhy-thms of life. of
The rhy - thms of life all the rhy-thms of life. of
come now lis - ten to the rhy - thm, all things chang-ing live with - in them. The rhy - thms of List-en to the rhy-thms of
42
life
life.
life,

12 Rounds and Canons

Four Part Round

10. Sing For Joy

Ken Langer

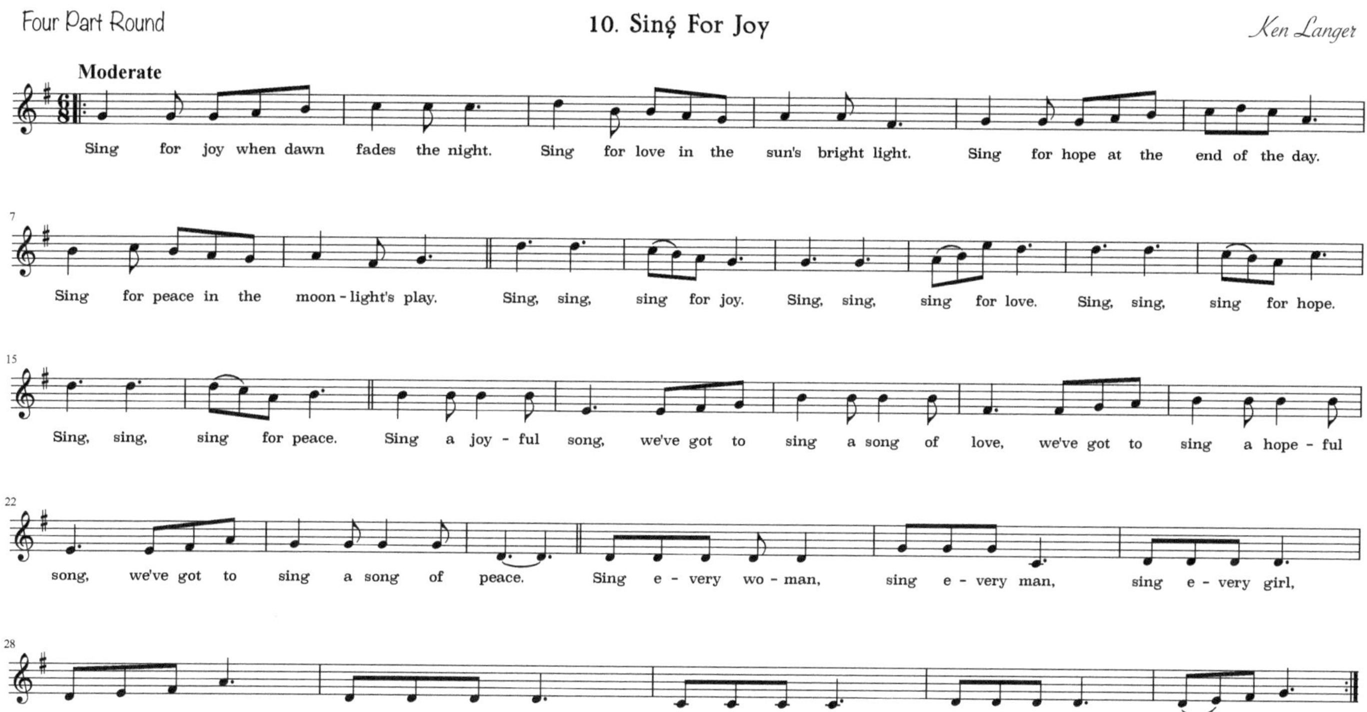

12 Rounds and Canons

Three Part Round — **11. There's a Presence** — *Ken Langer*

There's a pre - sence in the flow - ers and there's a pre - sence in the trees. There's a pre-sence in the moun - tains and there's a pre-sence

8 in the breeze. There's a my - stery all a-bout us no mat-ter where we may go of which all are a part but few take

17

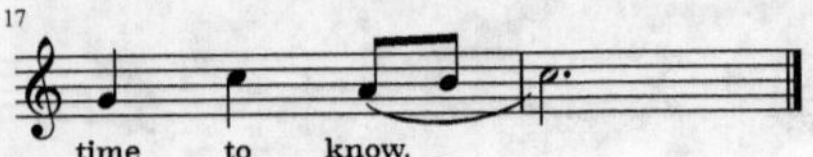

12 Rounds and Canons

Two Part Inversion Round **12. Turn It Around** *Ken Langer*

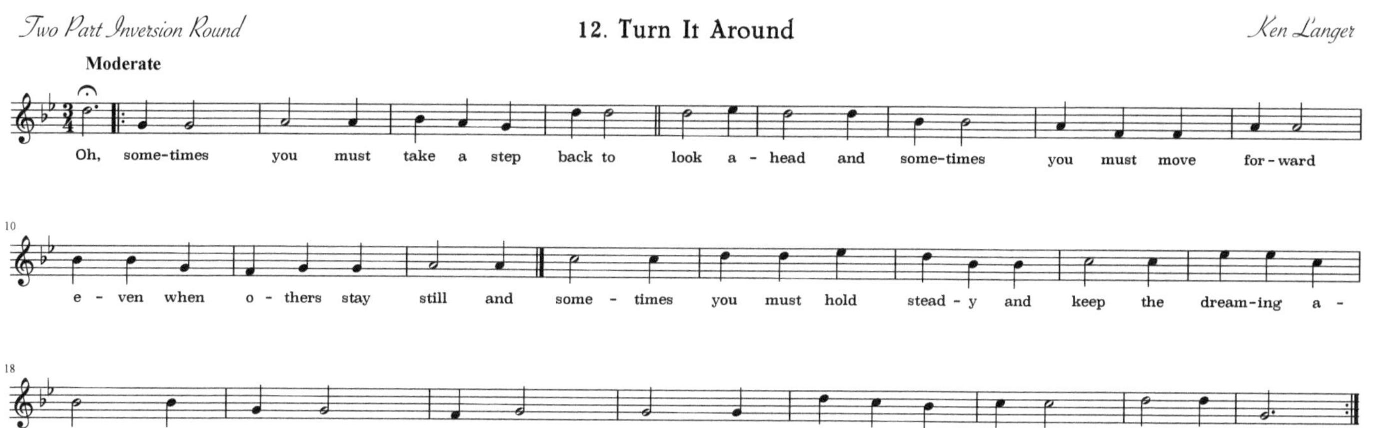

Note: The part beginning at the double bar at measure 13 is created by inverting the melody in measures 2- 12.

Ten Benedictions

1. This Be With You

Ken Langer

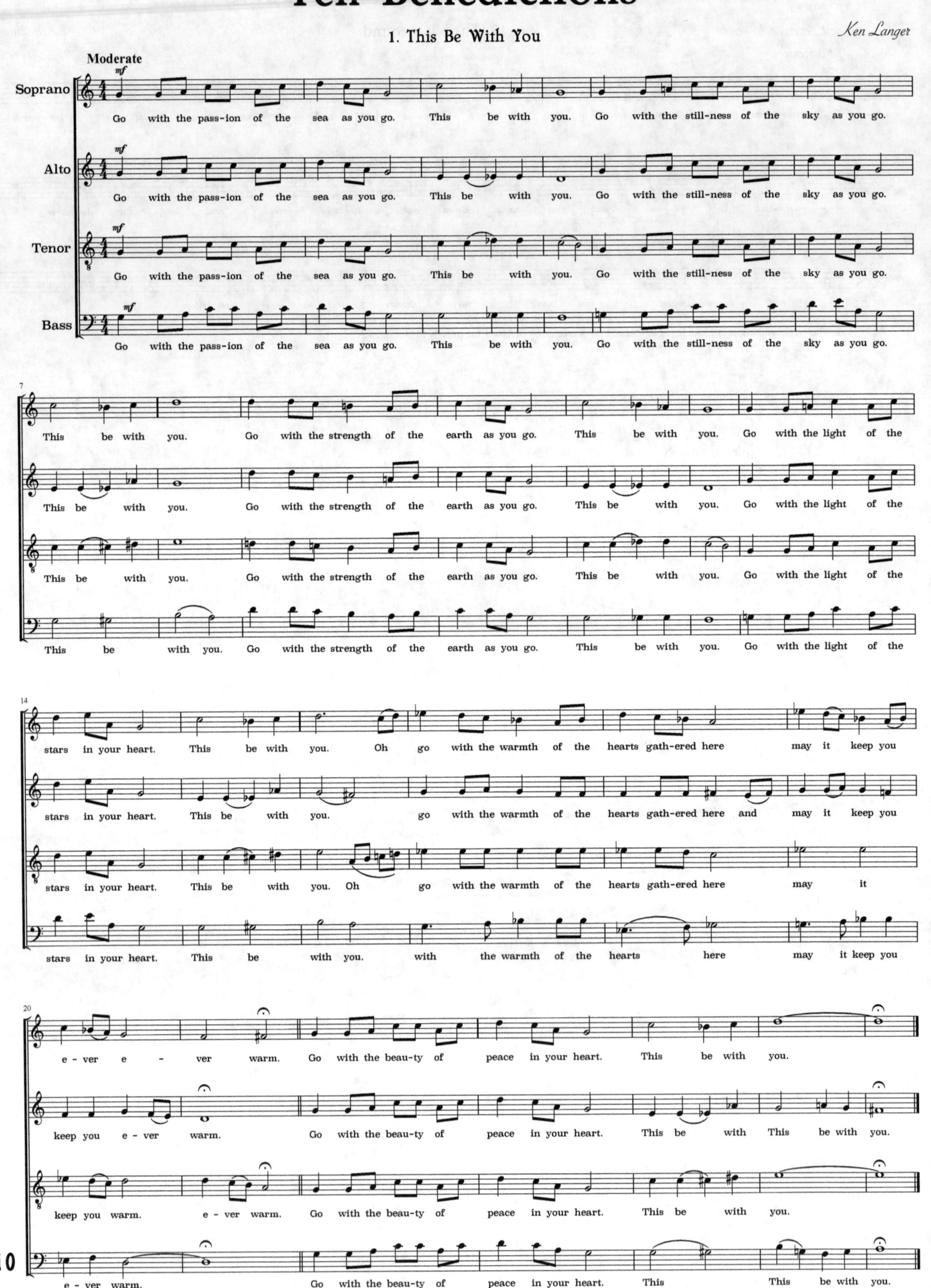

Ten Benedictions

2. Peace Be With You

Ken Langer

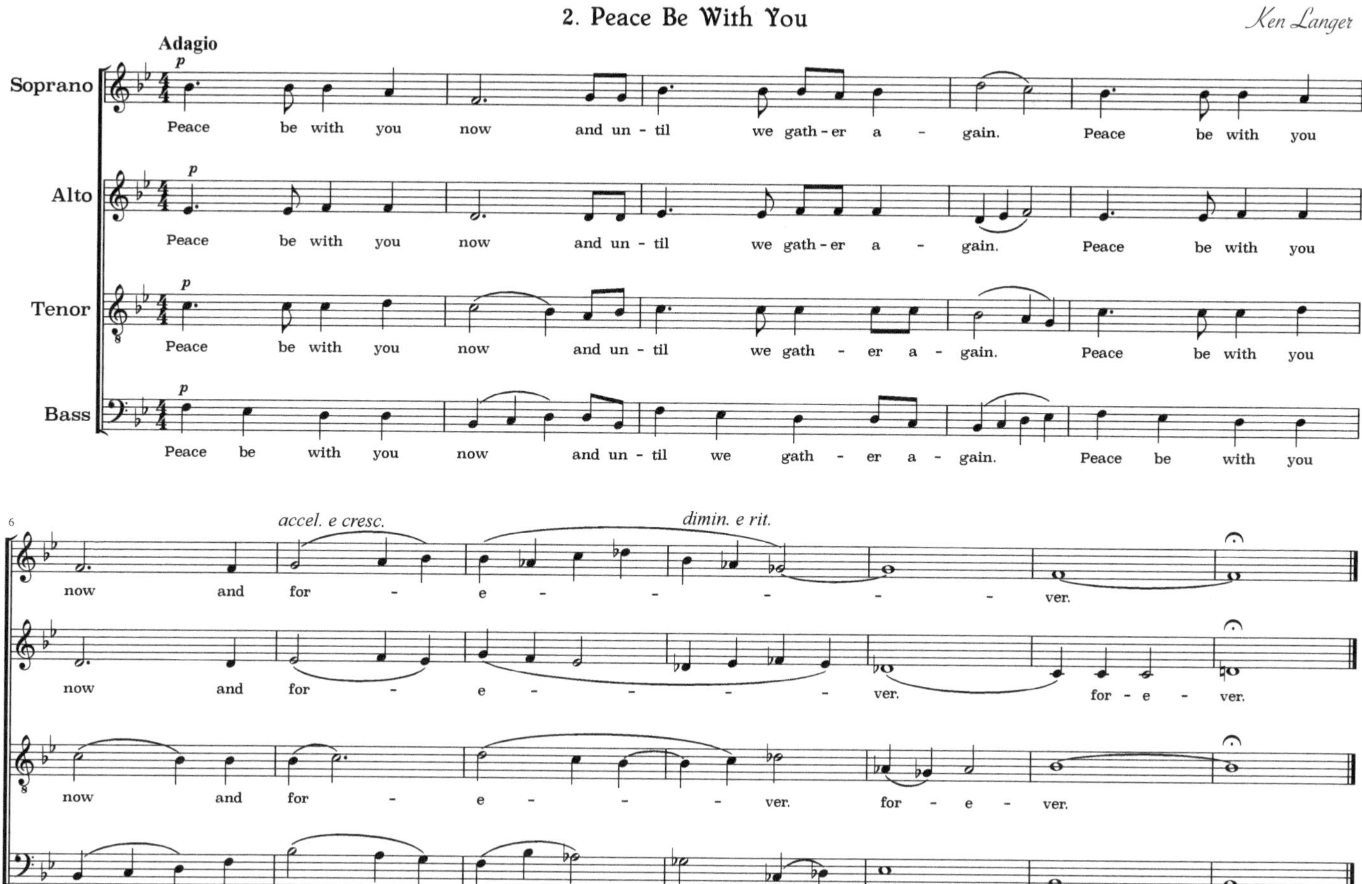

Ten Benedictions

3. Live Like Hope

Ken Langer

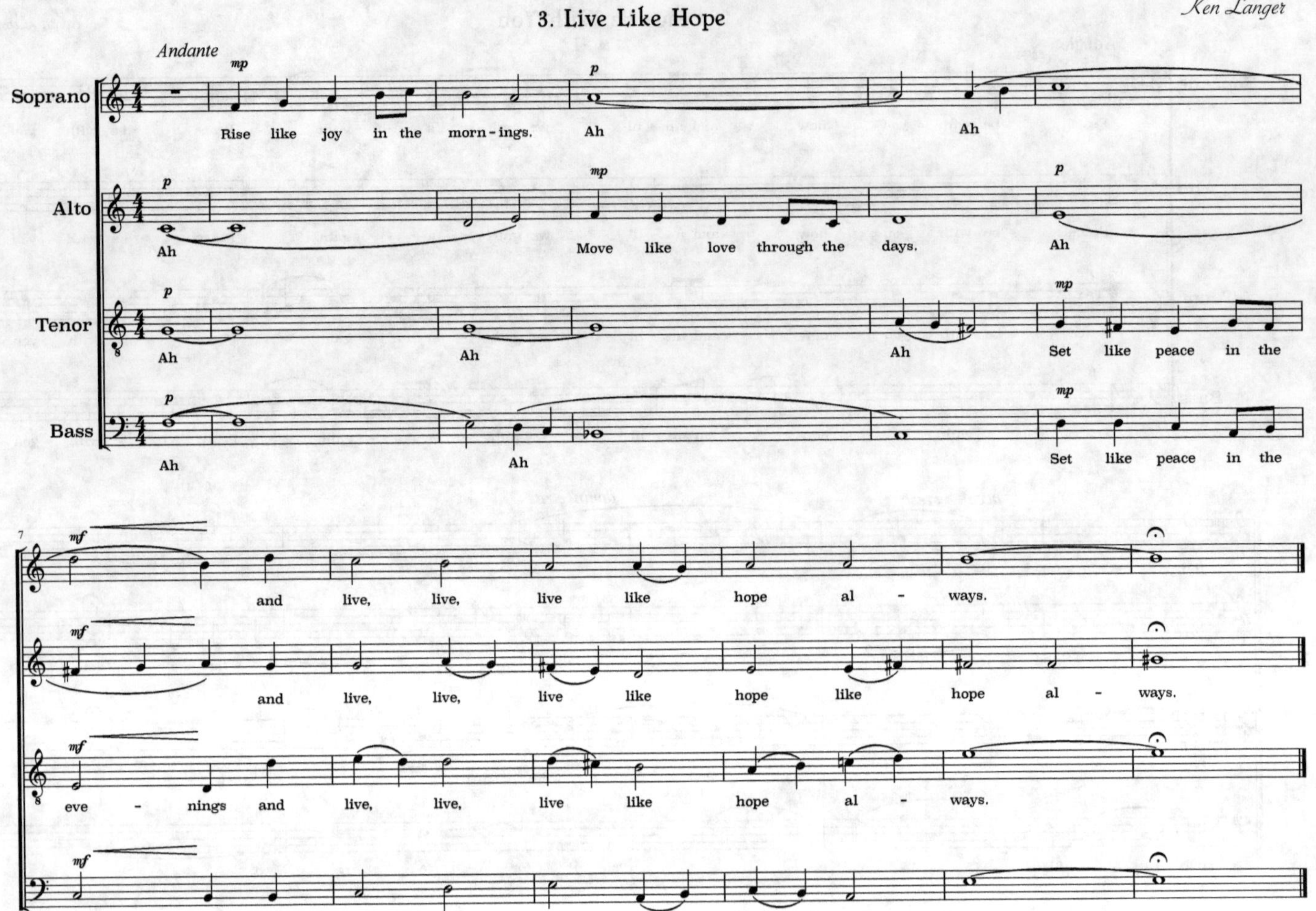

Ten Benedictions

4. Within You

Ken Langer

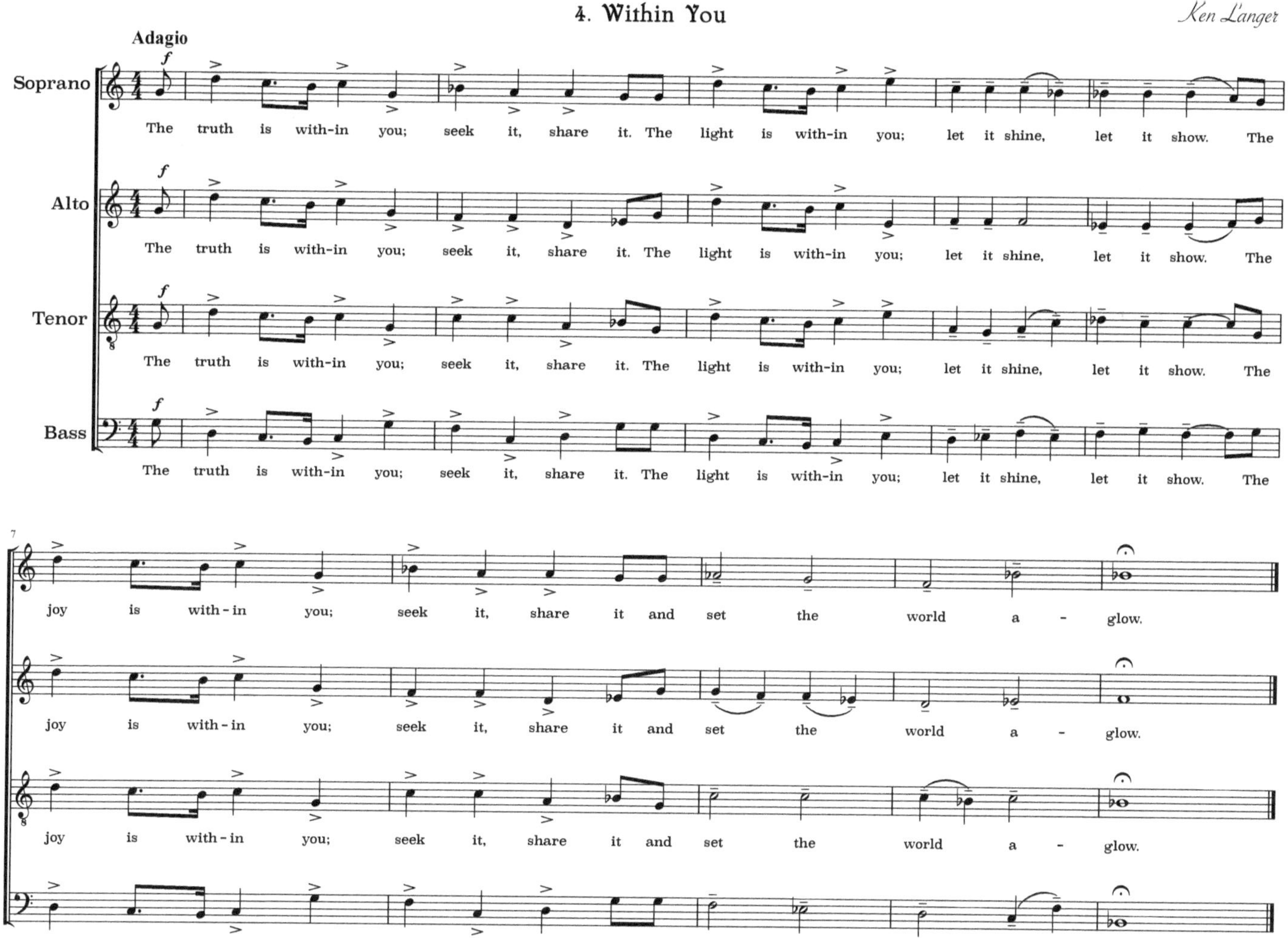

Ten Benedictions

5. Time To Go

Ken Langer

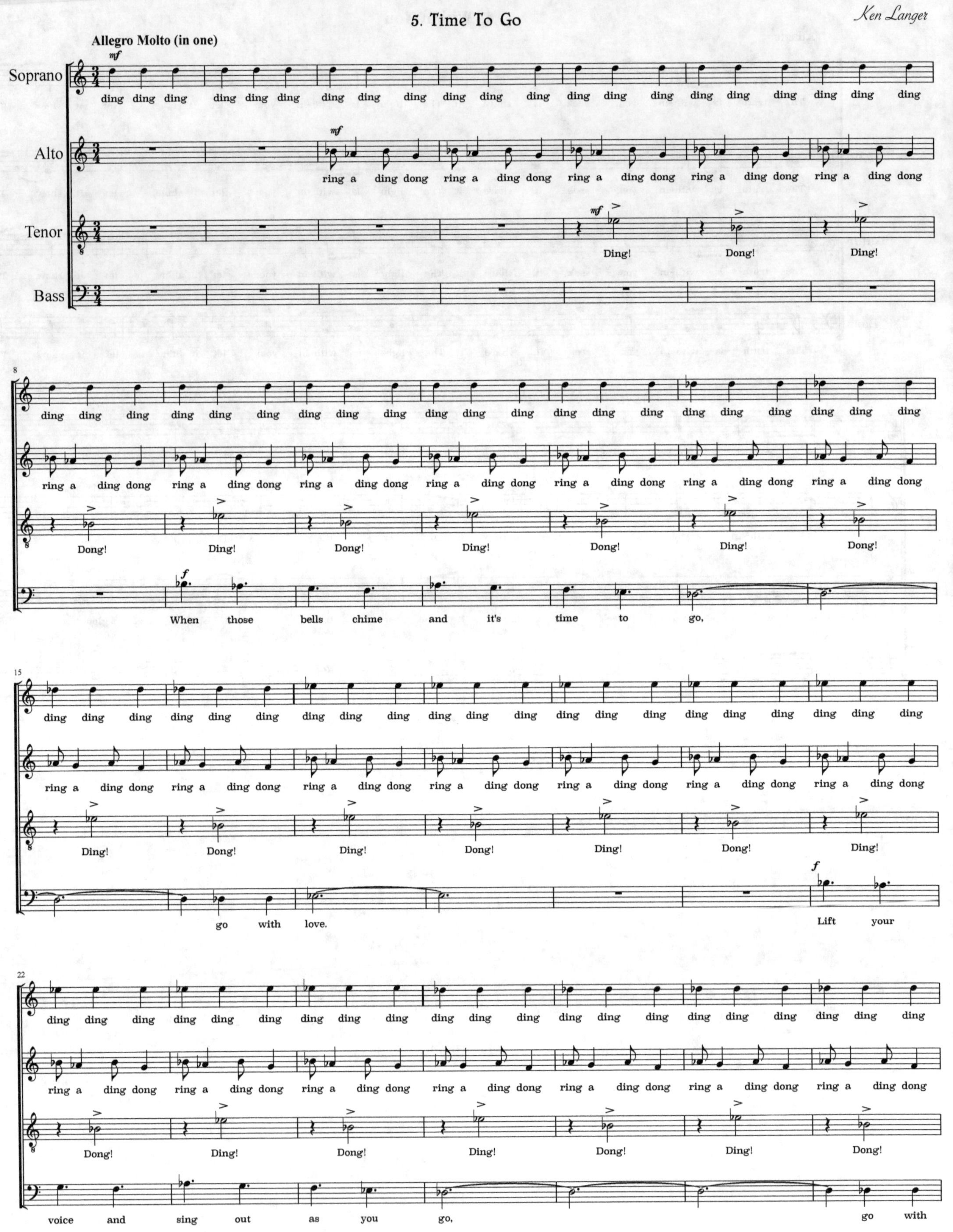

Ten Benedictions

4. Within You

Ken Langer

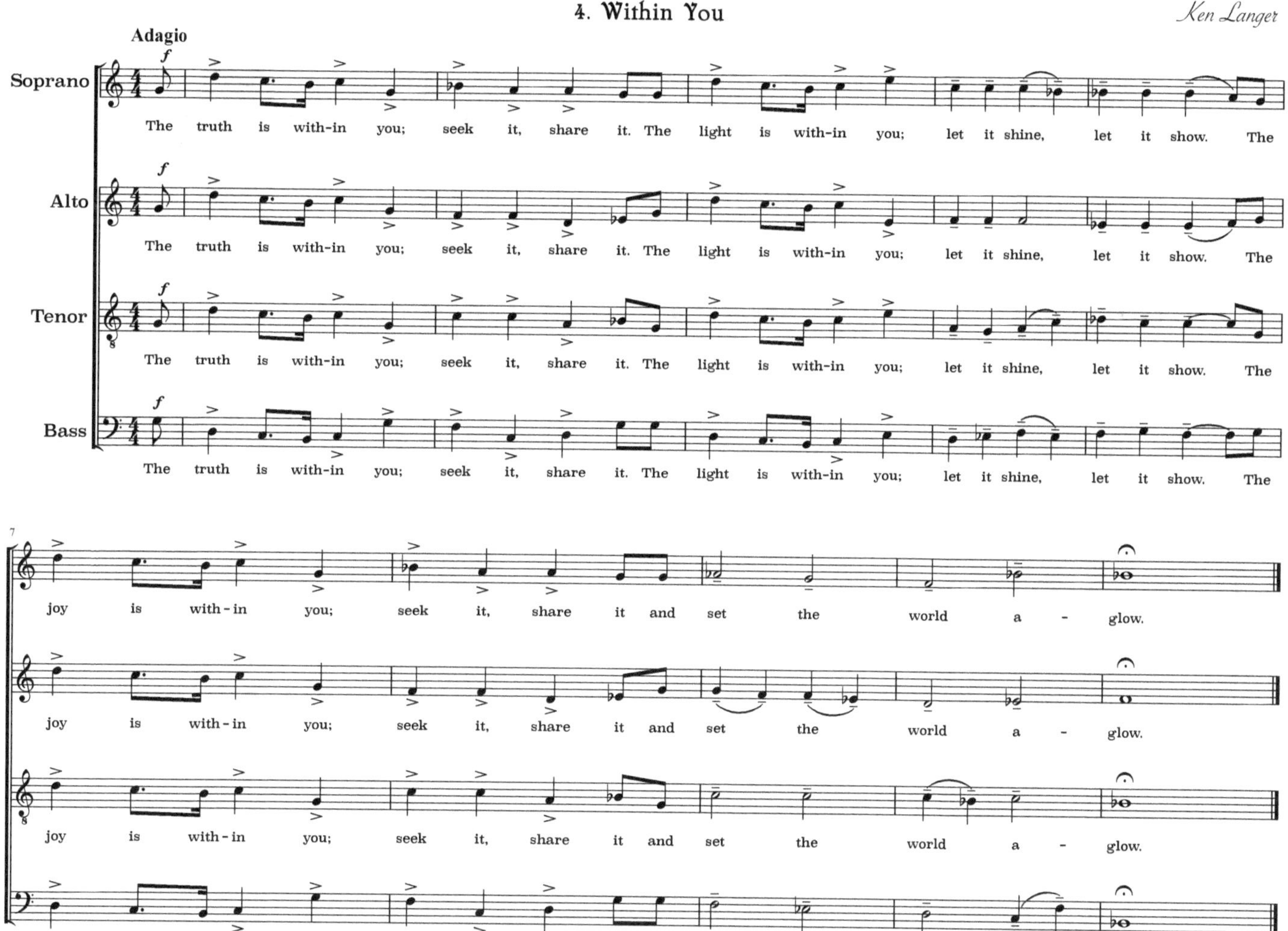

Ten Benedictions

5. Time To Go

Ken Langer

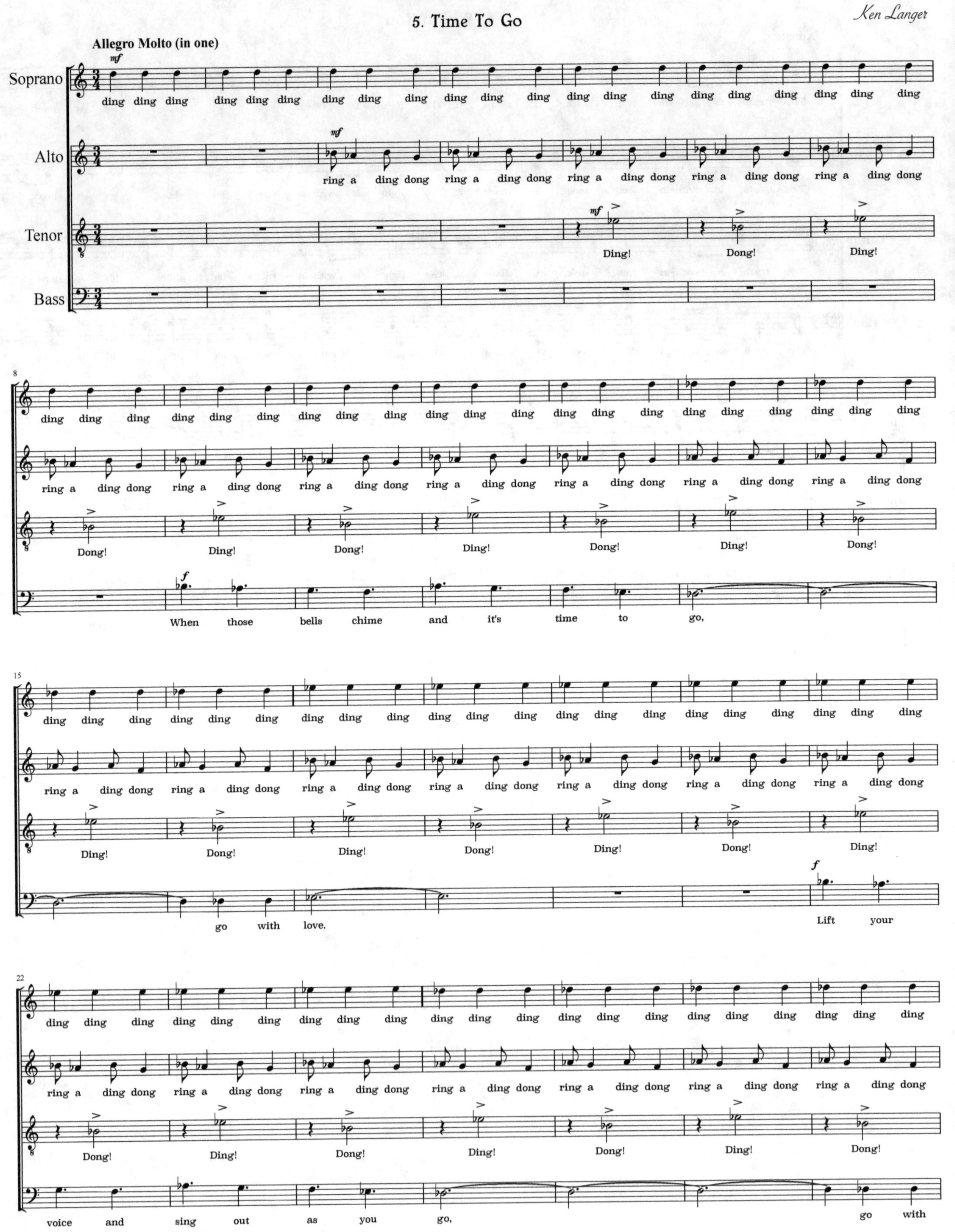

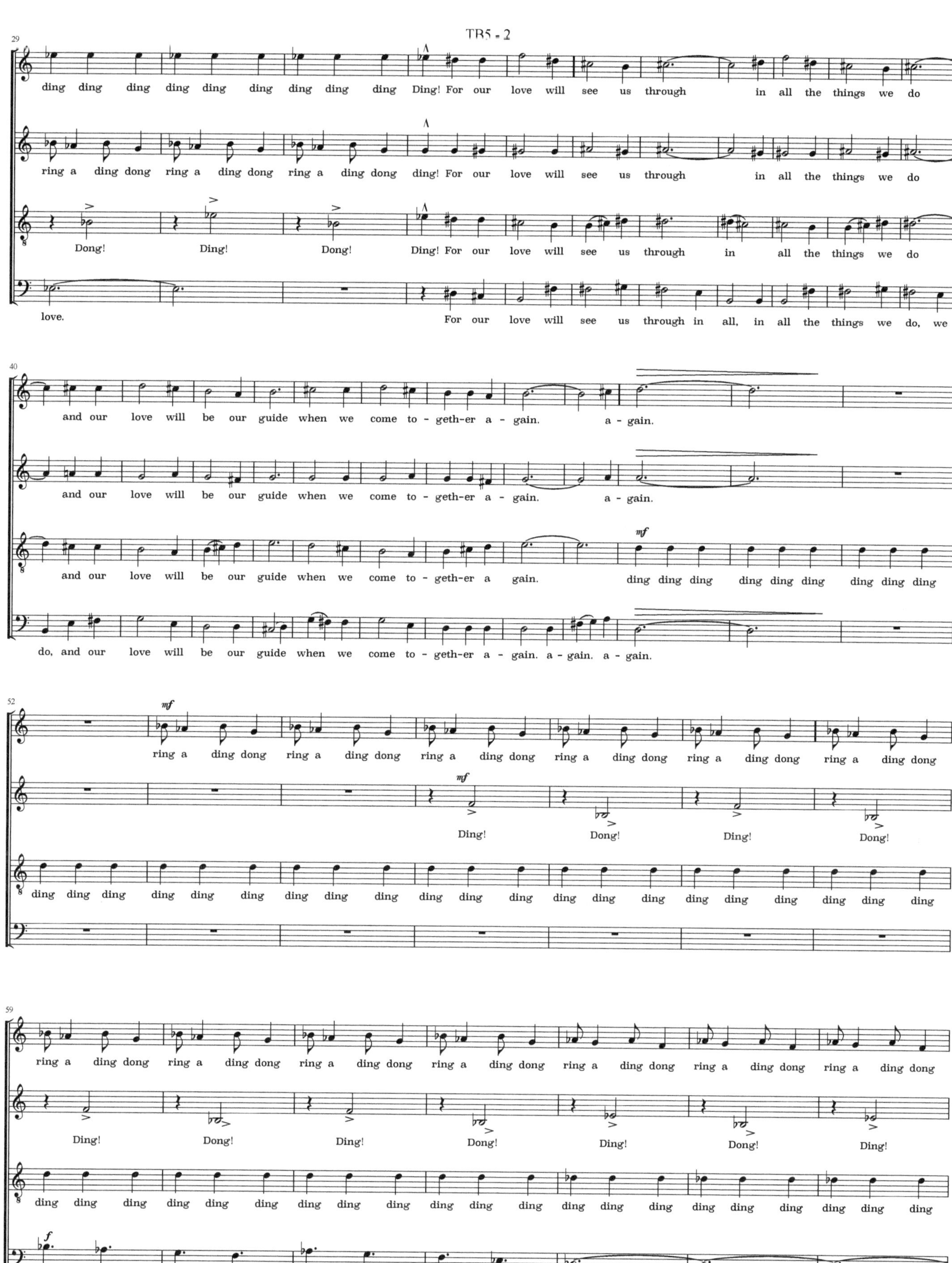
29
ding ding ding ding ding ding ding ding ding Ding! For our love will see us through in all the things we do
ring a ding dong ring a ding dong ring a ding dong ding! For our love will see us through in all the things we do
Dong! Ding! Dong! Ding! For our love will see us through in all the things we do
love. For our love will see us through in all, in all the things we do, we
40
and our love will be our guide when we come to - geth-er a - gain. a - gain.
and our love will be our guide when we come to - geth-er a - gain. a - gain.
and our love will be our guide when we come to - geth-er a gain. mf ding ding ding ding ding ding ding ding ding
do, and our love will be our guide when we come to - geth-er a - gain. a - gain. a - gain.
52
mf
ring a ding dong ring a ding dong ring a ding dong ring a ding dong ring a ding dong ring a ding dong
mf
Ding! Dong! Ding! Dong!
ding ding ding ding ding ding ding ding ding ding ding ding ding ding ding ding ding ding ding ding ding
59
ring a ding dong ring a ding dong ring a ding dong ring a ding dong ring a ding dong ring a ding dong ring a ding dong
Ding! Dong! Ding! Dong! Ding! Dong! Ding!
ding ding ding ding ding ding ding ding ding ding ding ding ding ding ding ding ding ding ding ding ding
f
When those bells chime and it's time to go,

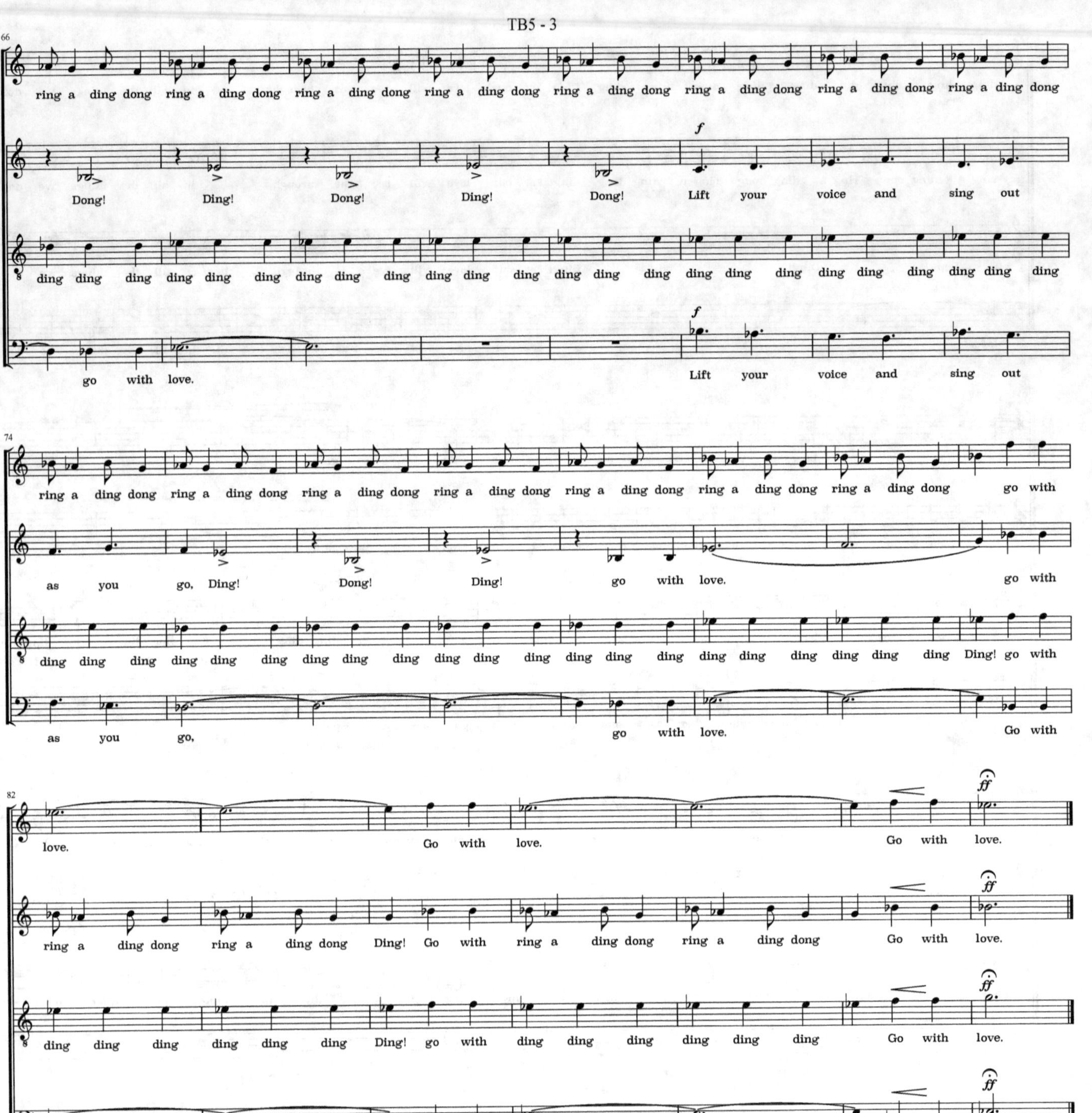
66
ring a ding dong ring a ding dong ring a ding dong ring a ding dong ring a ding dong ring a ding dong ring a ding dong ring a ding dong
f
Dong! Ding! Dong! Ding! Dong! Lift your voice and sing out
ding ding ding ding ding ding ding ding ding ding ding ding ding ding ding ding ding ding ding ding ding ding ding ding
f
go with love. Lift your voice and sing out
74
ring a ding dong ring a ding dong ring a ding dong ring a ding dong ring a ding dong ring a ding dong ring a ding dong go with
as you go, Ding! Dong! Ding! go with love. go with
ding ding ding ding ding ding ding ding ding ding ding ding ding ding ding ding ding ding ding ding ding Ding! go with
as you go, go with love. Go with
82
love. Go with love. Go with love.
ff
ring a ding dong ring a ding dong Ding! Go with ring a ding dong ring a ding dong Go with love.
ding ding ding ding ding ding Ding! go with ding ding ding ding ding ding Go with love.
love. Go with love. Go with love.

Ten Benedictions

6. Live Now

Ken Langer

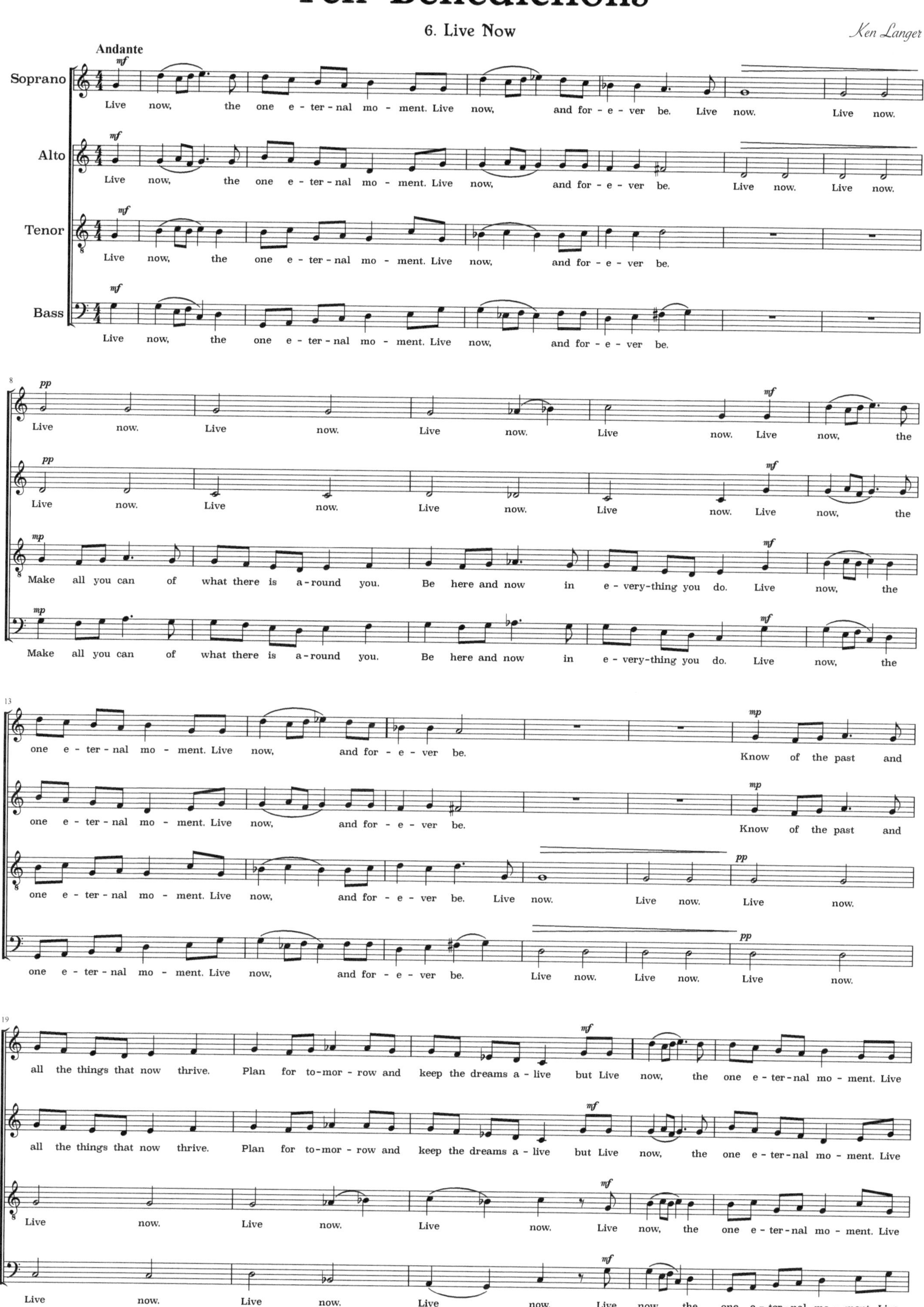

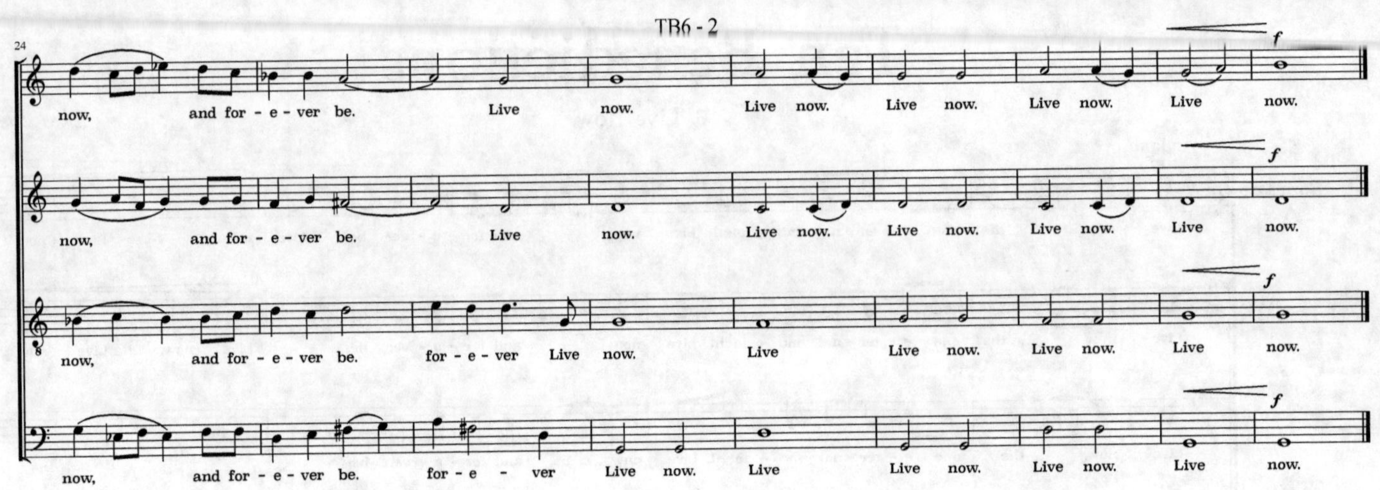
24
now, and for - e - ver be. Live now. Live now. Live now. Live now. Live now.
now, and for - e - ver be. Live now. Live now. Live now. Live now. Live now.
now, and for - e - ver be. for - e - ver Live now. Live Live now. Live now. Live now.
now, and for - e - ver be. for - e - ver Live now. Live Live now. Live now. Live now.
f
f
f
f

Ten Benedictions

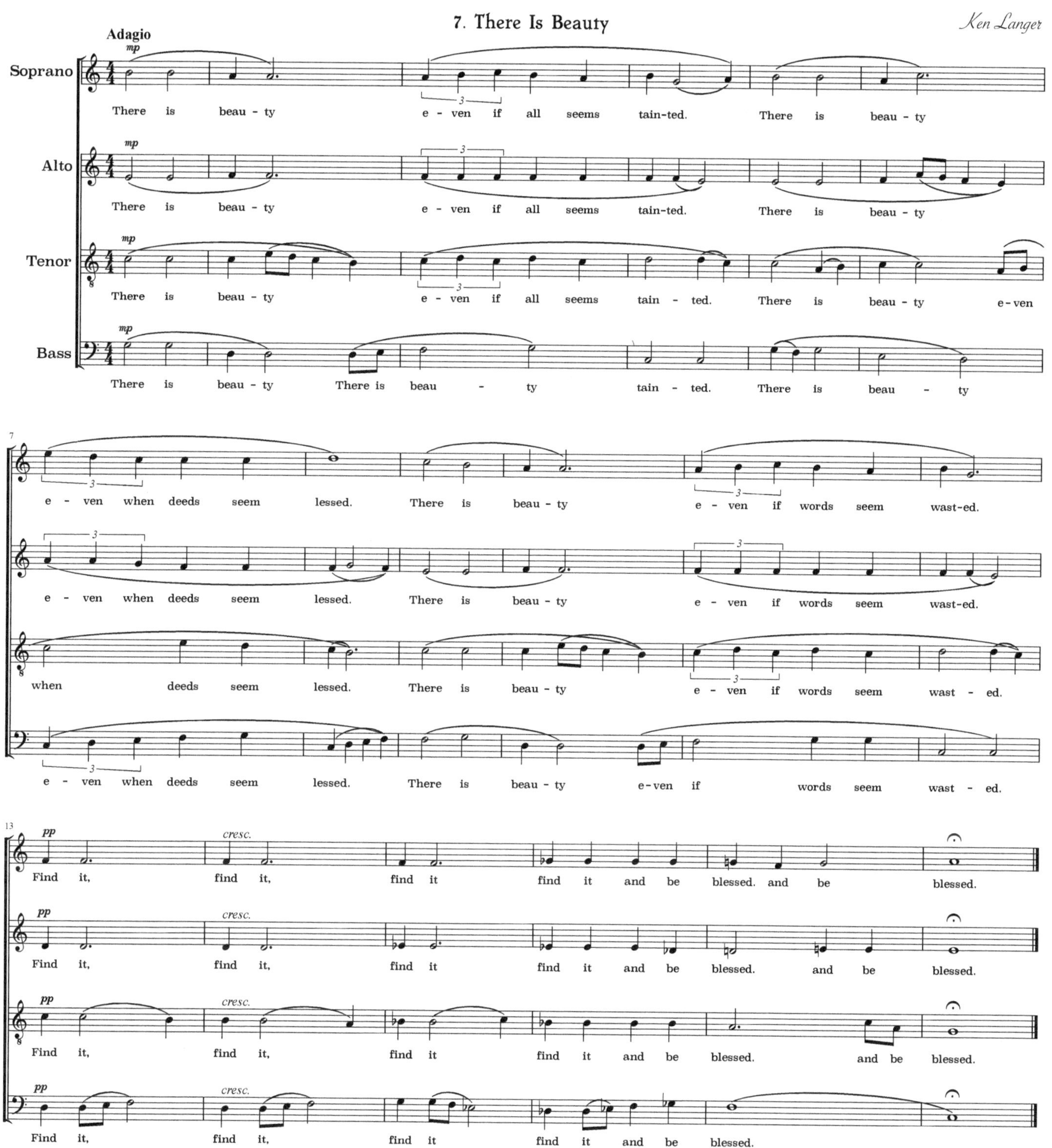

Ten Benedictions

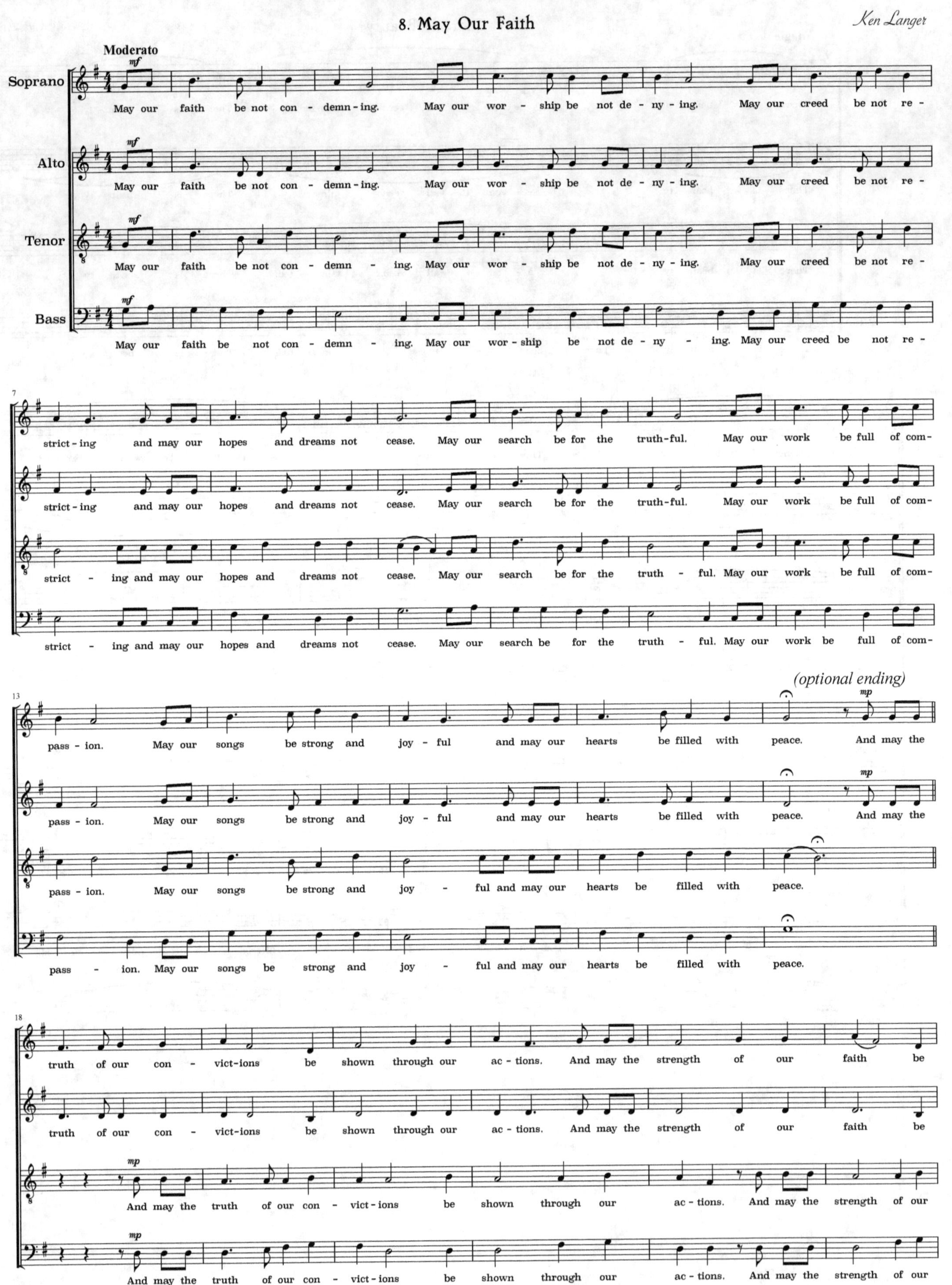

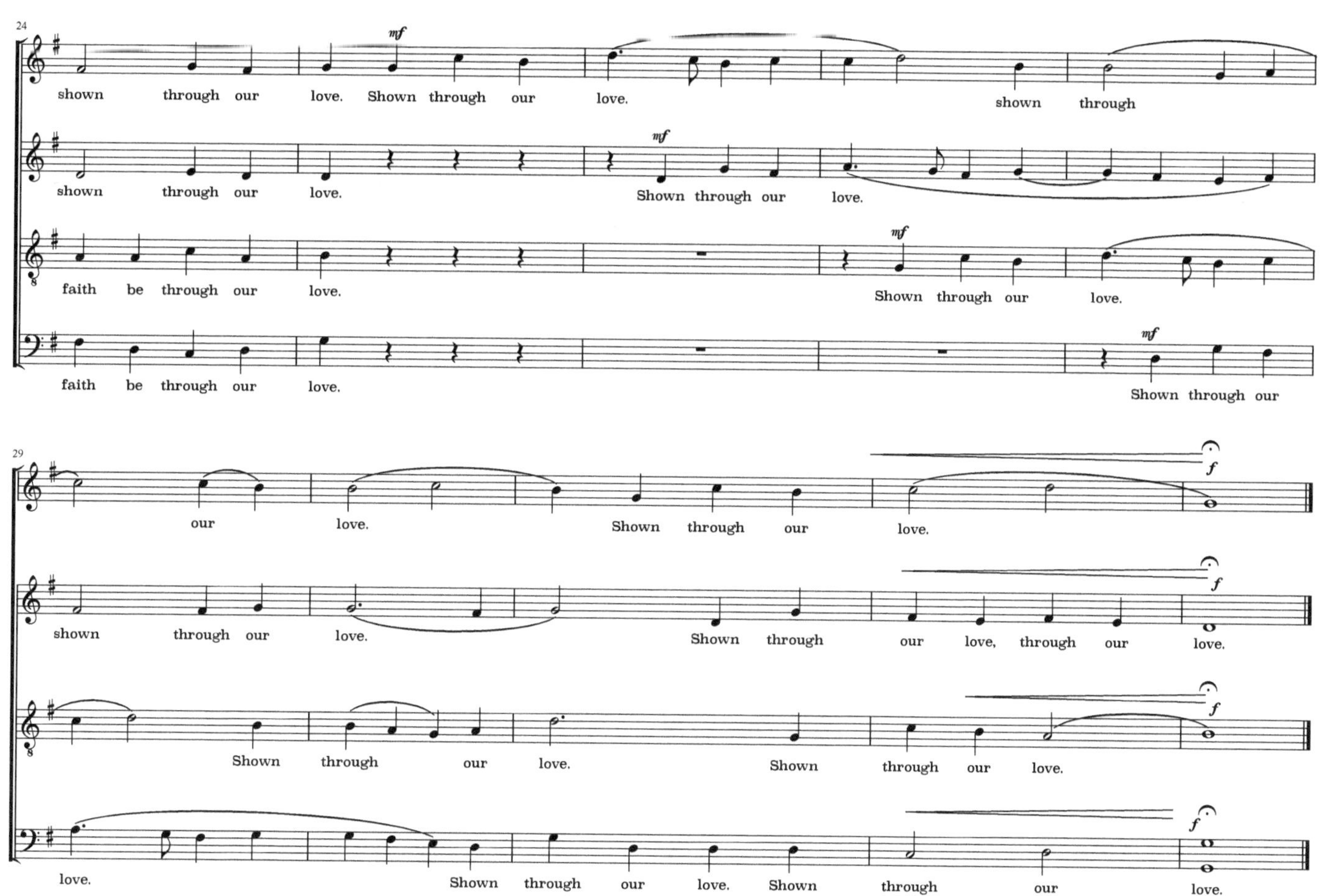
24
mf
shown through our love. Shown through our love. shown through
mf
shown through our love. Shown through our love.
mf
faith be through our love. Shown through our love.
mf
faith be through our love. Shown through our
29
f
our love. Shown through our love.
f
shown through our love. Shown through our love, through our love.
f
Shown through our love. Shown through our love.
f
love. Shown through our love. Shown through our love.

Ten Benedictions

Three Part Round — 9. Another Beginning — *Ken Langer*

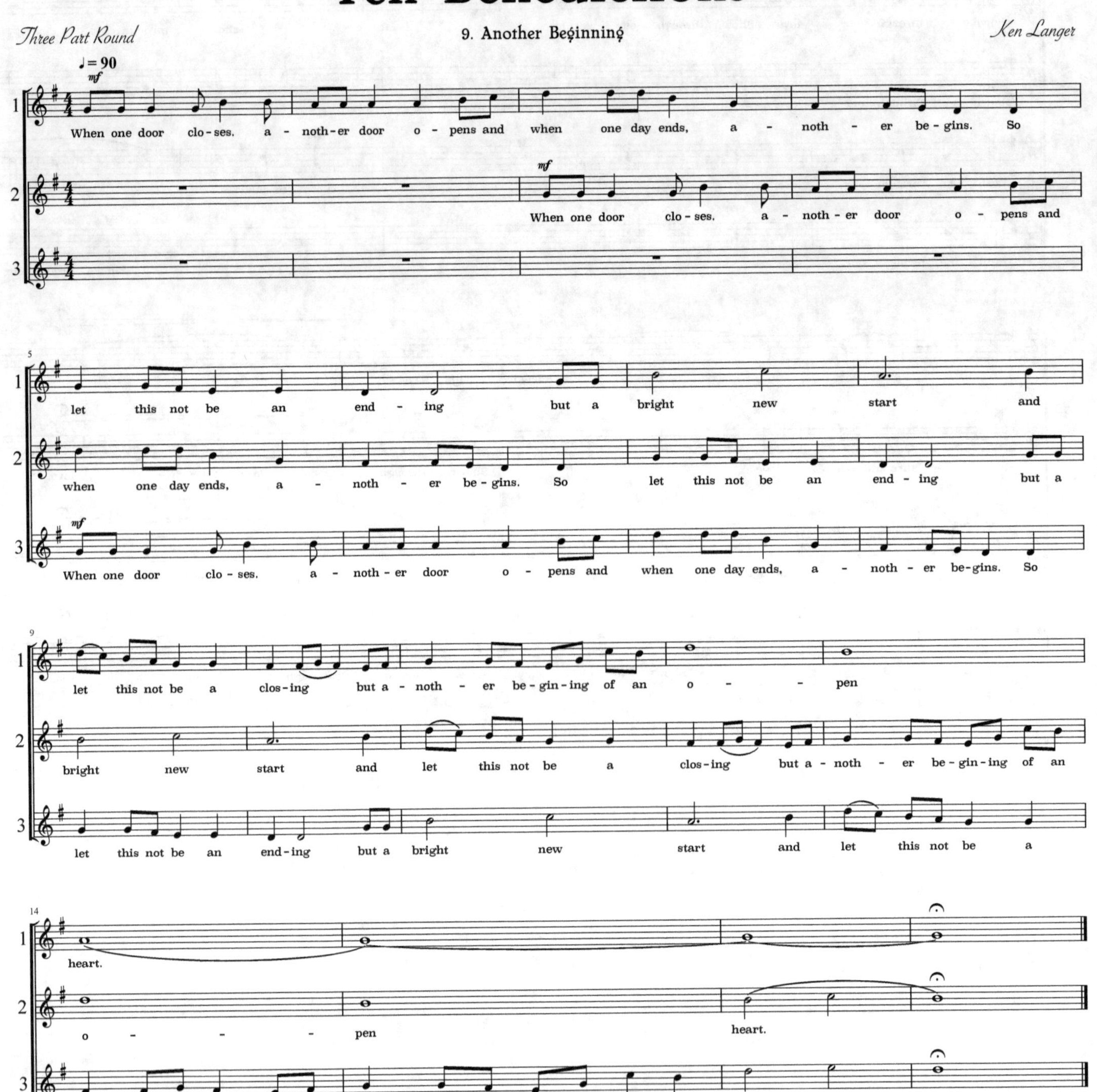

Ten Benedictions

10. Dream On

Ken Langer

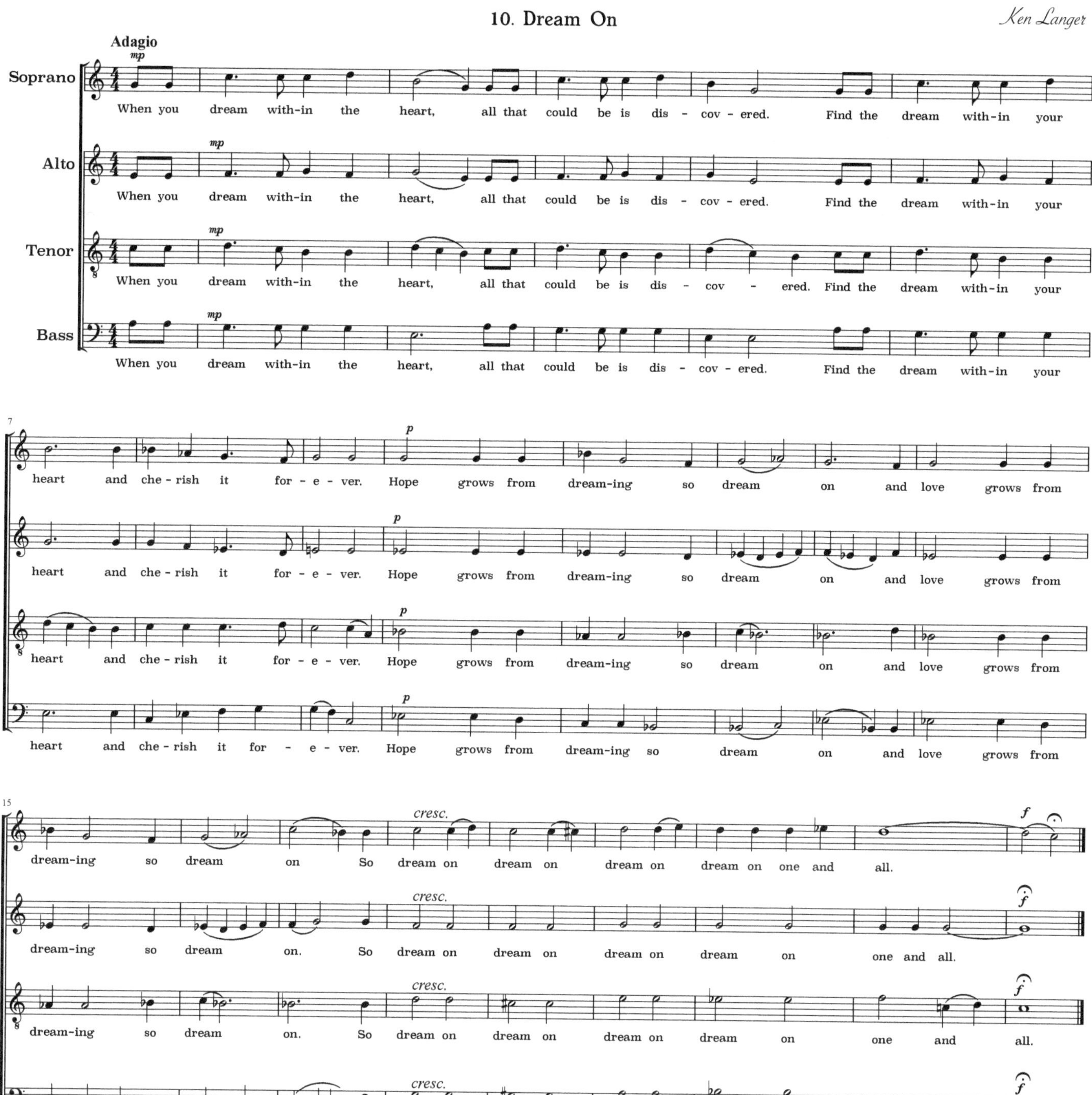

About The Composer

Dr. Kenneth Langer was born in the Pittsburgh area in 1959. He began playing trumpet in the 5th grade and decided in high school to make music his career.

Dr. Langer earned a Bachelor's Degree in Music Education at James Madison University in Harrisonburg, Virginia; a Master's of Music Degree at Radford University in Radford, Virginia; and a Ph.D. In Music Theory and Composition at Kent State University in Kent, Ohio. He has taught music at several small colleges.

He has also been the Director of Music and Arts at the Eno River Unitarian-Universalist Fellowship in Durham, North Carolina and the Assistant Conductor and Resident Composer at the Montpelier Unitarian-Universalist Church in Montpelier, Vermont.

During his twenty years of writing over 150 original works of music for various genres including brass, chorus, strings, orchestra, wind ensemble, and woodwinds; he has received numerous awards for his compositions including being named Vermont's Composer of the Year in the year 2000 and winning placement in several international composition contests. He has commercially published well over 30 compositions.

To perform any of these works please contact the composer at ken.langer@me.com or klangerdude@gmail.com

www.ingramcontent.com/pod-product-compliance
Lightning Source LLC
LaVergne TN
LVHW080922110826
845155LV00039B/179
* 9 7 8 1 9 4 9 4 6 4 0 4 7 *